T0022568

THE CHALLENGER DISASTER
TRAGEDY IN THE SKIES

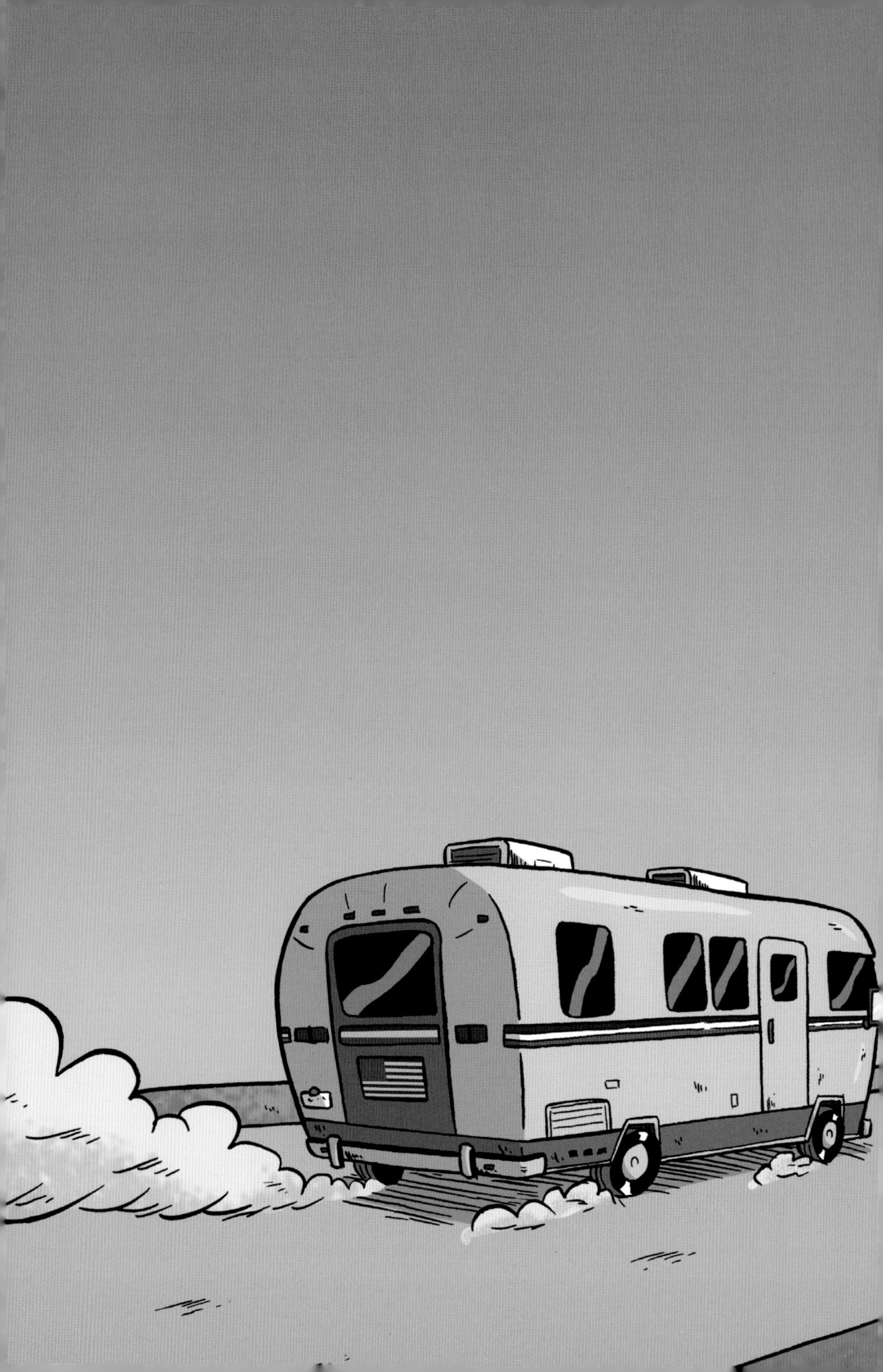

HISTORY COMICS

THE CHALLENGER DISASTER

TRAGEDY IN THE SKIES

Pranas T. Naujokaitis

Color by
Cassie Hart

:01
First Second
New York

First Second

Copyright © 2020 by Pranas T. Naujokaitis

Published by First Second
First Second is an imprint of Roaring Brook Press, a division of Holtzbrinck Publishing
Holdings Limited Partnership
120 Broadway, New York, NY 10271

Don't miss your next favorite book from First Second! For the latest updates go to
firstsecondnewsletter.com and sign up for our enewsletter.

Library of Congress Control Number: 2019948150

Paperback ISBN: 978-1-250-17430-7
Hardcover ISBN: 978-1-250-17429-1

Our books may be purchased in bulk for promotional, educational, or business use. Please
contact your local bookseller or the Macmillan Corporate and Premium Sales Department
at (800) 221-7945 ext. 5442 or by email at MacmillanSpecialMarkets@macmillan.com.

FIRST
EDITION

First edition, 2020
Edited by Dave Roman
Cover design by Kirk Benshoff
Interior book design by Sunny Lee
Color by Cassie Hart

Drawn on Strathmore 300 Series smooth Bristol board with pencil and inked with black
India ink using Hunt 102 and 107 nibs and various brushes. Panel borders inked with a
Copic Multiliner black pen size 0.5. Colored digitally in Photoshop.

Printed in China by 1010 Printing International Limited, North Point, Hong Kong
Paperback: 10 9 8 7 6 5 4 3 2 1
Hardcover: 10 9 8 7 6 5 4 3 2 1

D o your parents remember where they were when the Space Shuttle *Challenger* fragmented after launch on January 28, 1986? I was too young to have any real memories of it—I was only two years old when the orbiter carrying seven astronauts broke apart on its way out of the Earth's atmosphere. But that doesn't mean the event isn't imprinted on my memory. I can't remember a time when I *didn't* know that tragedy had befallen the *Challenger* crew. For those of us who love space, it is a defining moment in history.

The tragedy occurred at a time when the general public was falling out of love with space travel. Going to space and returning to Earth had become a routine event. But the Teacher in Space program reinvigorated public interest in space, and that's why millions of schoolchildren around the country were watching in awe and wonder as the orbiter took off toward the stars.

It's hard to describe the excitement around a rocket launch. Admittedly, the views are much, much better on your television set, because you aren't allowed to get very close in person. But if you do ever get the chance to see one with your own eyes, it's a magical experience. As the clock counts down and the launch window approaches, a nervous excitement ripples through the crowd. During those last few seconds before the rocket ignites, you can feel the energy rising.

And then . . . LIFTOFF! For the first few seconds, as the smoke bursts out from the rocket, it seems as if the spacecraft is going nowhere. Then, slowly, it begins to rise, and the flames burn as the rocket lifts off the pad. Even from miles away, you can see the bright orange fire contrasting against the blue sky (or sometimes even the night sky!) as the rocket climbs into the atmosphere. It's a sight so breathtaking that sometimes people even cry—I certainly have.

Usually, the rocket successfully makes it to orbit. But sometimes, as in the case of the *Challenger* on that fateful January morning, it doesn't. And in this case, the eyes of the entire nation, including children, were on that spacecraft as it broke apart after launch.

The Space Shuttle Program taught the National Aeronautics and Space Administration many things about going to space and living and working in orbit. Over the thirty years that the orbiters were flying, NASA successfully sent over 130 missions to space and brought them back home. On board *Columbia*, *Discovery*, *Endeavour*, *Atlantis*, and *Challenger*, astronauts conducted countless science experiments, deployed satellites, and even fixed the Hubble Space Telescope multiple times! It's hard to overestimate what

NASA learned from the program and how it will shape future space travel.

But the Space Shuttle Program also taught NASA how to recover after major setbacks and tragedies.

Nothing about spaceflight is routine. It's a fact that many people forget, given that it seems like every day, there is something new launching into space. But traveling to space, and especially launching humans into space and bringing them safely home, is an incredibly complicated and dangerous process. When you manage to do it successfully over and over again, as NASA did with the Space Shuttle Program, it's easy to forget how big the risks are.

Every evening around the world, when the sky goes dark and the stars begin to peek out from the night sky, children look at the cosmos and wonder what's out there. I was that child. Chances are that, if you're reading this, then you are that child as well. Spaceflight inspires our imaginations and reminds us to dream big. It tells us that we are capable of so much more than we think.

But when we look up at those stars, it's also important to remember the people who sacrificed so we could have these dreams. When it comes to spaceflight, it's easy to get lost in numbers and statistics, in the amazing technology on board these incredible craft. But we need to make sure we never lose sight of the human component as well.

In these pages, you'll read a lot about the technical components of the space shuttle and orbiter—after all, they were pretty amazing pieces of technology. But you'll also read about seven astronauts named Dick Scobee, Mike Smith, Ron McNair, Ellison Onizuka, Judy Resnik, Greg Jarvis, and Christa McAuliffe, who gave their lives to ensure we could continue to go to space. They are heroes, and after you finish this book, as you learn more about the space program and where we are now, it's so important to remember that we couldn't have ever gotten this far without them.

Ad astra per aspera (*through hardships to the stars*), and happy reading!

—**Swapna Krishna**, space, science, and tech writer
and former contributing writer at engadget.com

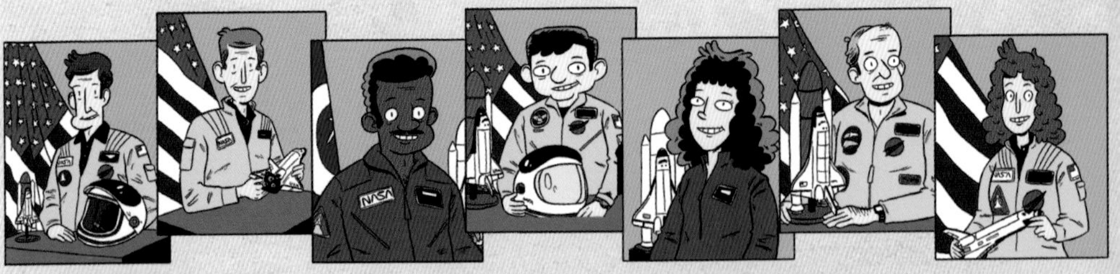
NASA

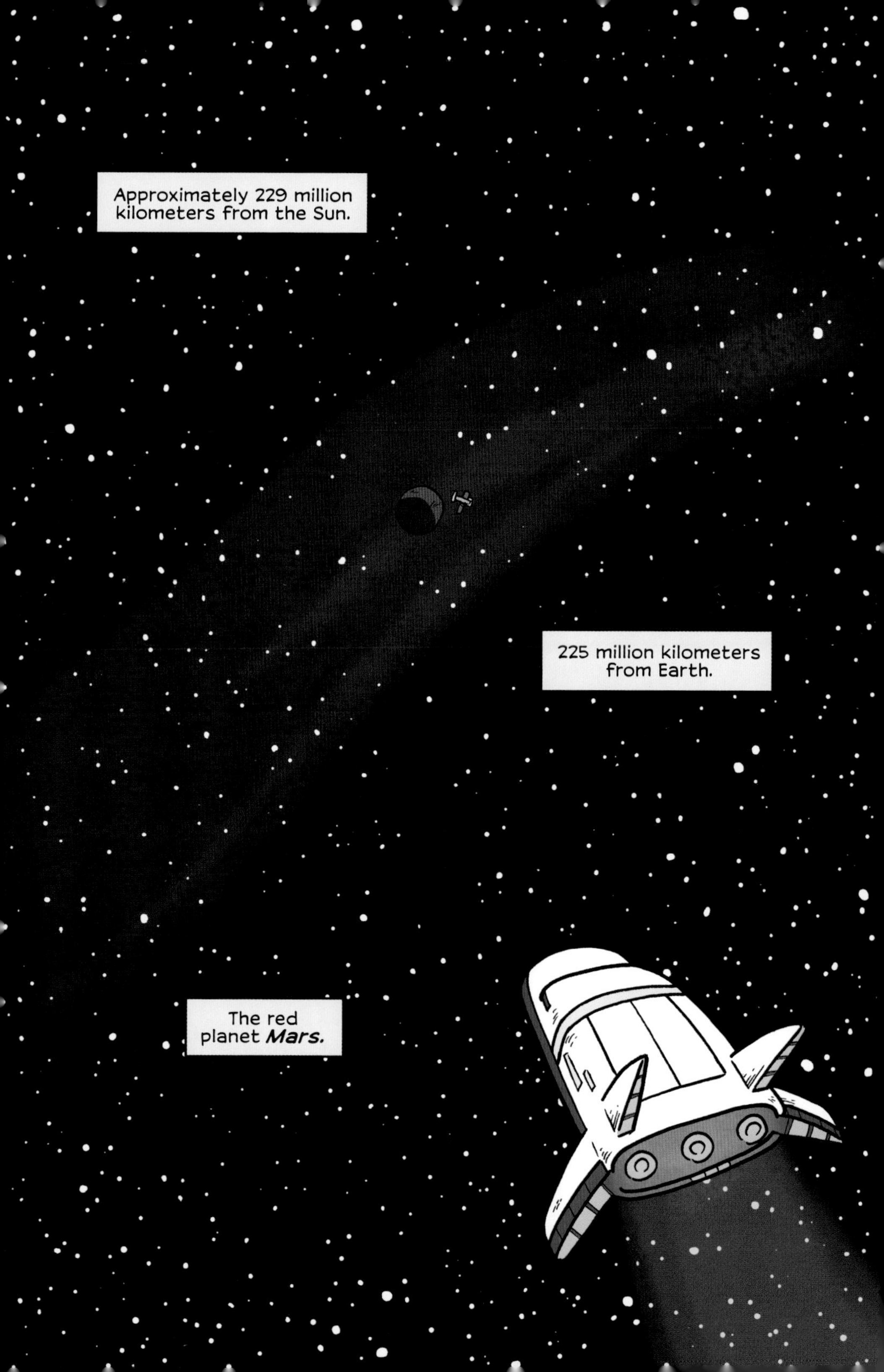
Approximately 229 million kilometers from the Sun.
225 million kilometers from Earth.
The red planet *Mars.*

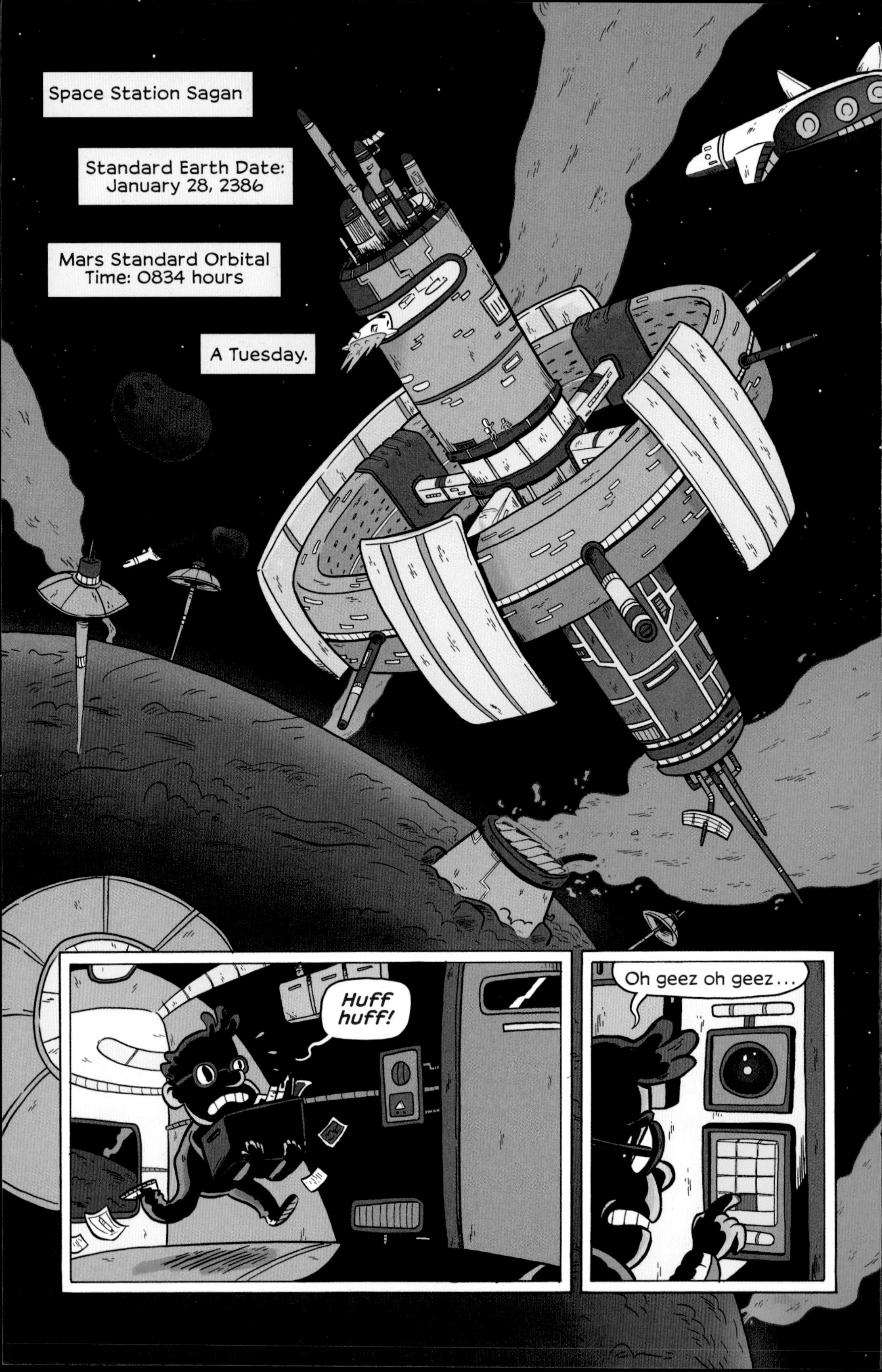
Space Station Sagan
Standard Earth Date: January 28, 2386
Mars Standard Orbital Time: 0834 hours
A Tuesday.
Huff huff!
Oh geez oh geez...

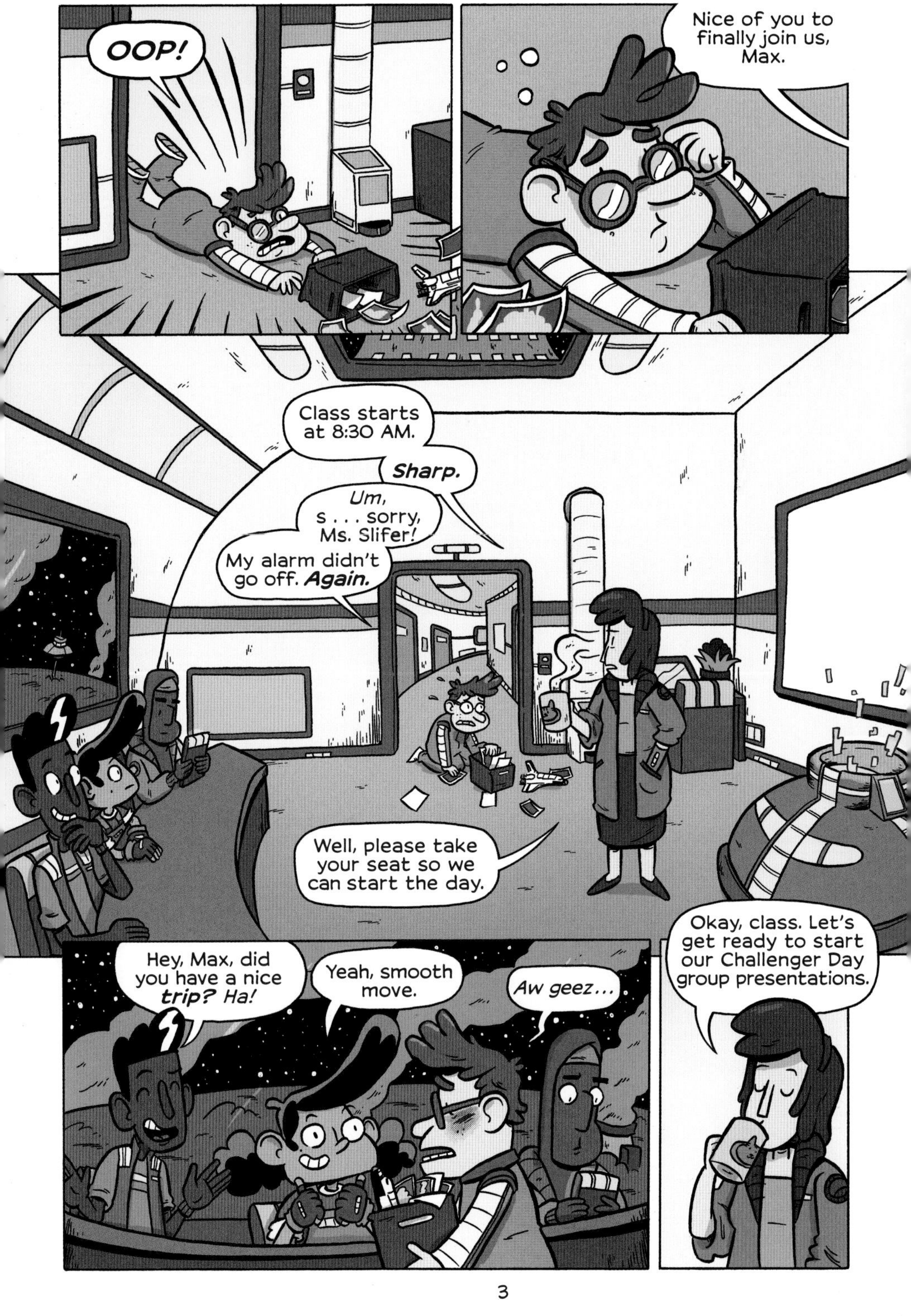

OOP!
Nice of you to finally join us, Max.
Class starts at 8:30 AM.
Sharp.
Um, s . . . sorry, Ms. Slifer!
My alarm didn't go off. Again.
Well, please take your seat so we can start the day.
Hey, Max, did you have a nice trip? Ha!
Yeah, smooth move.
Aw geez...
Okay, class. Let's get ready to start our Challenger Day group presentations.

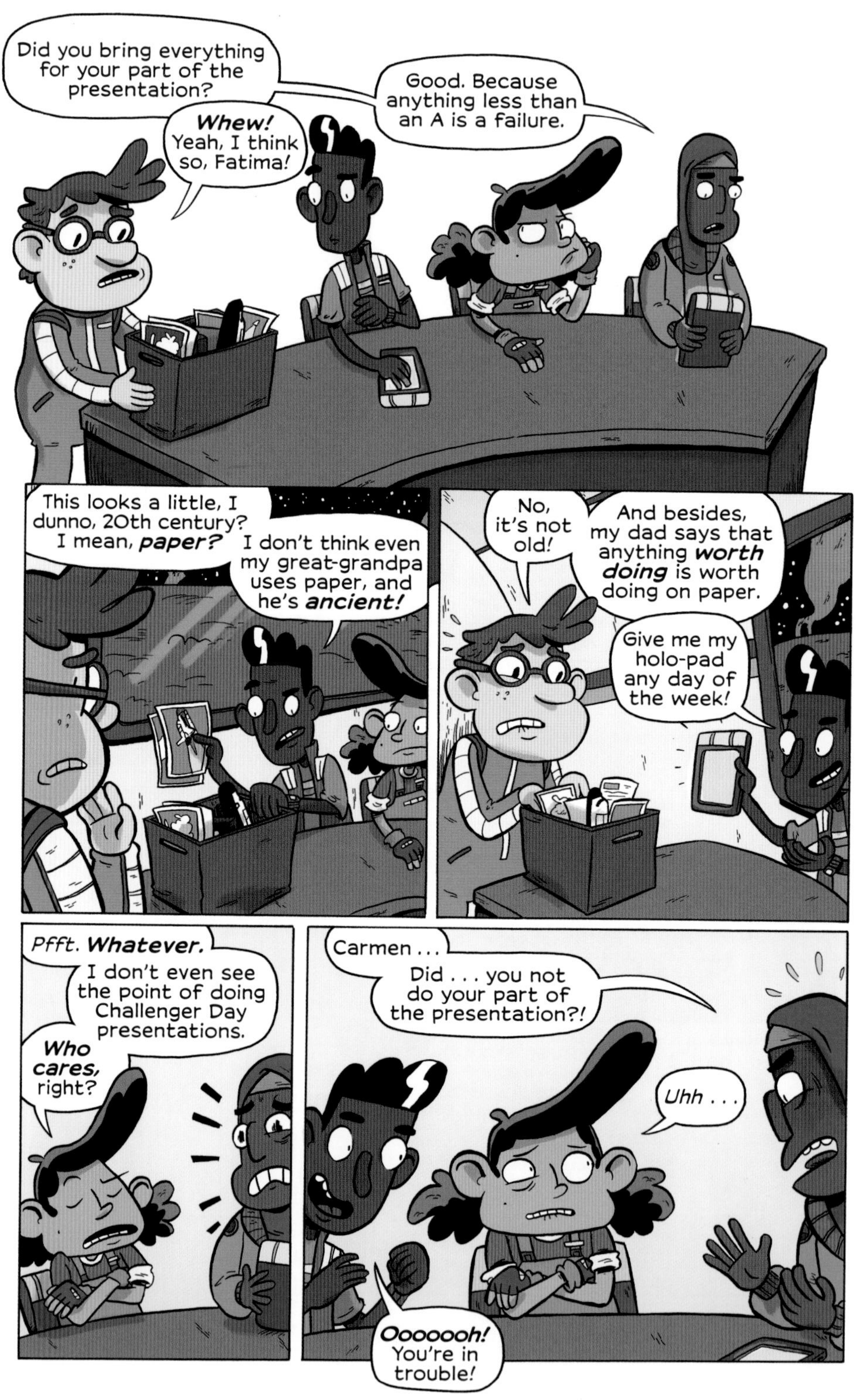
Did you bring everything for your part of the presentation?
Whew! Yeah, I think so, Fatima!
Good. Because anything less than an A is a failure.
This looks a little, I dunno, 20th century? I mean, paper?
I don't think even my great-grandpa uses paper, and he's ancient!
No, it's not old!
And besides, my dad says that anything worth doing is worth doing on paper.
Give me my holo-pad any day of the week!
Pfft. Whatever.
I don't even see the point of doing Challenger Day presentations.
Who cares, right?
Carmen . . .
Did . . . you not do your part of the presentation?!
Uhh . . .
Ooooooh! You're in trouble!

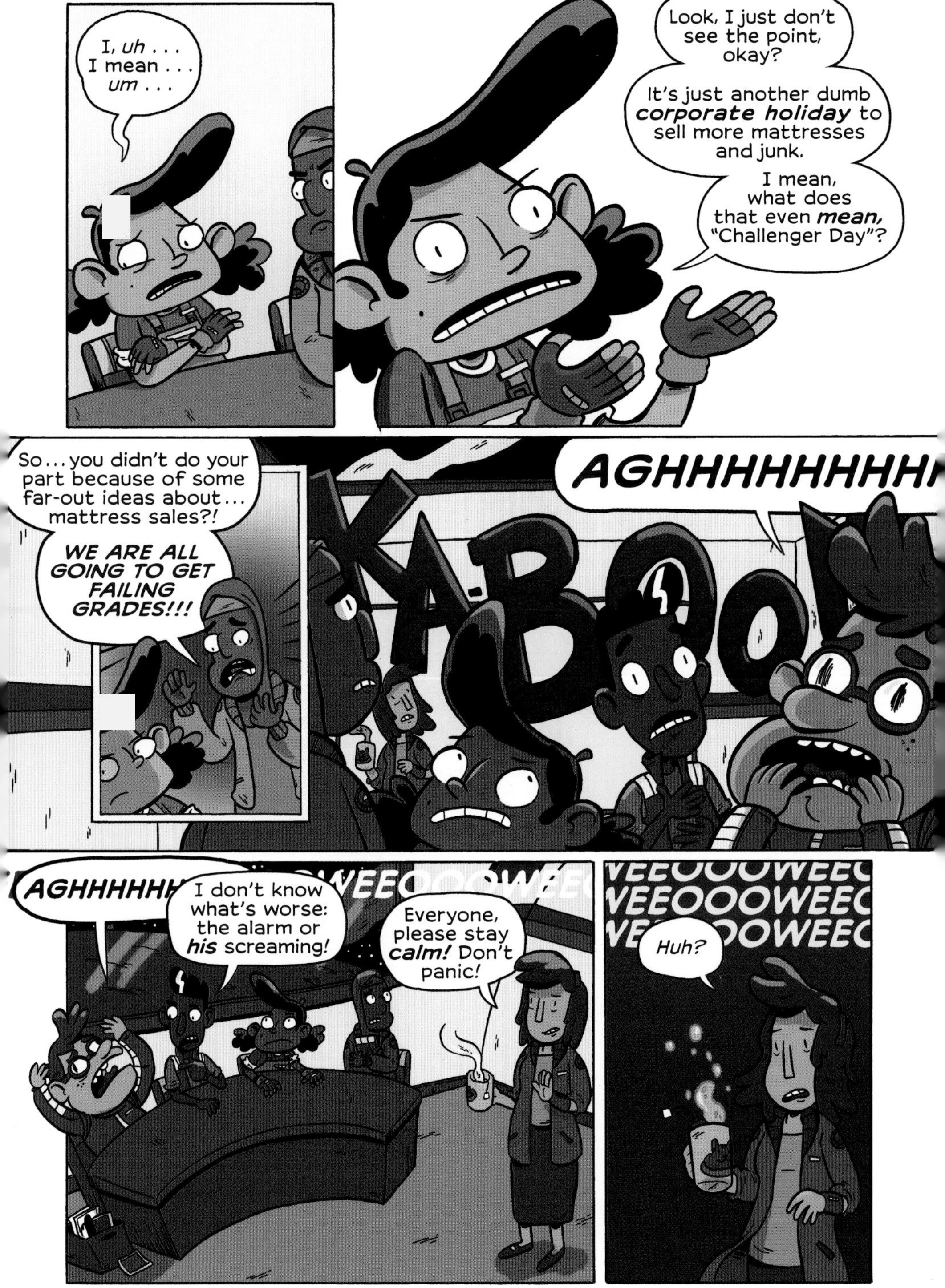
I, *uh* . . .
I mean . . .
um . . .
Look, I just don't see the point, okay?
It's just another dumb ***corporate holiday*** to sell more mattresses and junk.
I mean, what does that even ***mean,*** "Challenger Day"?
So . . . you didn't do your part because of some far-out ideas about . . . mattress sales?!
WE ARE ALL GOING TO GET FAILING GRADES!!!
KA-BOOM
AGHHHHHHHHH
AGHHHHHH
WEEOOOOWEE
I don't know what's worse: the alarm or ***his*** screaming!
Everyone, please stay ***calm!*** Don't panic!
WEEOOOWEE
WEEOOOWEE
OOWEE
Huh?

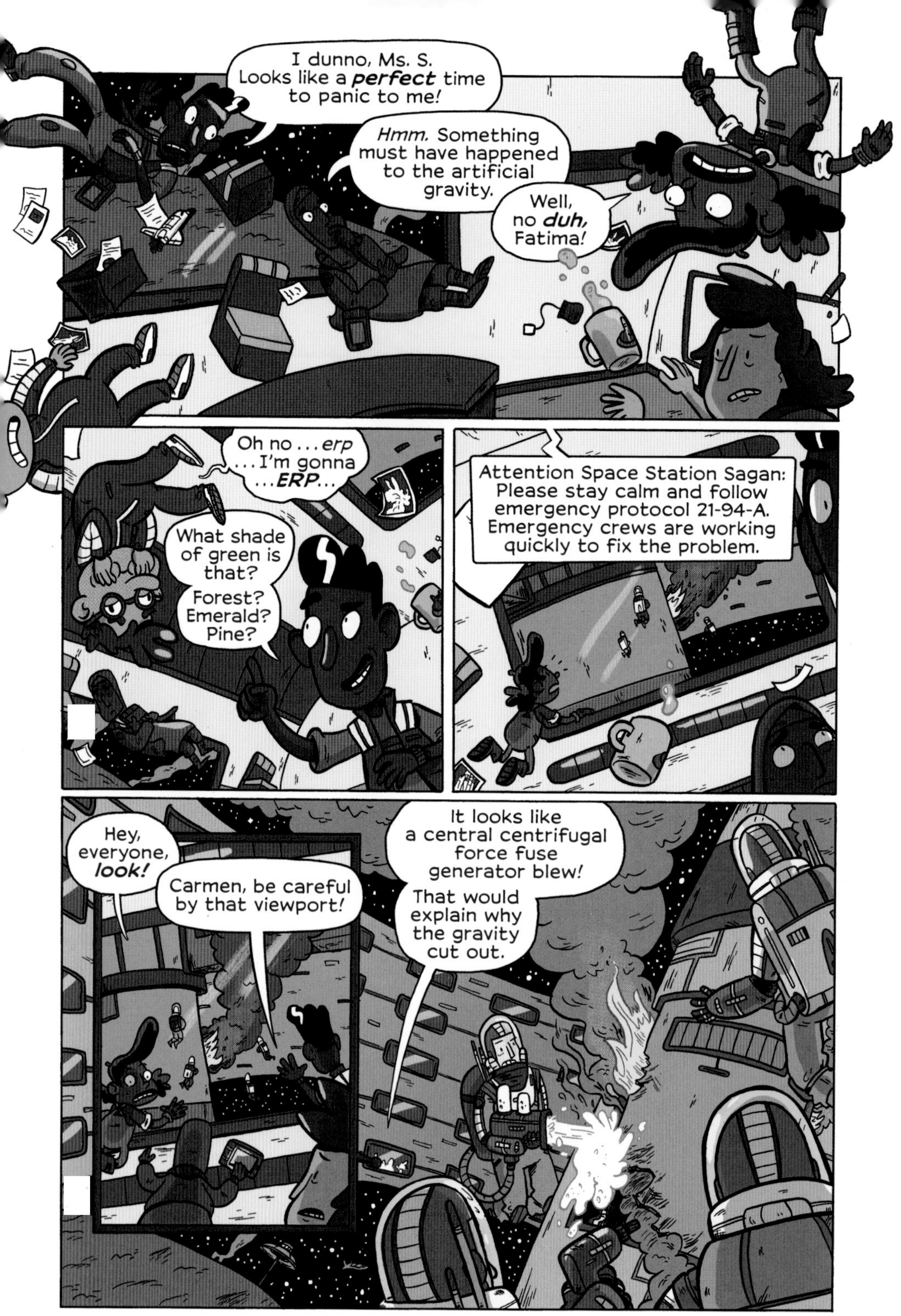
I dunno, Ms. S. Looks like a *perfect* time to panic to me!
Hmm. Something must have happened to the artificial gravity.
Well, no *duh,* Fatima!
Oh no . . . *erp* . . . I'm gonna . . . *ERP* . . .
What shade of green is that?
Forest? Emerald? Pine?
Attention Space Station Sagan: Please stay calm and follow emergency protocol 21-94-A. Emergency crews are working quickly to fix the problem.
Hey, everyone, *look!*
Carmen, be careful by that viewport!
It looks like a central centrifugal force fuse generator blew!
That would explain why the gravity cut out.

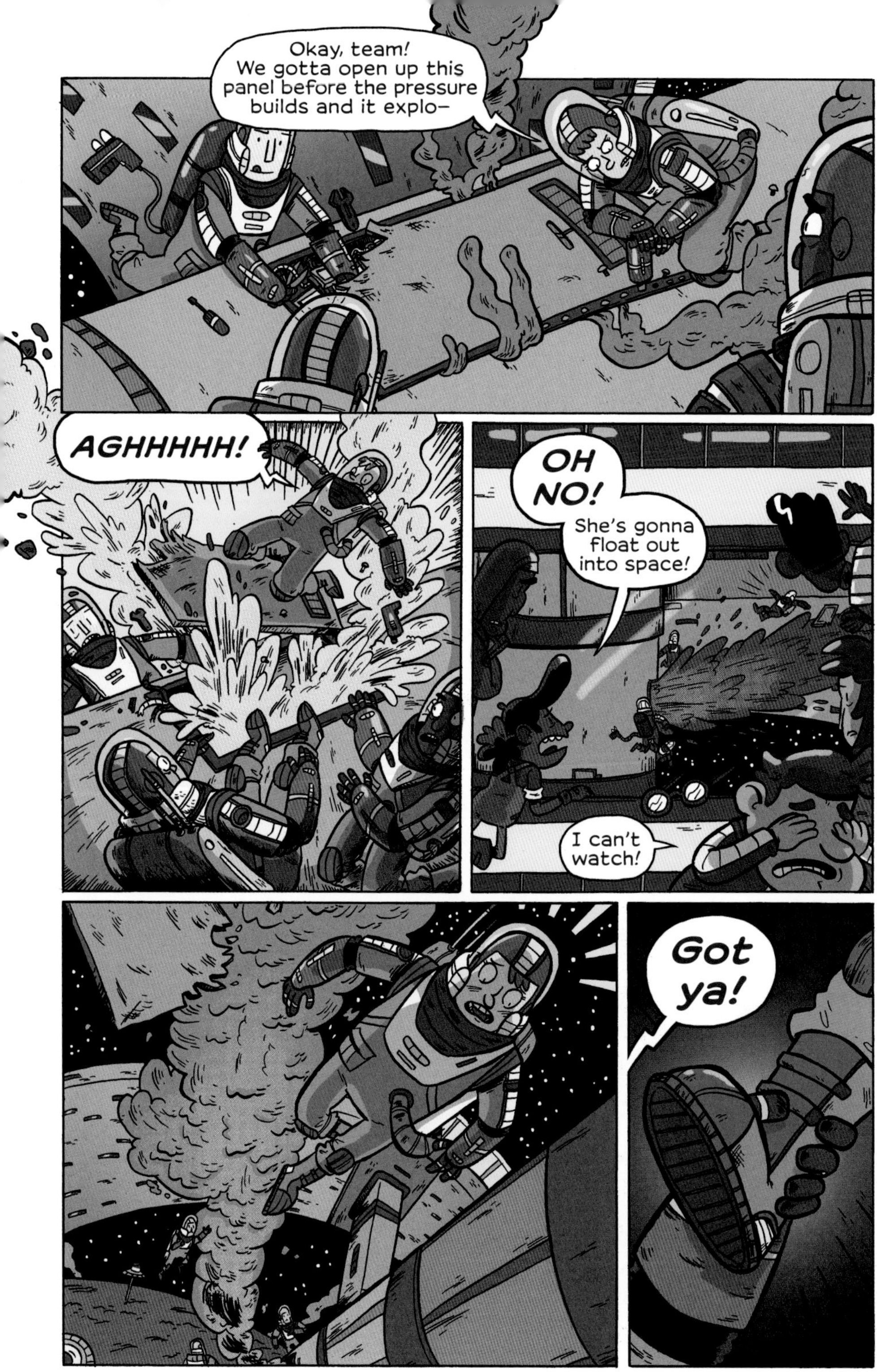
Okay, team! We gotta open up this panel before the pressure builds and it explo–
AGHHHHH!
OH NO!
She's gonna float out into space!
I can't watch!
Got ya!

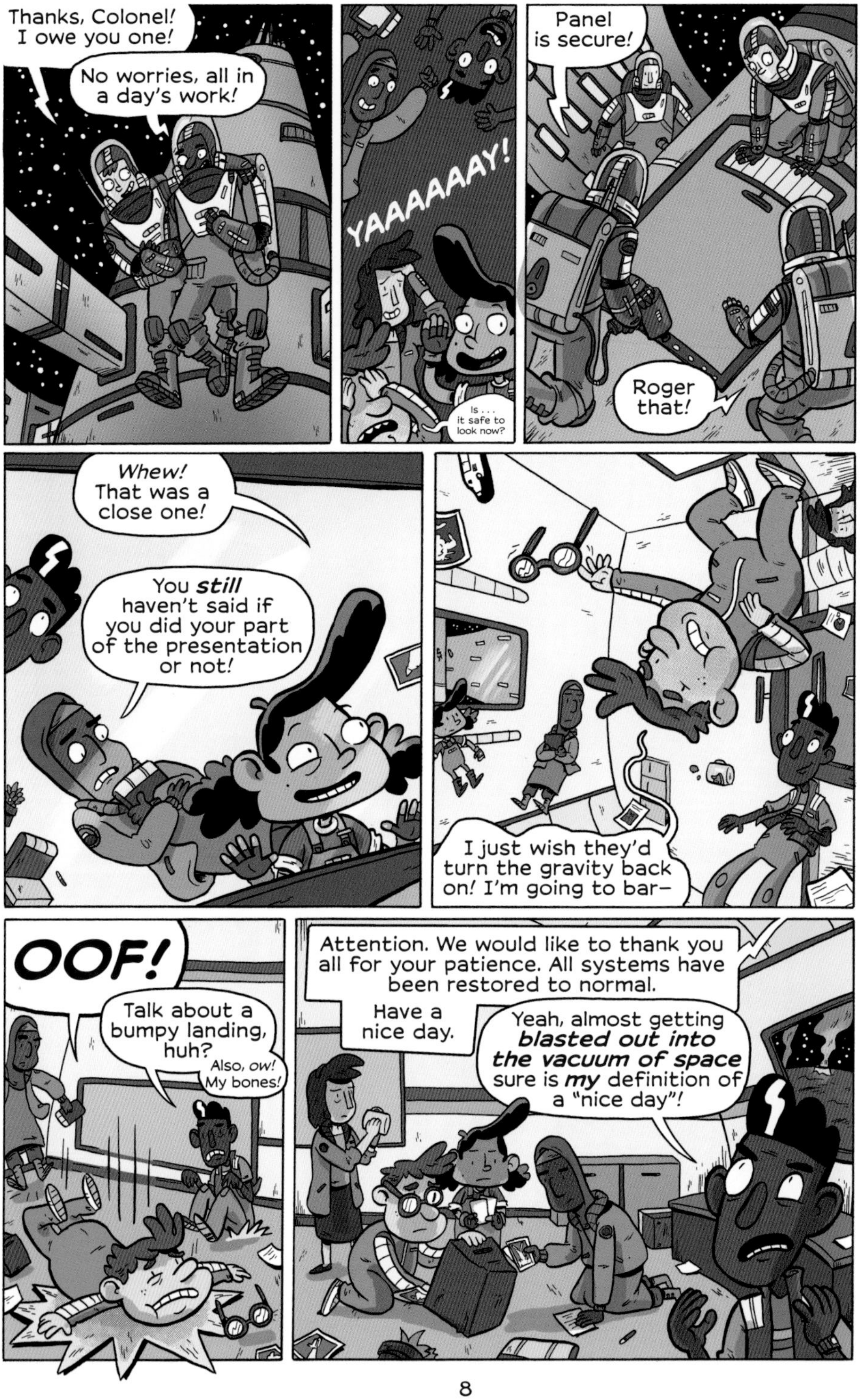

Thanks, Colonel! I owe you one!
No worries, all in a day's work!
YAAAAAAY!
Is . . . it safe to look now?
Panel is secure!
Roger that!
Whew! That was a close one!
You still haven't said if you did your part of the presentation or not!
I just wish they'd turn the gravity back on! I'm going to bar–
OOF!
Talk about a bumpy landing, huh?
Also, ow! My bones!
Attention. We would like to thank you all for your patience. All systems have been restored to normal.
Have a nice day.
Yeah, almost getting blasted out into the vacuum of space sure is my definition of a "nice day"!

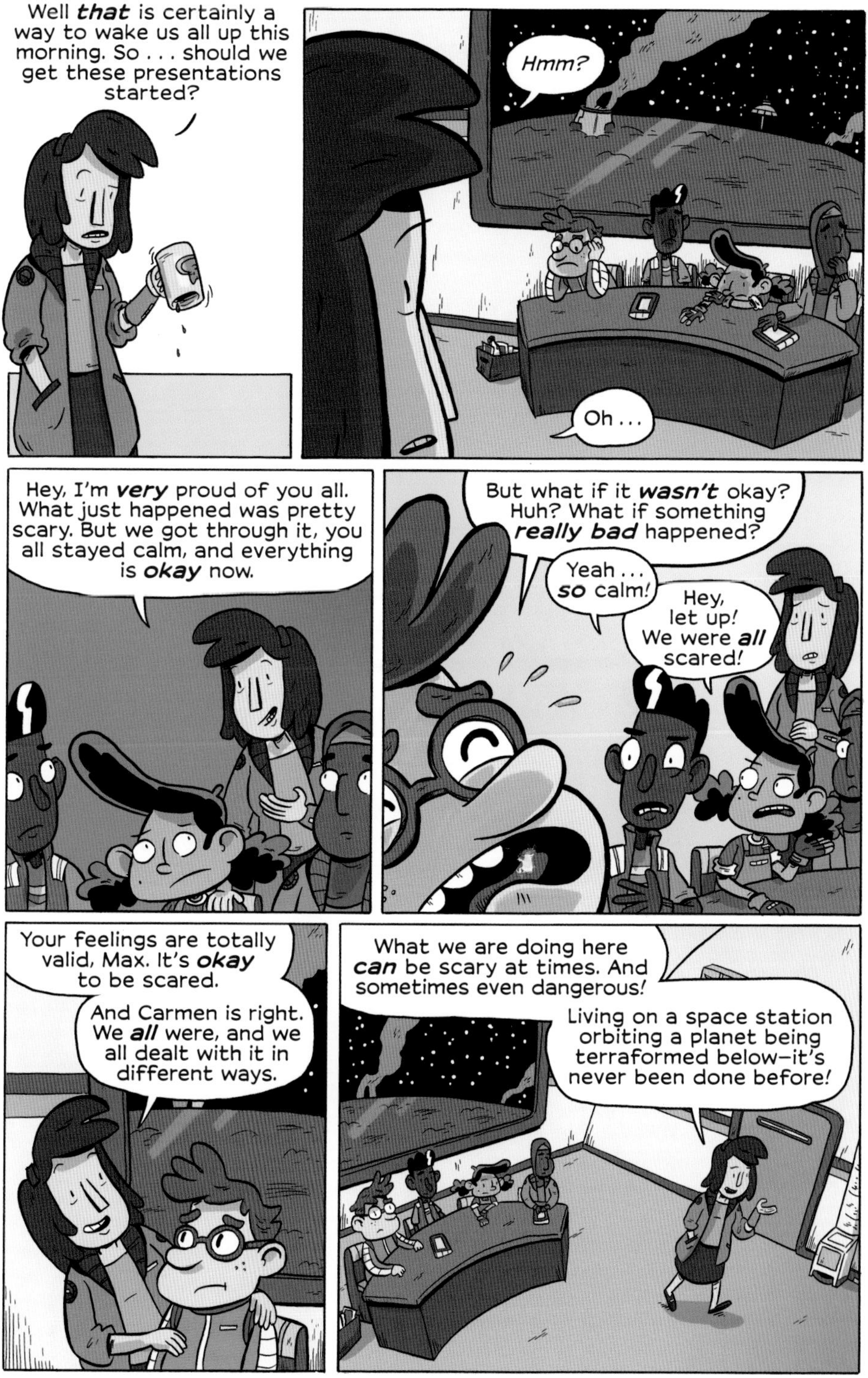
Well *that* is certainly a way to wake us all up this morning. So . . . should we get these presentations started?
Hmm?
Oh . . .
Hey, I'm *very* proud of you all. What just happened was pretty scary. But we got through it, you all stayed calm, and everything is *okay* now.
But what if it *wasn't* okay? Huh? What if something *really bad* happened?
Yeah . . . *so* calm!
Hey, let up! We were *all* scared!
Your feelings are totally valid, Max. It's *okay* to be scared.
And Carmen is right. We *all* were, and we all dealt with it in different ways.
What we are doing here *can* be scary at times. And sometimes even dangerous!
Living on a space station orbiting a planet being terraformed below—it's never been done before!

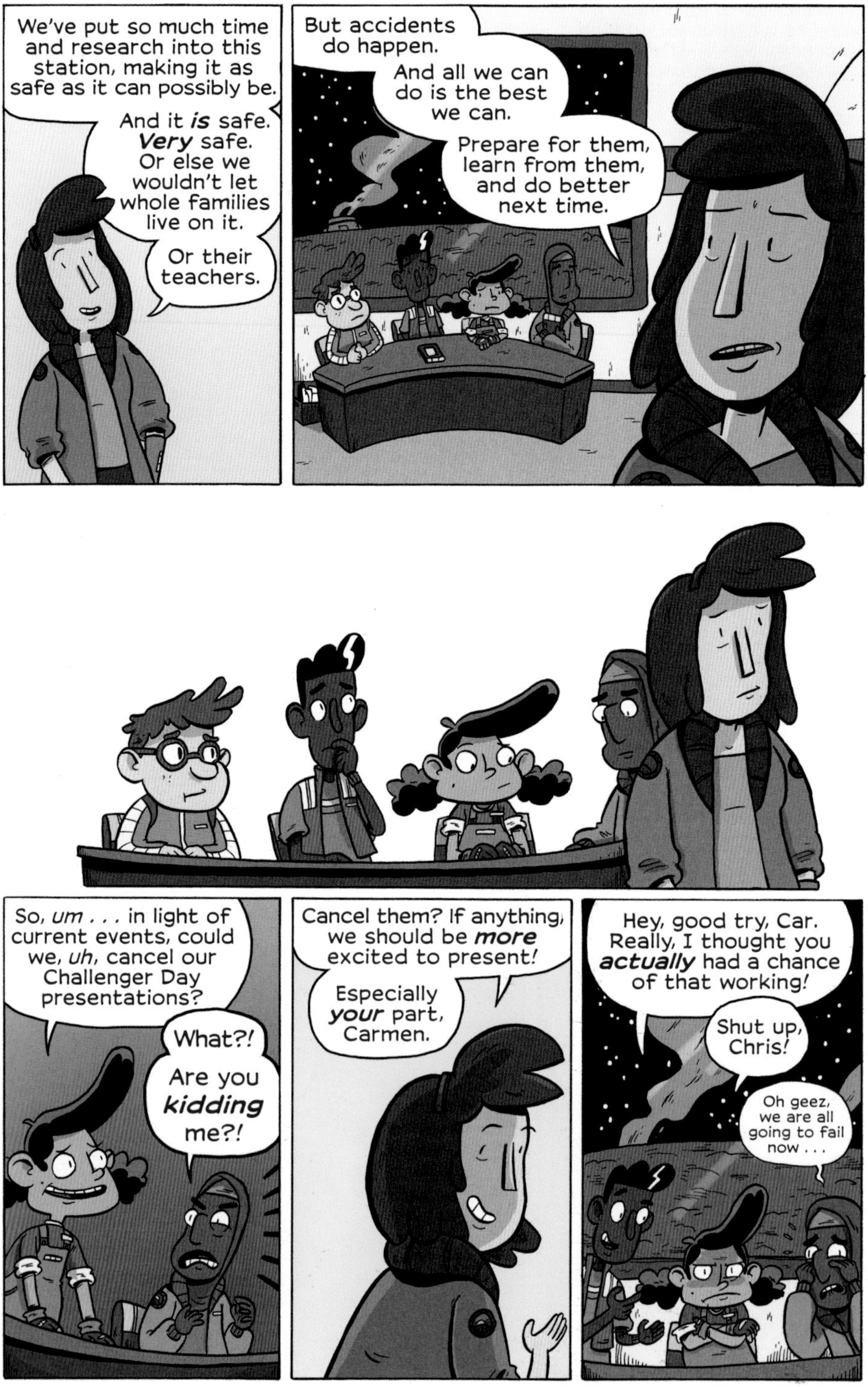
We've put so much time and research into this station, making it as safe as it can possibly be.
And it *is* safe. *Very* safe. Or else we wouldn't let whole families live on it.
Or their teachers.
But accidents do happen.
And all we can do is the best we can.
Prepare for them, learn from them, and do better next time.
So, *um . . .* in light of current events, could we, *uh*, cancel our Challenger Day presentations?
What?!
Are you *kidding* me?!
Cancel them? If anything, we should be *more* excited to present!
Especially *your* part, Carmen.
Hey, good try, Car. Really, I thought you *actually* had a chance of that working!
Shut up, Chris!
Oh geez, we are all going to fail now . . .

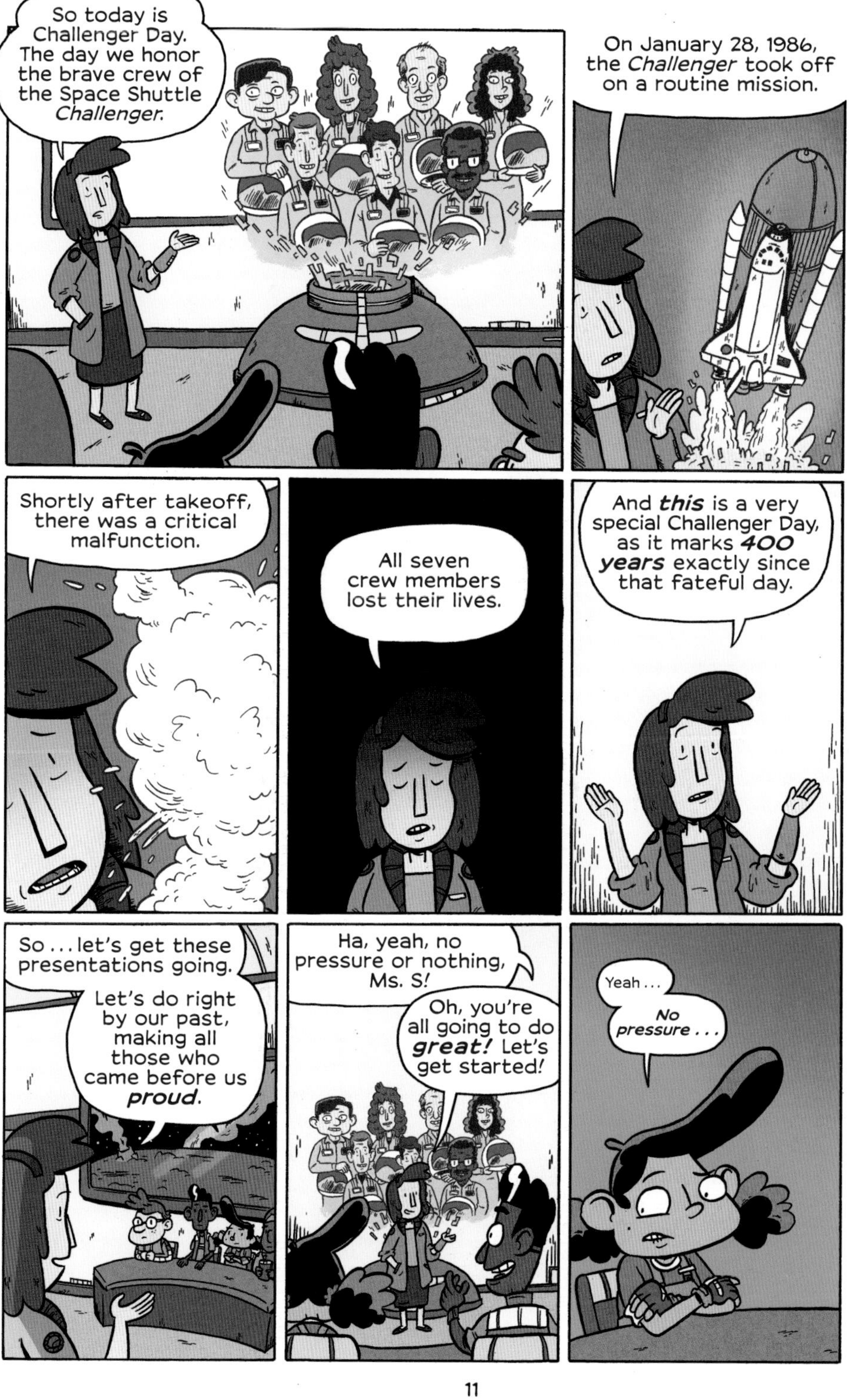

So today is Challenger Day. The day we honor the brave crew of the Space Shuttle *Challenger*.
On January 28, 1986, the *Challenger* took off on a routine mission.
Shortly after takeoff, there was a critical malfunction.
All seven crew members lost their lives.
And ***this*** is a very special Challenger Day, as it marks ***400 years*** exactly since that fateful day.
So . . . let's get these presentations going.
Let's do right by our past, making all those who came before us ***proud***.
Ha, yeah, no pressure or nothing, Ms. S!
Oh, you're all going to do ***great!*** Let's get started!
Yeah . . .
No pressure . . .

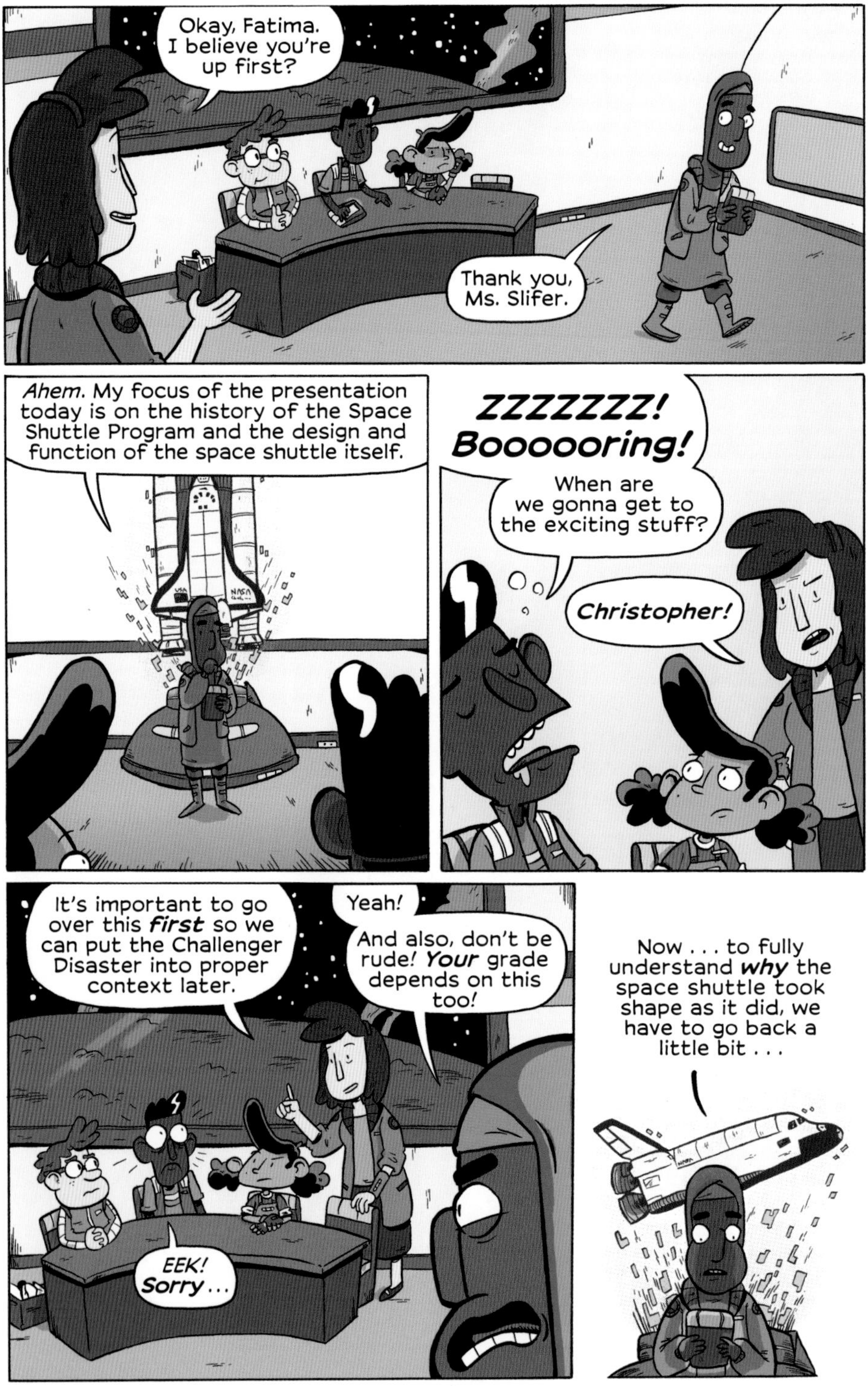
Okay, Fatima. I believe you're up first?
Thank you, Ms. Slifer.
Ahem. My focus of the presentation today is on the history of the Space Shuttle Program and the design and function of the space shuttle itself.
ZZZZZZZ! Boooooring!
When are we gonna get to the exciting stuff?
Christopher!
It's important to go over this ***first*** so we can put the Challenger Disaster into proper context later.
Yeah!
And also, don't be rude! ***Your*** grade depends on this too!
EEK! Sorry . . .
Now . . . to fully understand ***why*** the space shuttle took shape as it did, we have to go back a little bit . . .

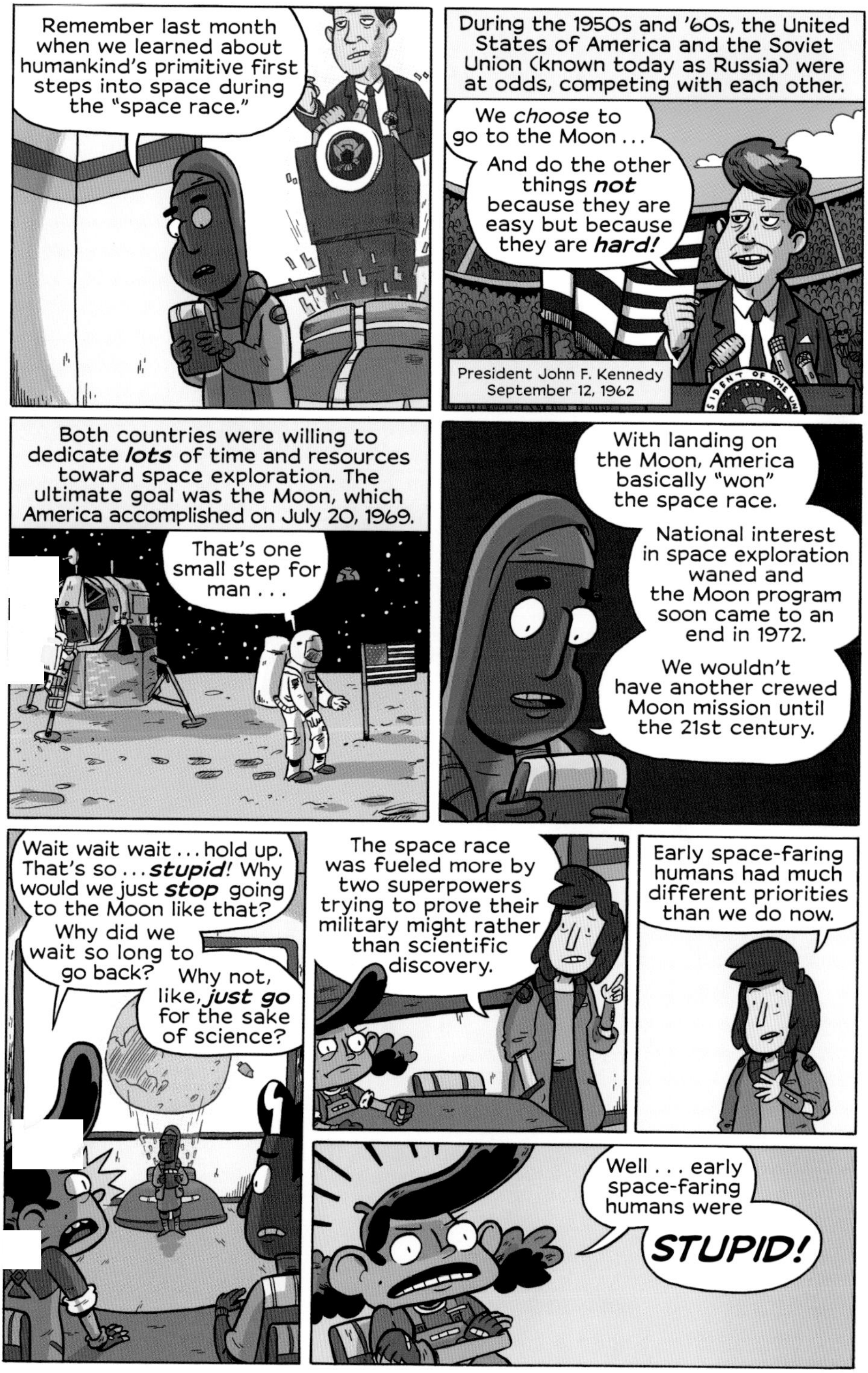
Remember last month when we learned about humankind's primitive first steps into space during the "space race."
During the 1950s and '60s, the United States of America and the Soviet Union (known today as Russia) were at odds, competing with each other.
We *choose* to go to the Moon . . .
And do the other things ***not*** because they are easy but because they are ***hard!***
President John F. Kennedy September 12, 1962
Both countries were willing to dedicate ***lots*** of time and resources toward space exploration. The ultimate goal was the Moon, which America accomplished on July 20, 1969.
That's one small step for man . . .
With landing on the Moon, America basically "won" the space race.
National interest in space exploration waned and the Moon program soon came to an end in 1972.
We wouldn't have another crewed Moon mission until the 21st century.
Wait wait wait . . . hold up. That's so . . . ***stupid!*** Why would we just ***stop*** going to the Moon like that?
Why did we wait so long to go back?
Why not, like, ***just go*** for the sake of science?
The space race was fueled more by two superpowers trying to prove their military might rather than scientific discovery.
Early space-faring humans had much different priorities than we do now.
Well . . . early space-faring humans were
STUPID!

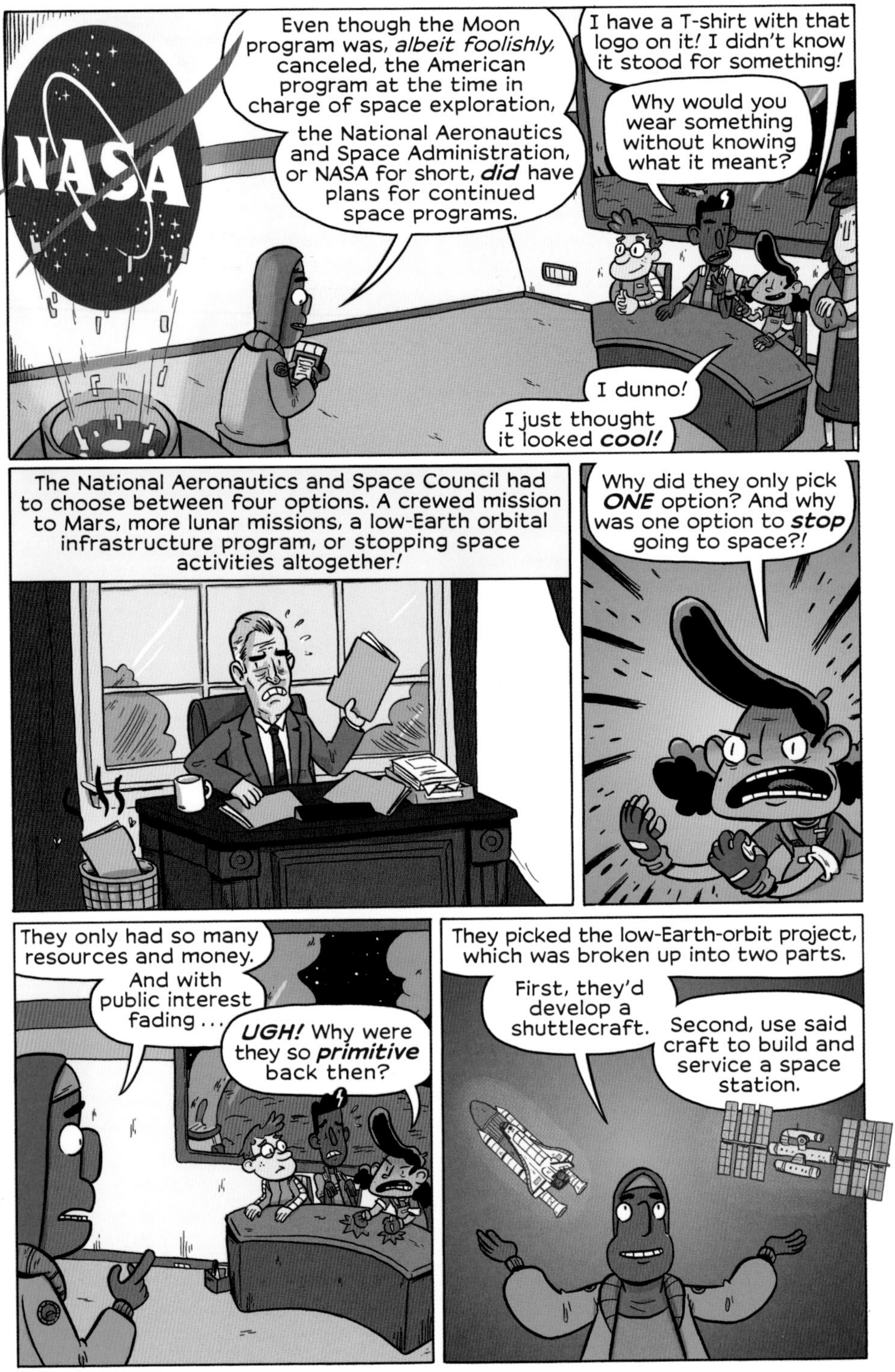
NASA
Even though the Moon program was, *albeit foolishly,* canceled, the American program at the time in charge of space exploration,
the National Aeronautics and Space Administration, or NASA for short, ***did*** have plans for continued space programs.
I have a T-shirt with that logo on it! I didn't know it stood for something!
Why would you wear something without knowing what it meant?
I dunno!
I just thought it looked ***cool!***
The National Aeronautics and Space Council had to choose between four options. A crewed mission to Mars, more lunar missions, a low-Earth orbital infrastructure program, or stopping space activities altogether!
Why did they only pick ***ONE*** option? And why was one option to ***stop*** going to space?!
They only had so many resources and money.
And with public interest fading . . .
UGH! Why were they so ***primitive*** back then?
They picked the low-Earth-orbit project, which was broken up into two parts.
First, they'd develop a shuttlecraft.
Second, use said craft to build and service a space station.

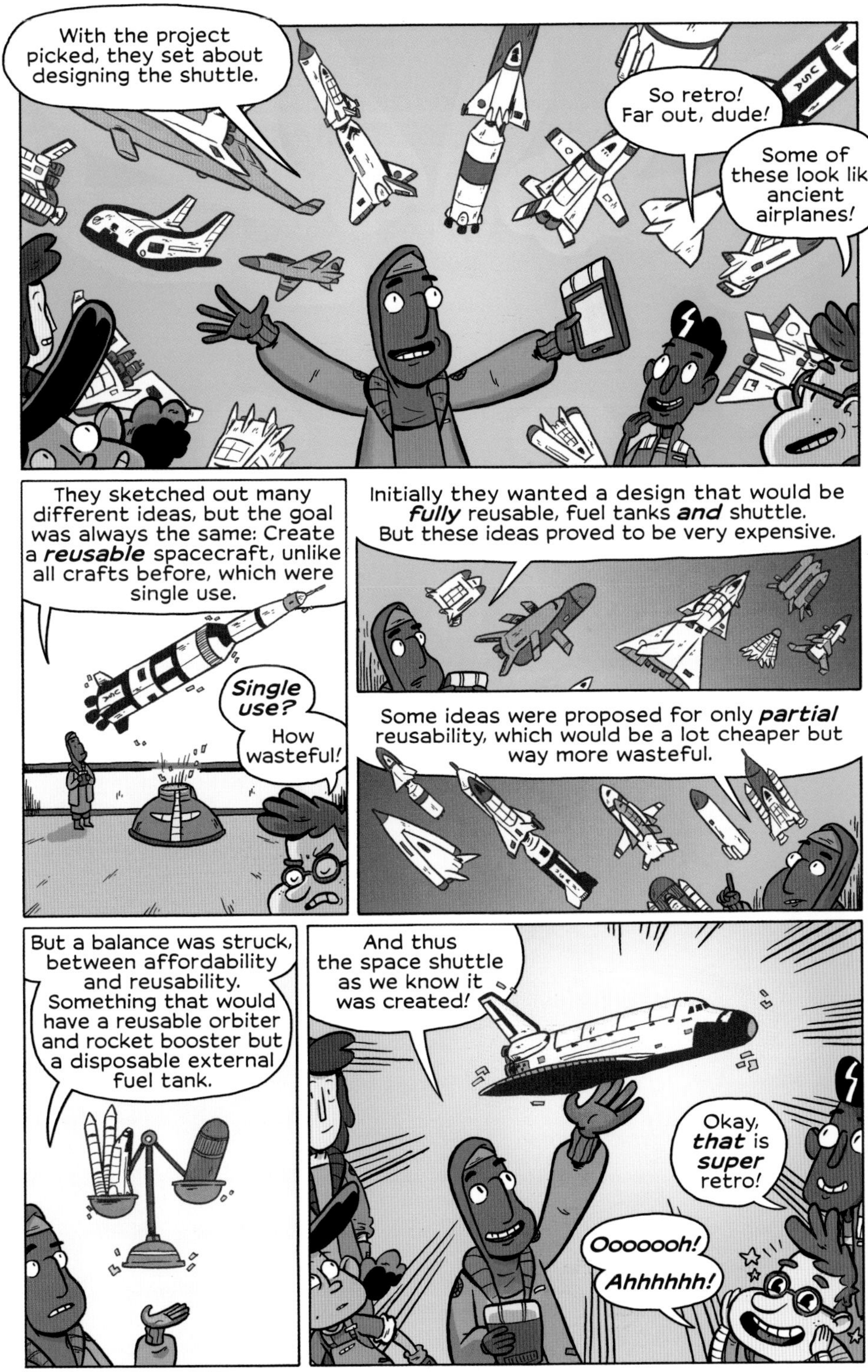
With the project picked, they set about designing the shuttle.
So retro! Far out, dude!
Some of these look like ancient airplanes!
They sketched out many different ideas, but the goal was always the same: Create a ***reusable*** spacecraft, unlike all crafts before, which were single use.
Single use? How wasteful!
Initially they wanted a design that would be ***fully*** reusable, fuel tanks ***and*** shuttle. But these ideas proved to be very expensive.
Some ideas were proposed for only ***partial*** reusability, which would be a lot cheaper but way more wasteful.
But a balance was struck, between affordability and reusability. Something that would have a reusable orbiter and rocket booster but a disposable external fuel tank.
And thus the space shuttle as we know it was created!
Okay, ***that*** is ***super*** retro!
Ooooooh!
Ahhhhhh!

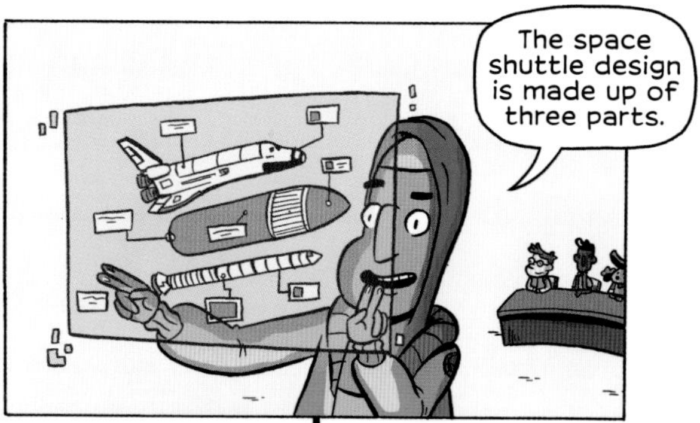
The space shuttle design is made up of three parts.

The two ***solid rocket boosters,*** or SRBs for short. They provided the initial liftoff with a burn time of just over two minutes. As the name suggests, they are filled with ***solid*** fuel, which does not burn as evenly as liquid fuel.

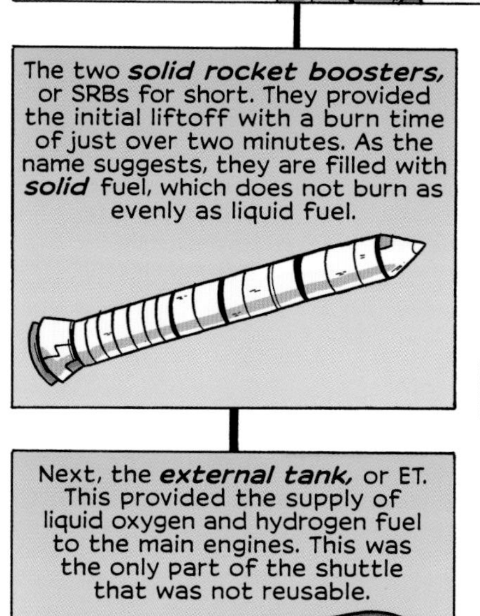

Next, the ***external tank,*** or ET. This provided the supply of liquid oxygen and hydrogen fuel to the main engines. This was the only part of the shuttle that was not reusable.

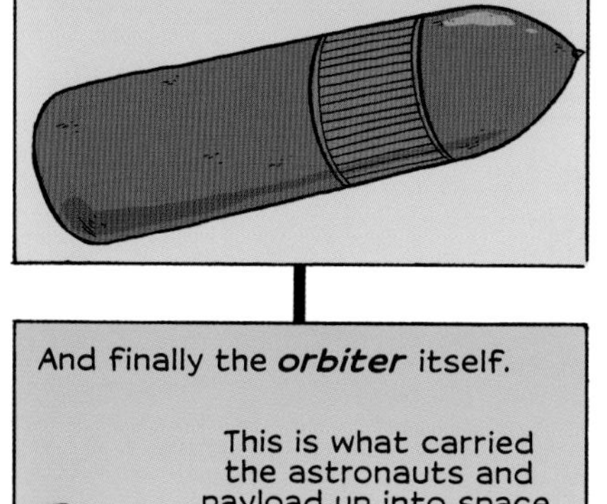

And finally the ***orbiter*** itself.

This is what carried the astronauts and payload up into space.

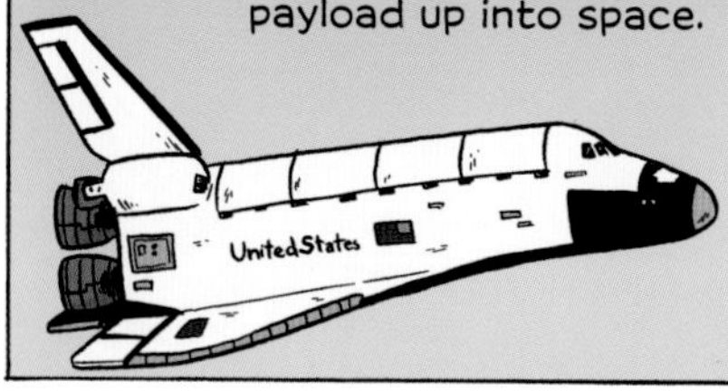
United States

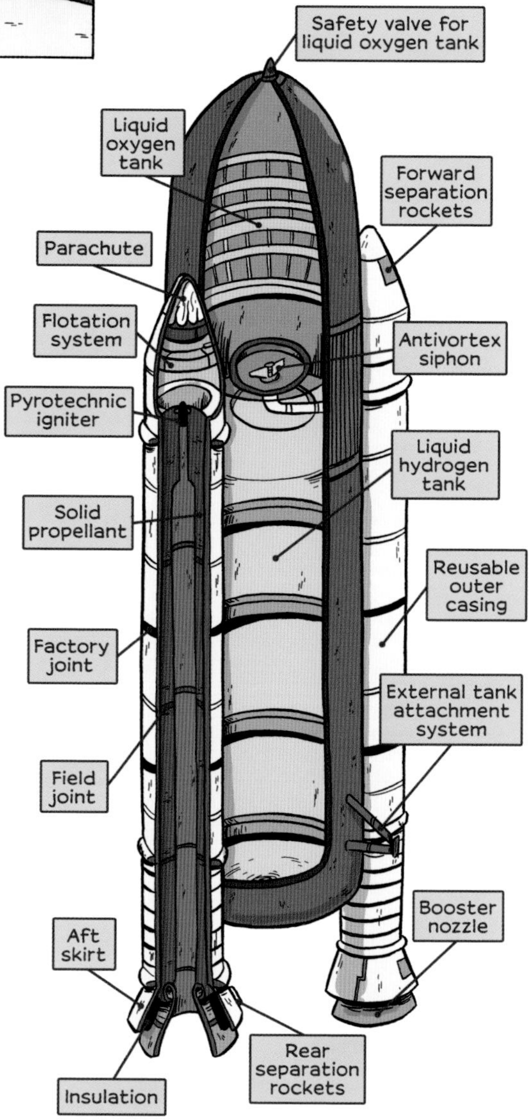
Safety valve for liquid oxygen tank
Liquid oxygen tank
Forward separation rockets
Parachute
Flotation system
Antivortex siphon
Pyrotechnic igniter
Liquid hydrogen tank
Solid propellant
Reusable outer casing
Factory joint
External tank attachment system
Field joint
Booster nozzle
Aft skirt
Rear separation rockets
Insulation

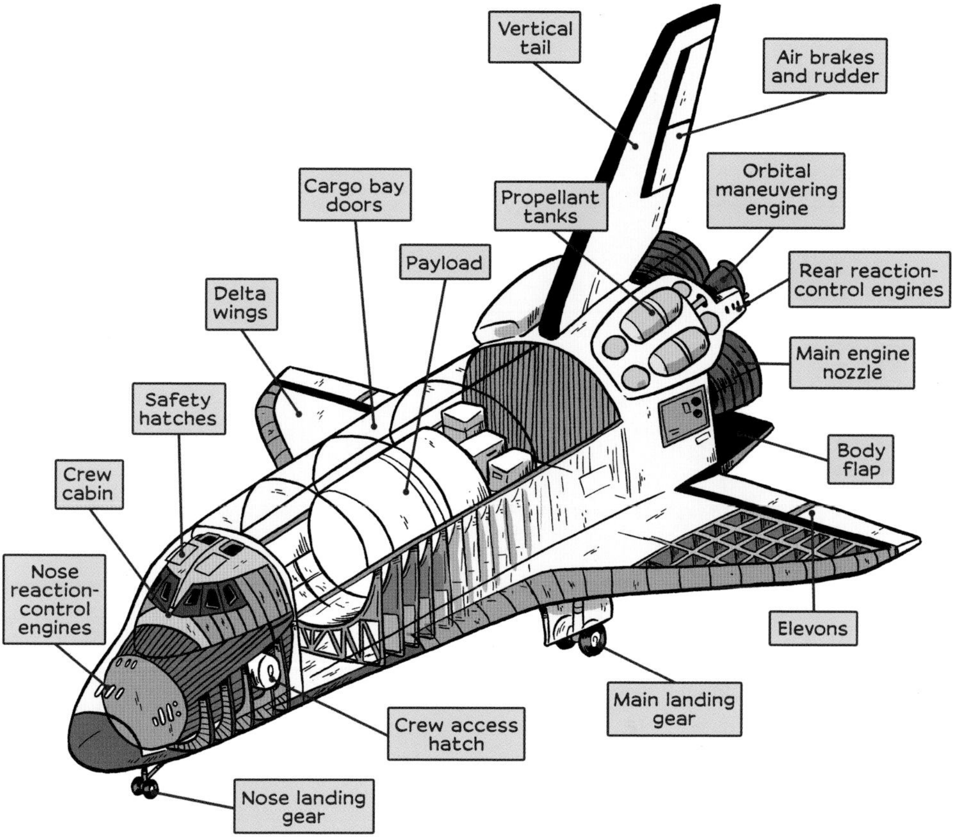
Vertical tail
Air brakes and rudder
Orbital maneuvering engine
Cargo bay doors
Propellant tanks
Payload
Rear reaction-control engines
Delta wings
Main engine nozzle
Safety hatches
Body flap
Crew cabin
Nose reaction-control engines
Elevons
Main landing gear
Crew access hatch
Nose landing gear

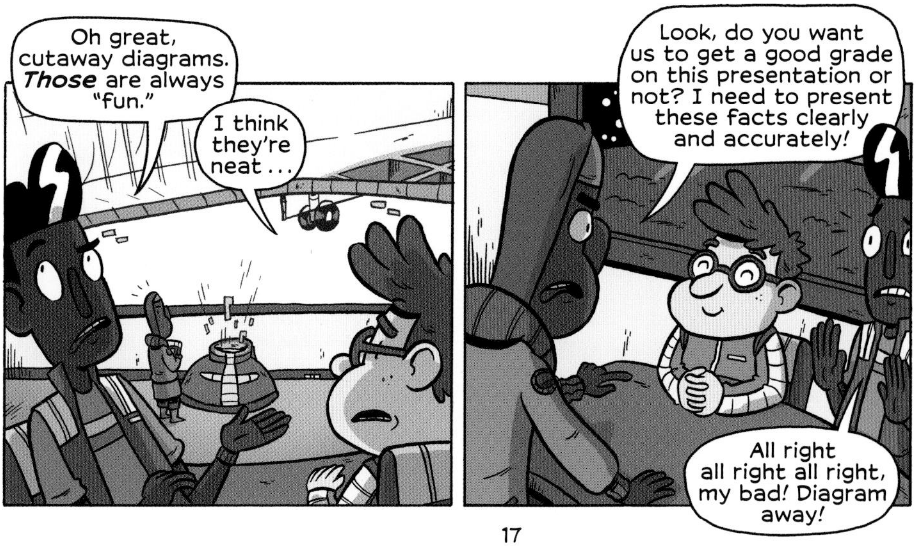
Oh great, cutaway diagrams. *Those* are always "fun."
I think they're neat . . .
Look, do you want us to get a good grade on this presentation or not? I need to present these facts clearly and accurately!
All right all right all right, my bad! Diagram away!

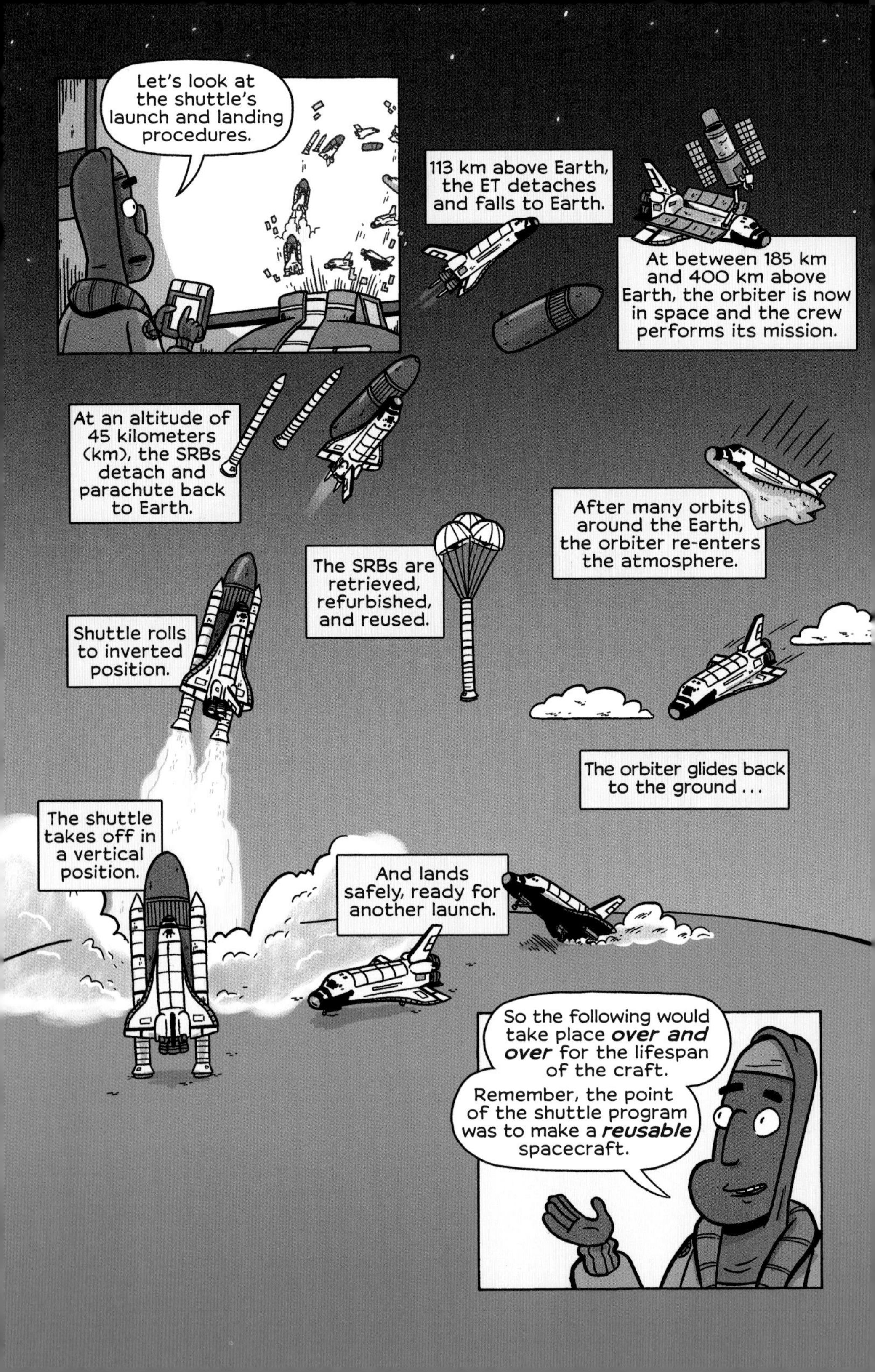
Let's look at the shuttle's launch and landing procedures.
The shuttle takes off in a vertical position.
Shuttle rolls to inverted position.
At an altitude of 45 kilometers (km), the SRBs detach and parachute back to Earth.
The SRBs are retrieved, refurbished, and reused.
113 km above Earth, the ET detaches and falls to Earth.
At between 185 km and 400 km above Earth, the orbiter is now in space and the crew performs its mission.
After many orbits around the Earth, the orbiter re-enters the atmosphere.
The orbiter glides back to the ground . . .
And lands safely, ready for another launch.
So the following would take place *over and over* for the lifespan of the craft.
Remember, the point of the shuttle program was to make a *reusable* spacecraft.

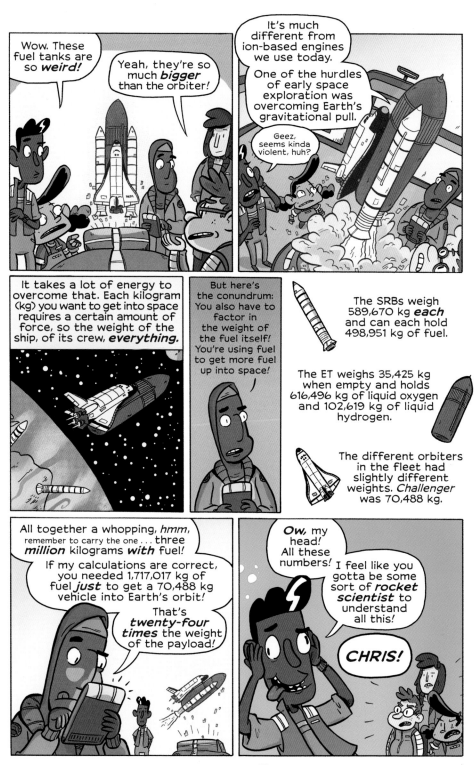

Wow. These fuel tanks are so *weird!*

Yeah, they're so much *bigger* than the orbiter!

It's much different from ion-based engines we use today.

One of the hurdles of early space exploration was overcoming Earth's gravitational pull.

Geez, seems kinda violent, huh?

It takes a lot of energy to overcome that. Each kilogram (kg) you want to get into space requires a certain amount of force, so the weight of the ship, of its crew, *everything*.

But here's the conundrum: You also have to factor in the weight of the fuel itself! You're using fuel to get more fuel up into space!

The SRBs weigh 589,670 kg *each* and can each hold 498,951 kg of fuel.

The ET weighs 35,425 kg when empty and holds 616,496 kg of liquid oxygen and 102,619 kg of liquid hydrogen.

The different orbiters in the fleet had slightly different weights. *Challenger* was 70,488 kg.

All together a whopping, hmm, remember to carry the one ... three *million* kilograms *with* fuel!

If my calculations are correct, you needed 1,717,017 kg of fuel *just* to get a 70,488 kg vehicle into Earth's orbit!

That's *twenty-four times* the weight of the payload!

Ow, my head! All these numbers! I feel like you gotta be some sort of *rocket scientist* to understand all this!

CHRIS!

19

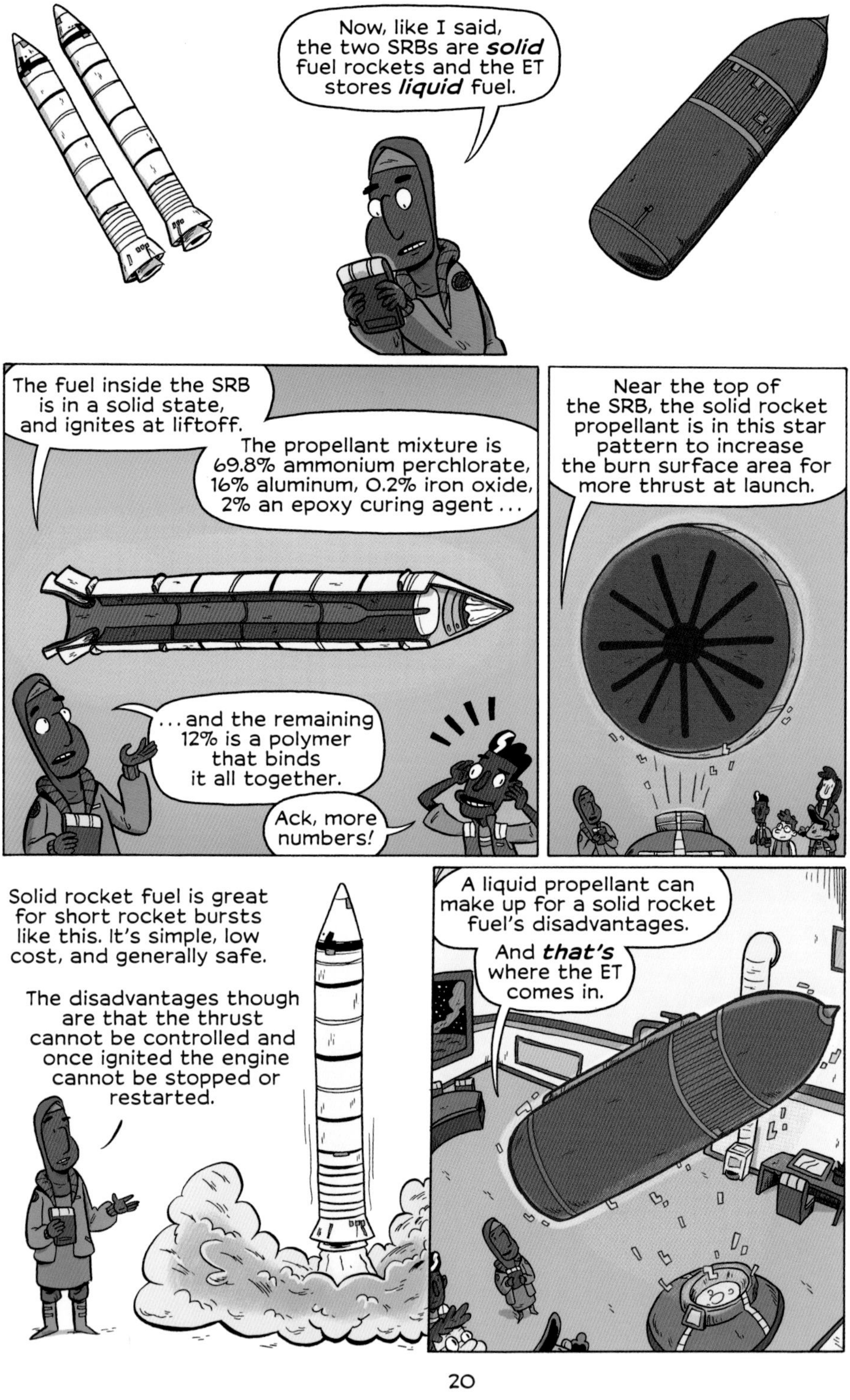

Now, like I said, the two SRBs are ***solid*** fuel rockets and the ET stores ***liquid*** fuel.
The fuel inside the SRB is in a solid state, and ignites at liftoff.
The propellant mixture is 69.8% ammonium perchlorate, 16% aluminum, 0.2% iron oxide, 2% an epoxy curing agent . . .
. . . and the remaining 12% is a polymer that binds it all together.
Ack, more numbers!
Near the top of the SRB, the solid rocket propellant is in this star pattern to increase the burn surface area for more thrust at launch.
Solid rocket fuel is great for short rocket bursts like this. It's simple, low cost, and generally safe.
The disadvantages though are that the thrust cannot be controlled and once ignited the engine cannot be stopped or restarted.
A liquid propellant can make up for a solid rocket fuel's disadvantages.
And ***that's*** where the ET comes in.

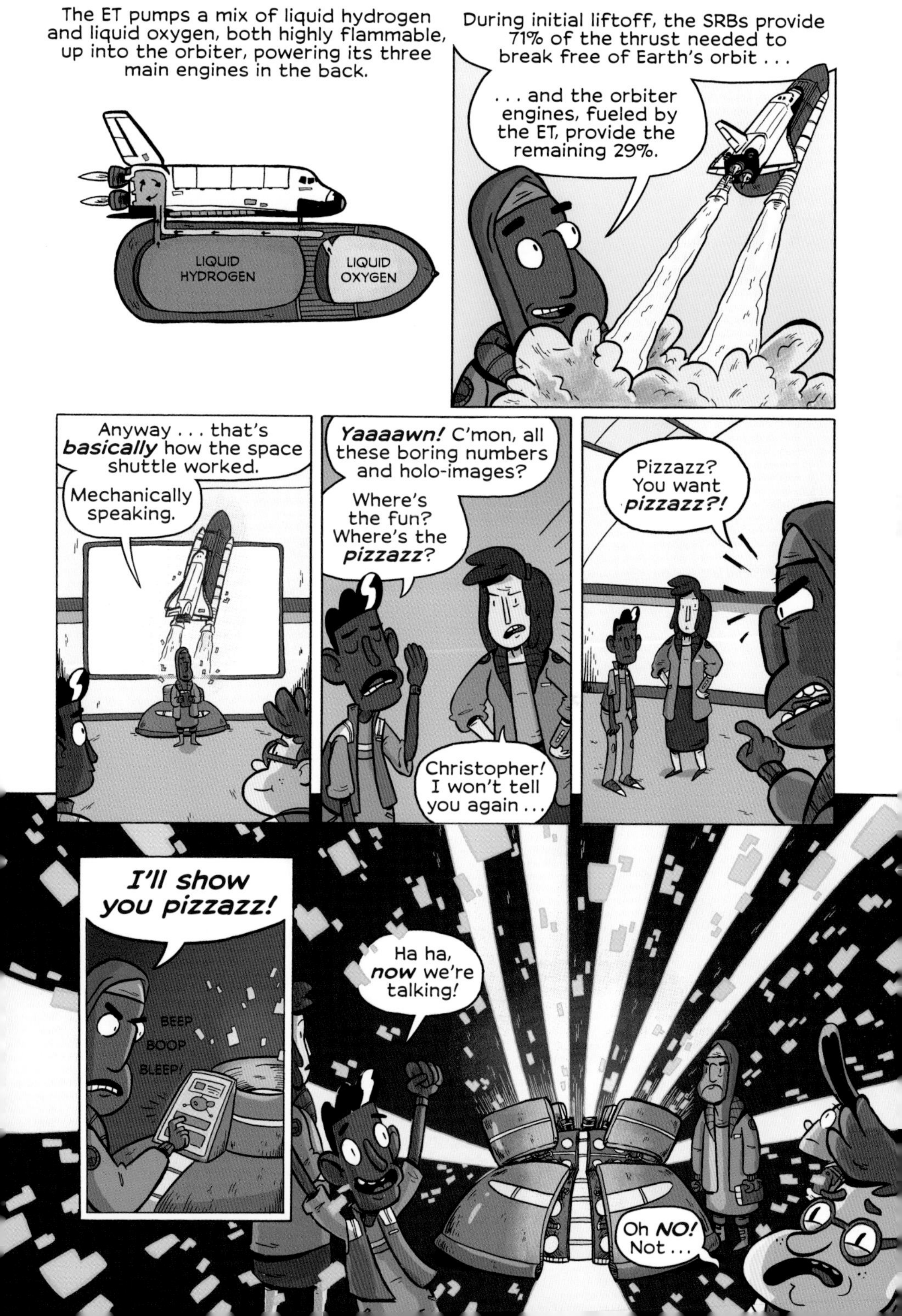

The ET pumps a mix of liquid hydrogen and liquid oxygen, both highly flammable, up into the orbiter, powering its three main engines in the back.
LIQUID HYDROGEN
LIQUID OXYGEN
During initial liftoff, the SRBs provide 71% of the thrust needed to break free of Earth's orbit . . .
. . . and the orbiter engines, fueled by the ET, provide the remaining 29%.
Anyway . . . that's ***basically*** how the space shuttle worked.
Mechanically speaking.
Yaaaawn! C'mon, all these boring numbers and holo-images?
Where's the fun? Where's the ***pizzazz***?
Christopher! I won't tell you again . . .
Pizzazz? You want ***pizzazz?!***
I'll show you pizzazz!
BEEP
BOOP
BLEEP!
Ha ha, ***now*** we're talking!
Oh ***NO!*** Not . . .

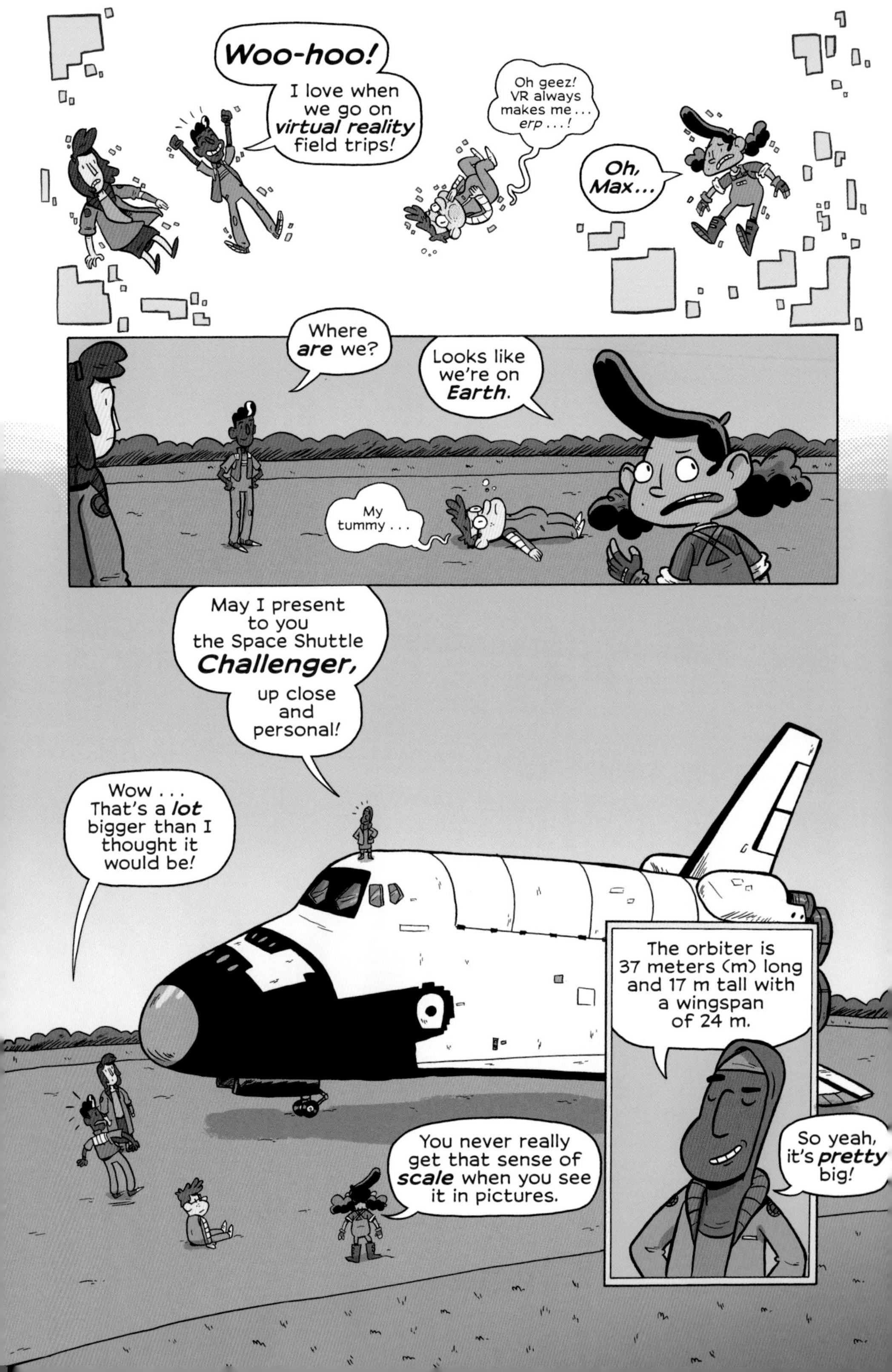
Woo-hoo! I love when we go on virtual reality field trips!
Oh geez! VR always makes me . . . erp . . . !
Oh, Max...
Where are we?
Looks like we're on Earth.
My tummy . . .
May I present to you the Space Shuttle Challenger, up close and personal!
Wow . . . That's a lot bigger than I thought it would be!
The orbiter is 37 meters (m) long and 17 m tall with a wingspan of 24 m.
You never really get that sense of scale when you see it in pictures.
So yeah, it's pretty big!

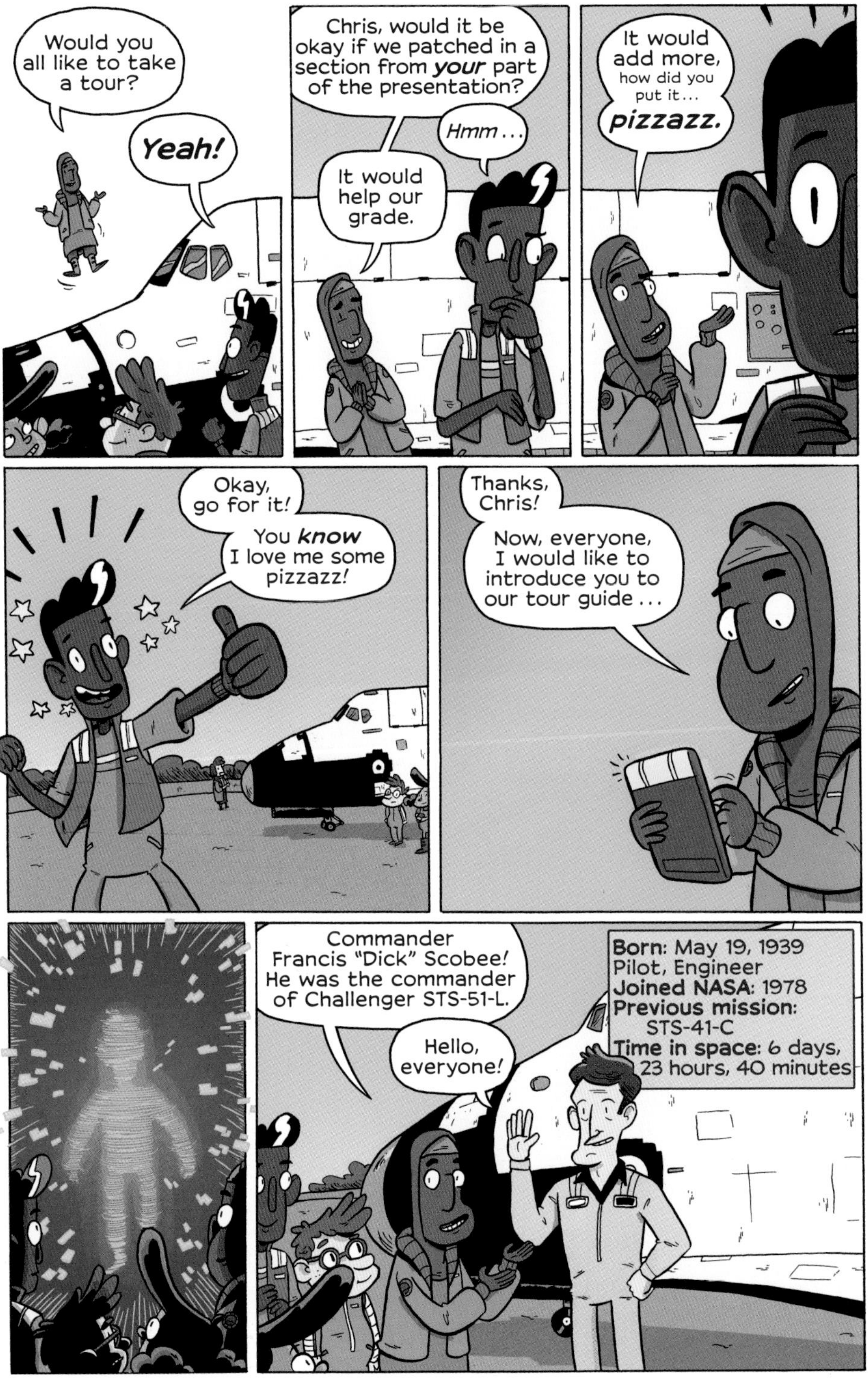
Would you all like to take a tour?
Yeah!
Chris, would it be okay if we patched in a section from *your* part of the presentation?
Hmm . . .
It would help our grade.
It would add more, how did you put it . . . **pizzazz.**
Okay, go for it!
You *know* I love me some pizzazz!
Thanks, Chris!
Now, everyone, I would like to introduce you to our tour guide . . .
Commander Francis "Dick" Scobee! He was the commander of Challenger STS-51-L.
Hello, everyone!
Born: May 19, 1939
Pilot, Engineer
Joined NASA: 1978
Previous mission: STS-41-C
Time in space: 6 days, 23 hours, 40 minutes

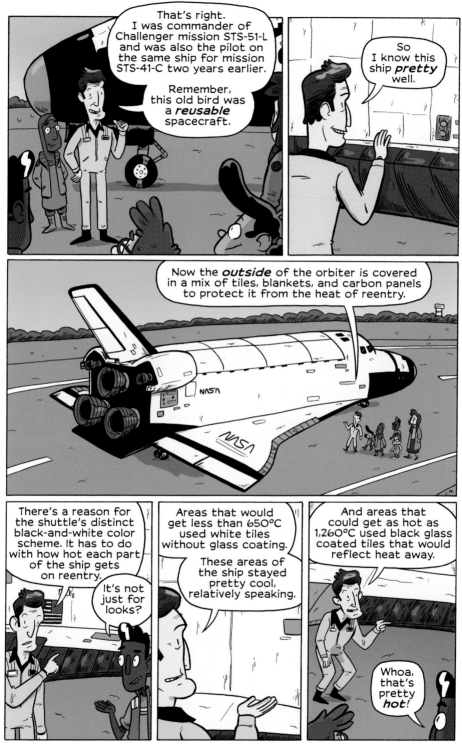

That's right. I was commander of Challenger mission STS-51-L and was also the pilot on the same ship for mission STS-41-C two years earlier.

Remember, this old bird was a *reusable* spacecraft.

So I know this ship *pretty* well.

Now the *outside* of the orbiter is covered in a mix of tiles, blankets, and carbon panels to protect it from the heat of reentry.

There's a reason for the shuttle's distinct black-and-white color scheme. It has to do with how hot each part of the ship gets on reentry.

It's not just for looks?

Areas that would get less than 650°C used white tiles without glass coating.

These areas of the ship stayed pretty cool, relatively speaking.

And areas that could get as hot as 1,260°C used black glass coated tiles that would reflect heat away.

Whoa, that's pretty *hot!*

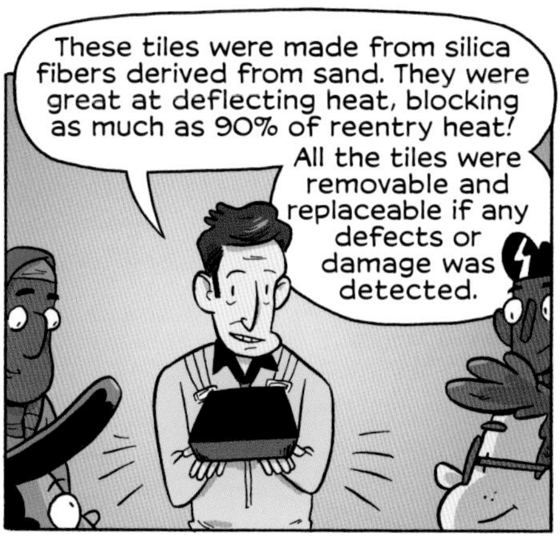
These tiles were made from silica fibers derived from sand. They were great at deflecting heat, blocking as much as 90% of reentry heat!
All the tiles were removable and replaceable if any defects or damage was detected.

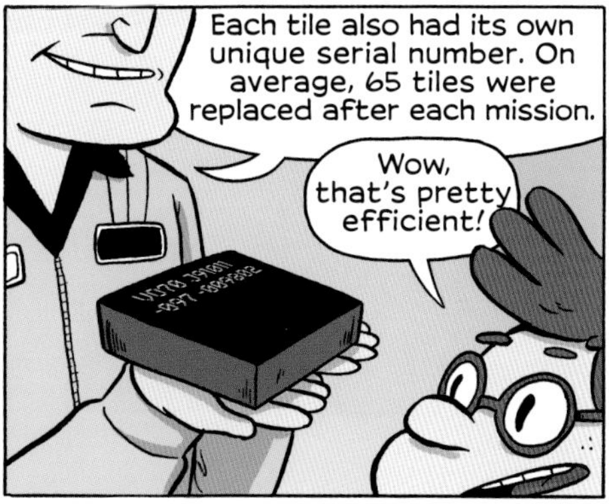
Each tile also had its own unique serial number. On average, 65 tiles were replaced after each mission.
Wow, that's pretty efficient!

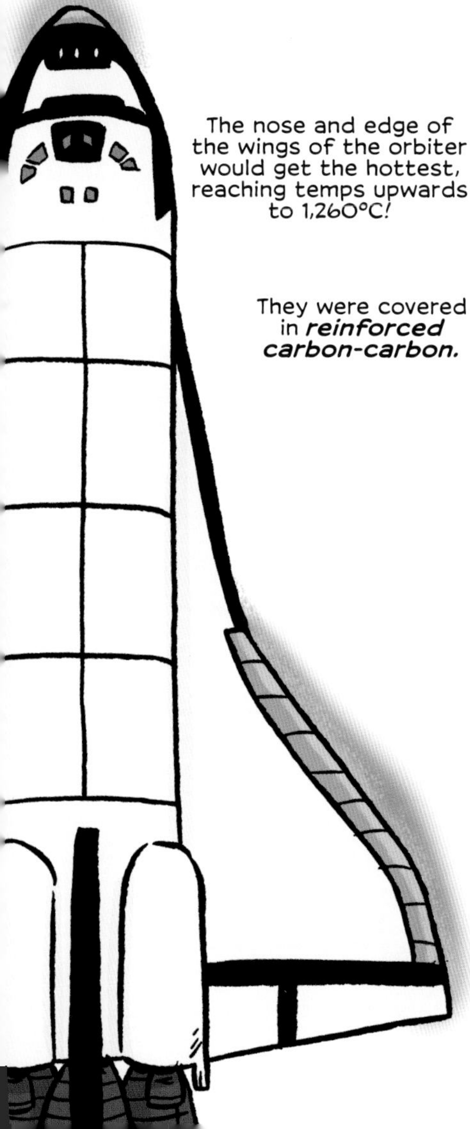
The nose and edge of the wings of the orbiter would get the hottest, reaching temps upwards to 1,260°C!
They were covered in ***reinforced carbon-carbon.***

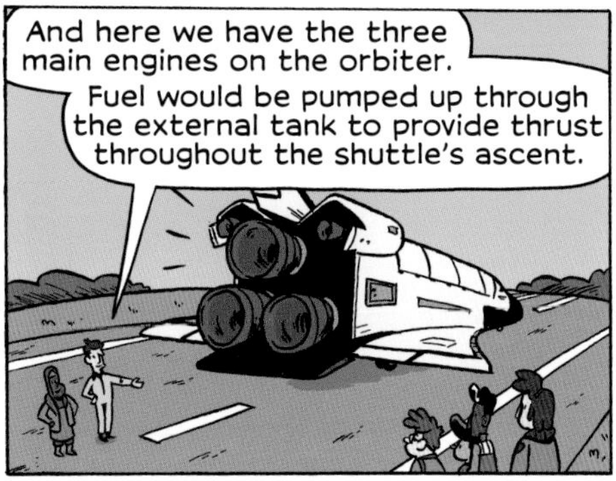
And here we have the three main engines on the orbiter.
Fuel would be pumped up through the external tank to provide thrust throughout the shuttle's ascent.

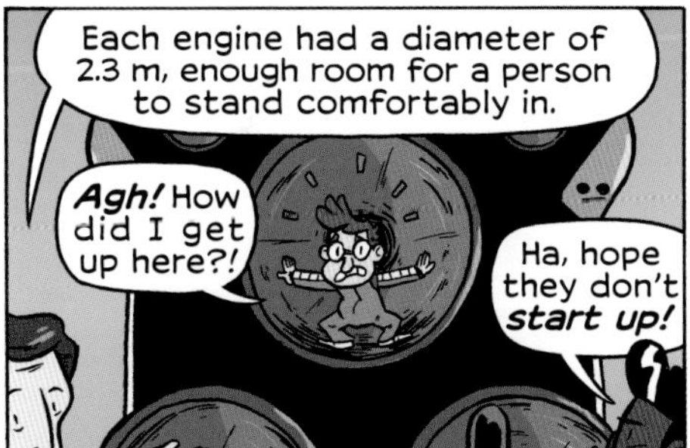
Each engine had a diameter of 2.3 m, enough room for a person to stand comfortably in.
Agh! How did I get up here?!
Ha, hope they don't ***start up!***

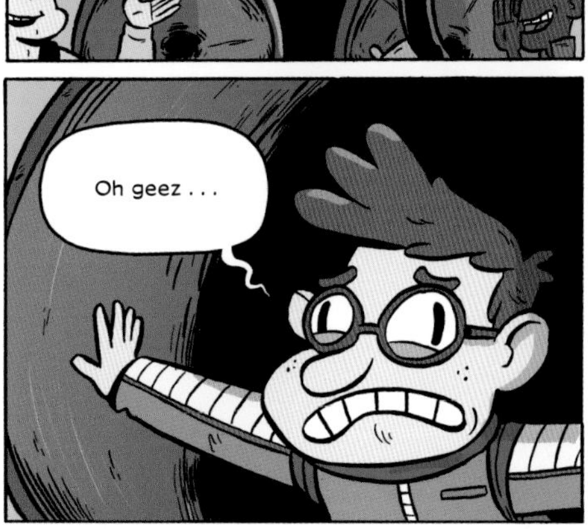
Oh geez . . .

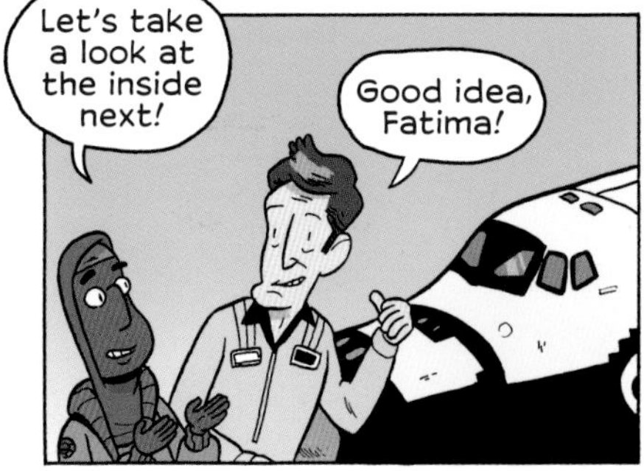
Let's take a look at the inside next!
Good idea, Fatima!

The ***crew compartment*** took up only the front part of the orbiter. It has 708 cubic meters (m^3) of space, or 800 m^3 if you put the moveable airlock on the outside of the ship.

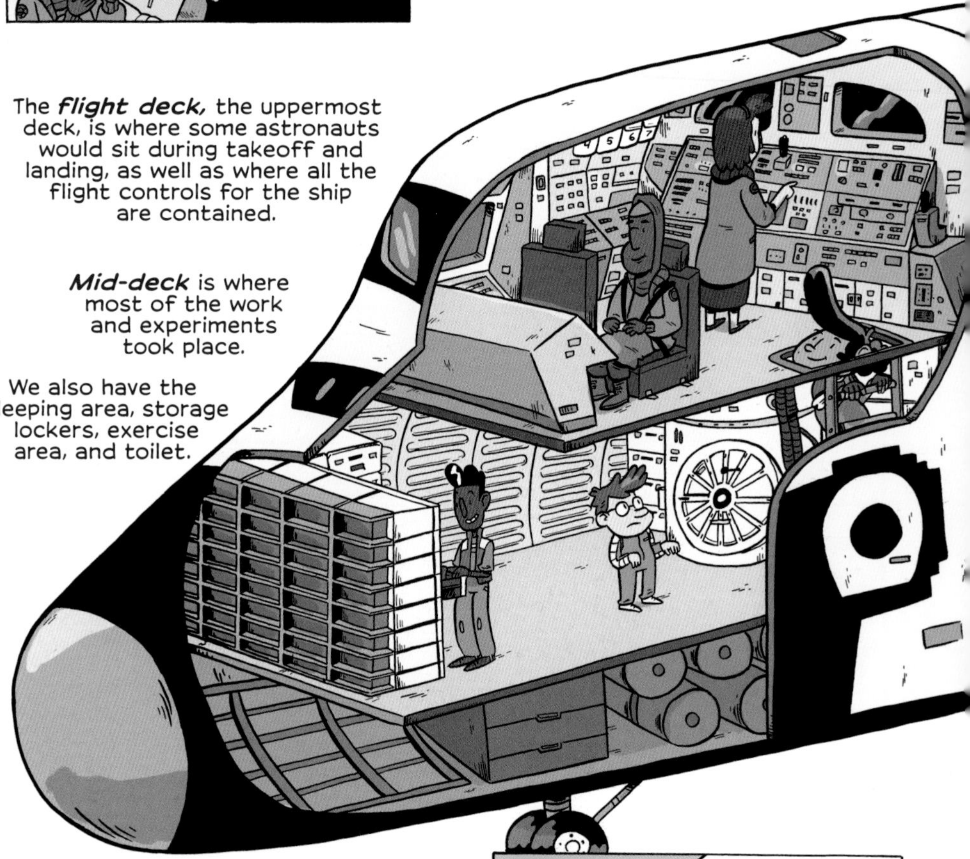

The ***flight deck,*** the uppermost deck, is where some astronauts would sit during takeoff and landing, as well as where all the flight controls for the ship are contained.

Mid-deck is where most of the work and experiments took place.

We also have the sleeping area, storage lockers, exercise area, and toilet.

And finally at the bottom is the appropriately named ***lower deck.*** It's mainly where life support equipment and electrical items are kept.

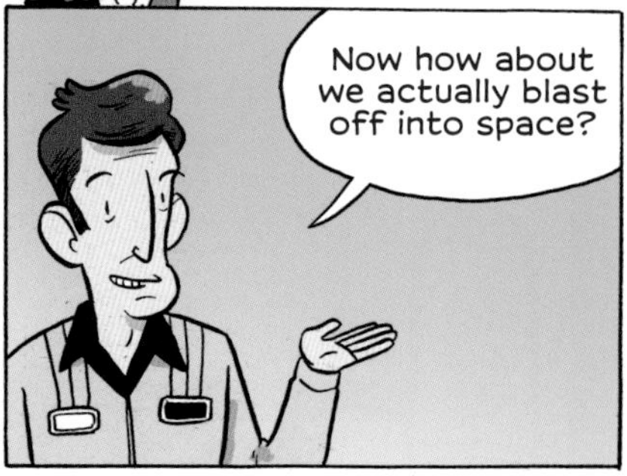
Now how about we actually blast off into space?

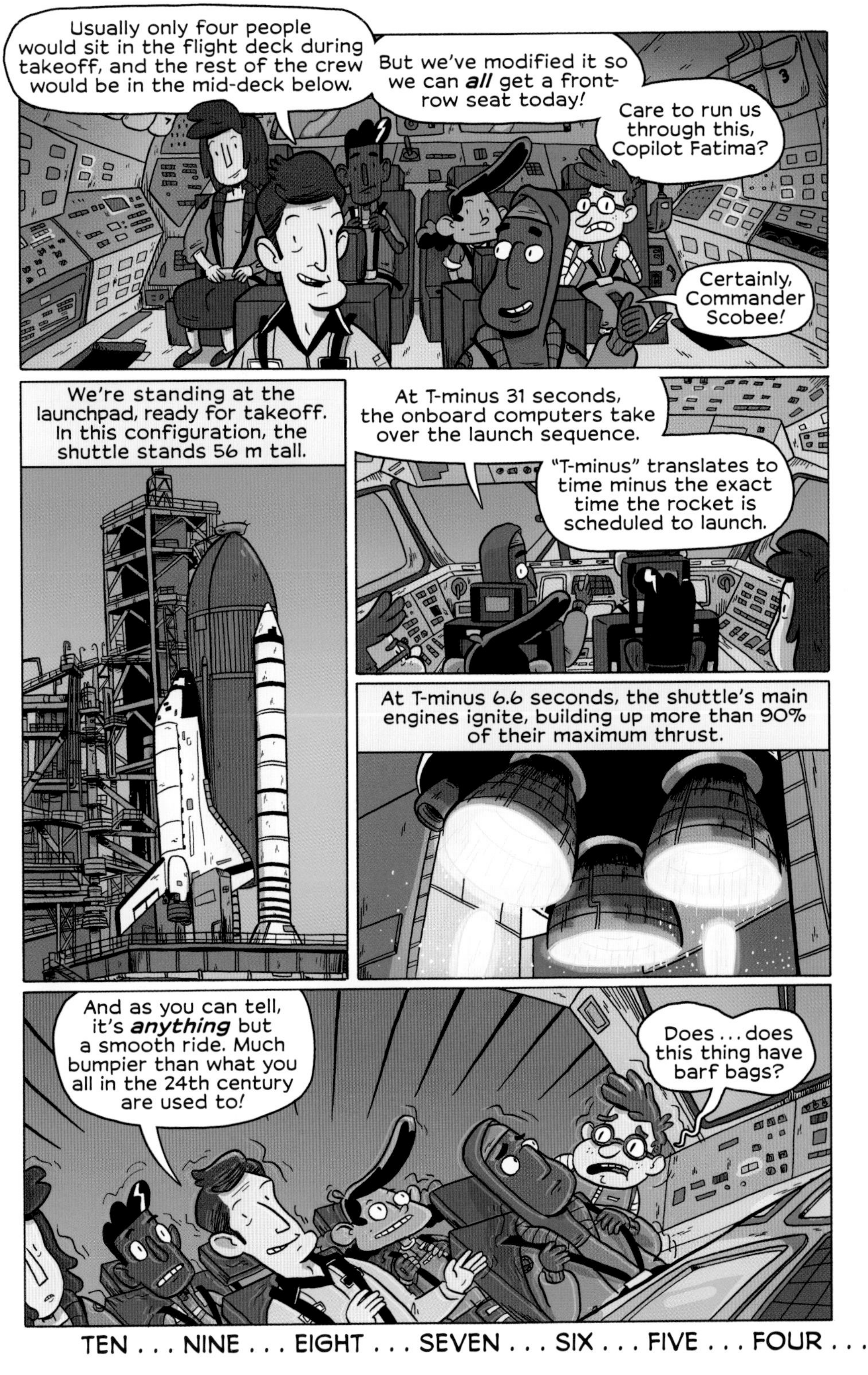
Usually only four people would sit in the flight deck during takeoff, and the rest of the crew would be in the mid-deck below.
But we've modified it so we can ***all*** get a front-row seat today!
Care to run us through this, Copilot Fatima?
Certainly, Commander Scobee!
We're standing at the launchpad, ready for takeoff. In this configuration, the shuttle stands 56 m tall.
At T-minus 31 seconds, the onboard computers take over the launch sequence.
"T-minus" translates to time minus the exact time the rocket is scheduled to launch.
At T-minus 6.6 seconds, the shuttle's main engines ignite, building up more than 90% of their maximum thrust.
And as you can tell, it's ***anything*** but a smooth ride. Much bumpier than what you all in the 24th century are used to!
Does . . . does this thing have barf bags?

TEN . . . NINE . . . EIGHT . . . SEVEN . . . SIX . . . FIVE . . . FOUR . . .

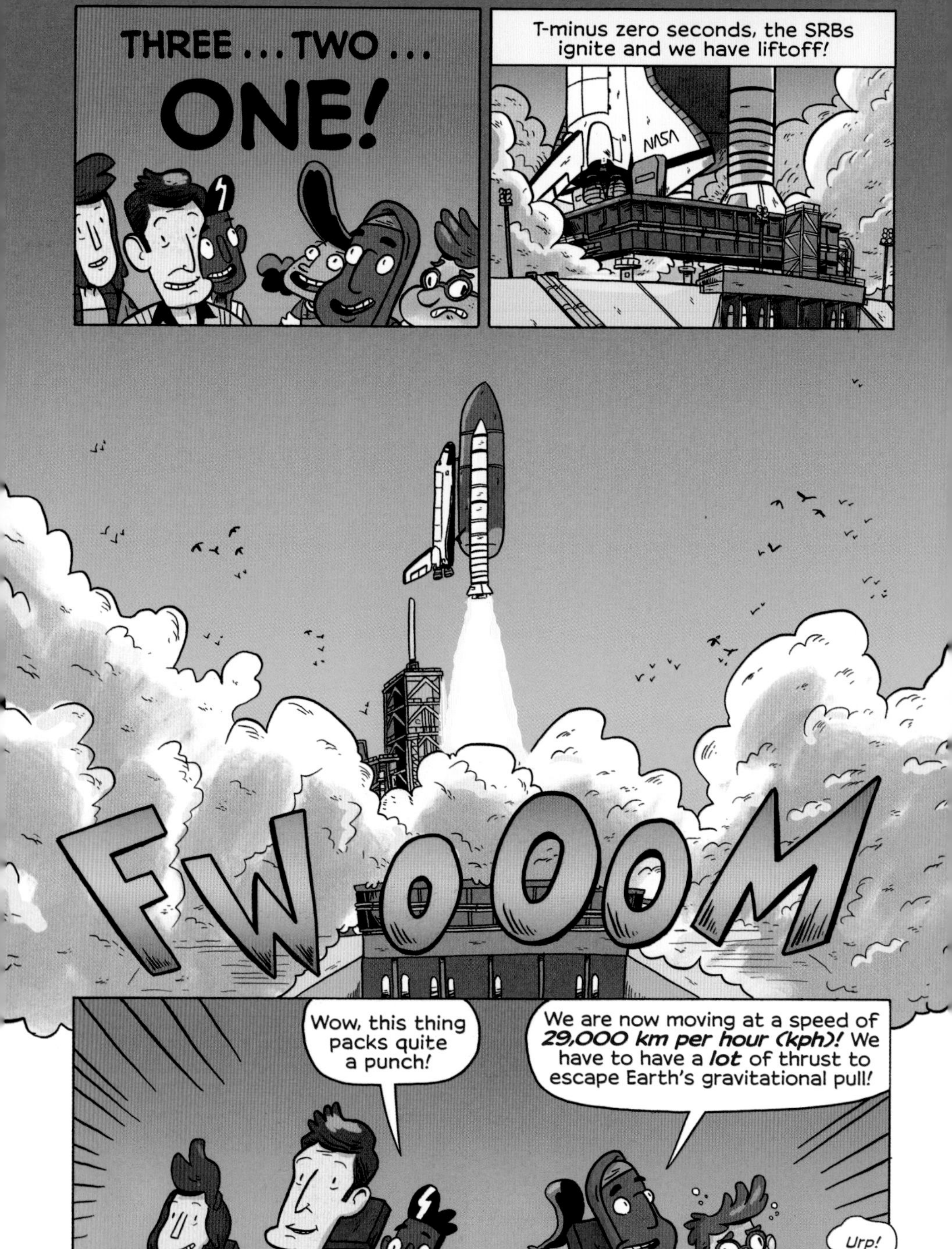
THREE . . . TWO . . .
ONE!
T-minus zero seconds, the SRBs ignite and we have liftoff!
NASA
FWOOOM
Wow, this thing packs quite a punch!
We are now moving at a speed of **29,000 km per hour (kph)!** We have to have a ***lot*** of thrust to escape Earth's gravitational pull!
Urp!

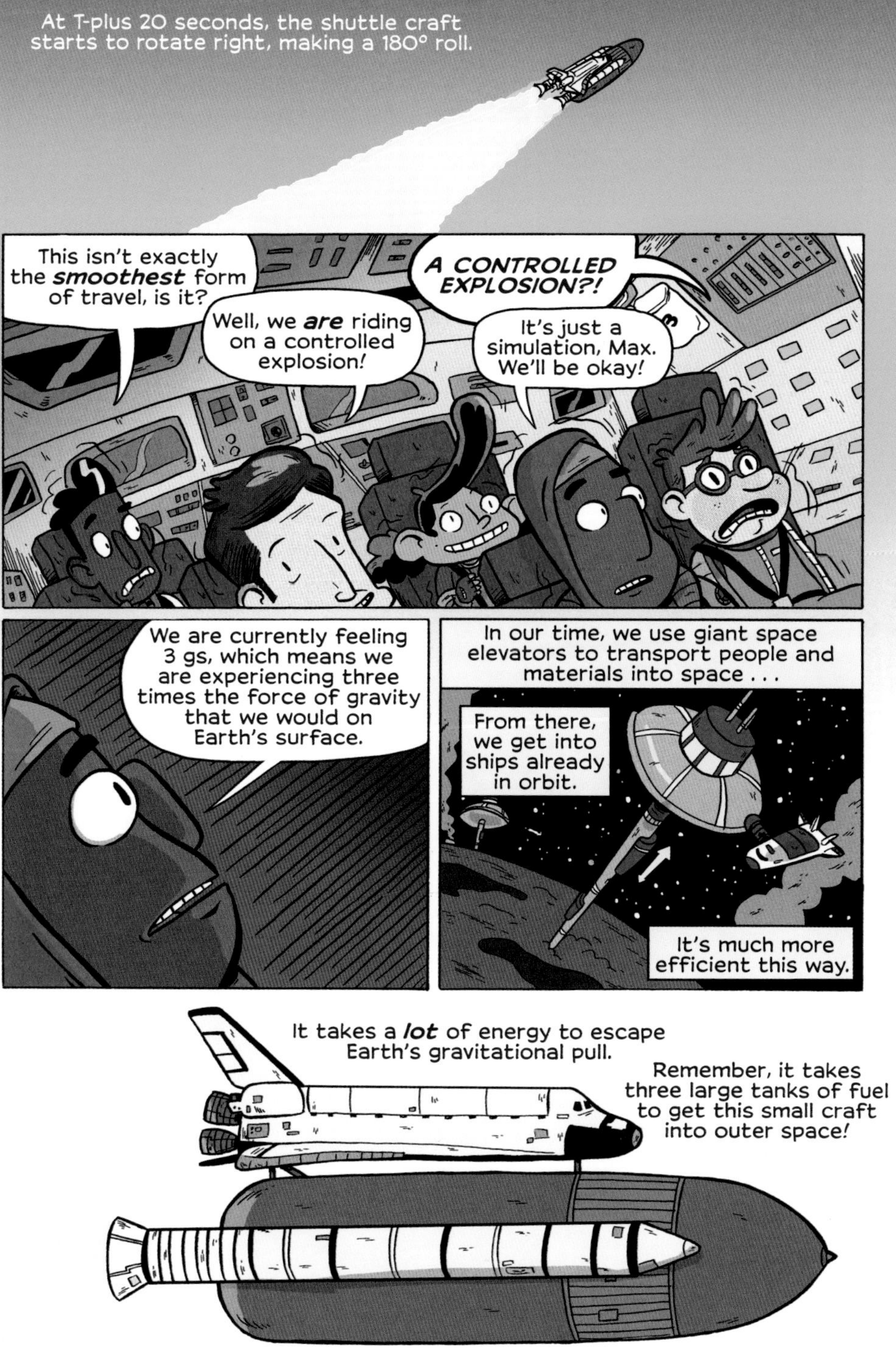
At T-plus 20 seconds, the shuttle craft starts to rotate right, making a 180° roll.
This isn't exactly the *smoothest* form of travel, is it?
Well, we ***are*** riding on a controlled explosion!
A CONTROLLED EXPLOSION?!
It's just a simulation, Max. We'll be okay!
We are currently feeling 3 gs, which means we are experiencing three times the force of gravity that we would on Earth's surface.
In our time, we use giant space elevators to transport people and materials into space . . .
From there, we get into ships already in orbit.
It's much more efficient this way.
It takes a ***lot*** of energy to escape Earth's gravitational pull.
Remember, it takes three large tanks of fuel to get this small craft into outer space!

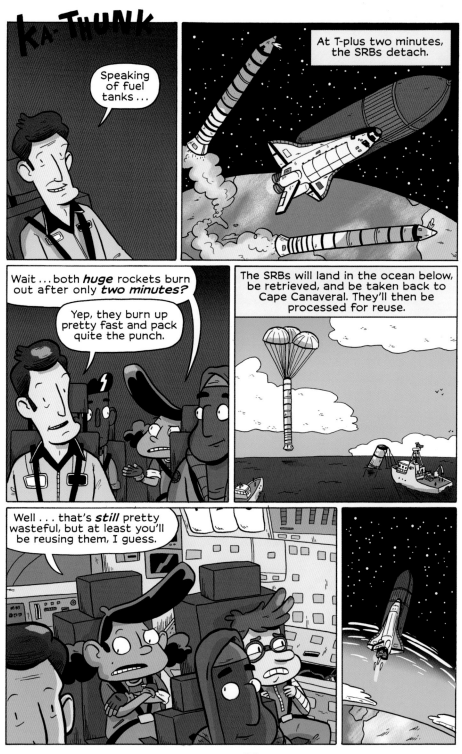

KA-THUNK

Speaking of fuel tanks...

At T-plus two minutes, the SRBs detach.

Wait...both *huge* rockets burn out after only *two minutes?*

Yep, they burn up pretty fast and pack quite the punch.

The SRBs will land in the ocean below, be retrieved, and be taken back to Cape Canaveral. They'll then be processed for reuse.

Well...that's *still* pretty wasteful, but at least you'll be reusing them, I guess.

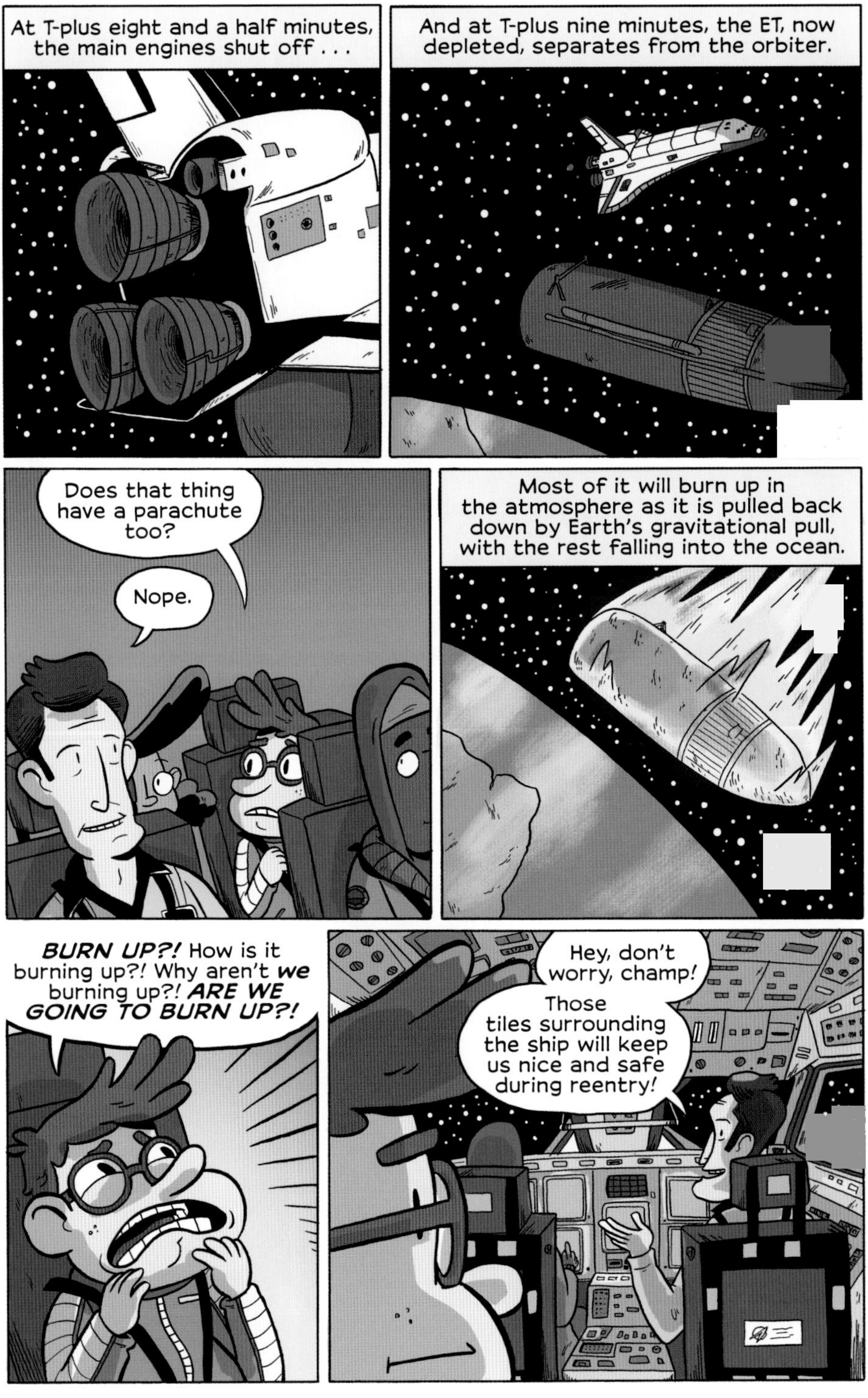

At T-plus eight and a half minutes, the main engines shut off . . .
And at T-plus nine minutes, the ET, now depleted, separates from the orbiter.
Does that thing have a parachute too?
Nope.
Most of it will burn up in the atmosphere as it is pulled back down by Earth's gravitational pull, with the rest falling into the ocean.
BURN UP?! How is it burning up?! Why aren't *we* burning up?! *ARE WE GOING TO BURN UP?!*
Hey, don't worry, champ!
Those tiles surrounding the ship will keep us nice and safe during reentry!

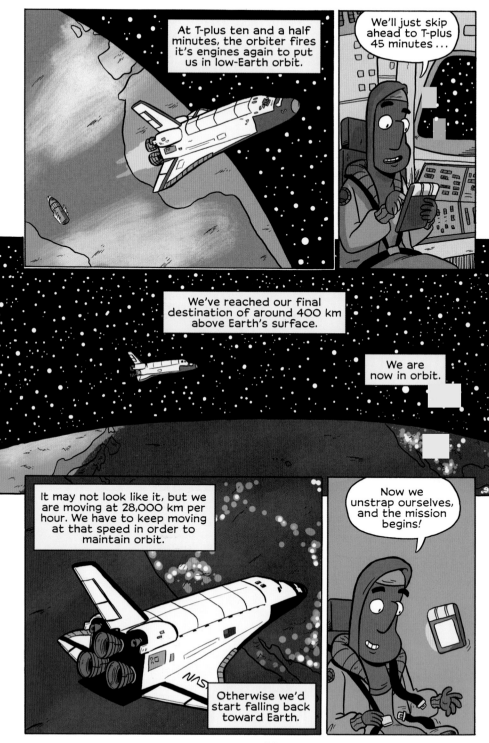

At T-plus ten and a half minutes, the orbiter fires it's engines again to put us in low-Earth orbit.

We'll just skip ahead to T-plus 45 minutes...

We've reached our final destination of around 400 km above Earth's surface.

We are now in orbit.

It may not look like it, but we are moving at 28,000 km per hour. We have to keep moving at that speed in order to maintain orbit.

Otherwise we'd start falling back toward Earth.

Now we unstrap ourselves, and the mission begins!

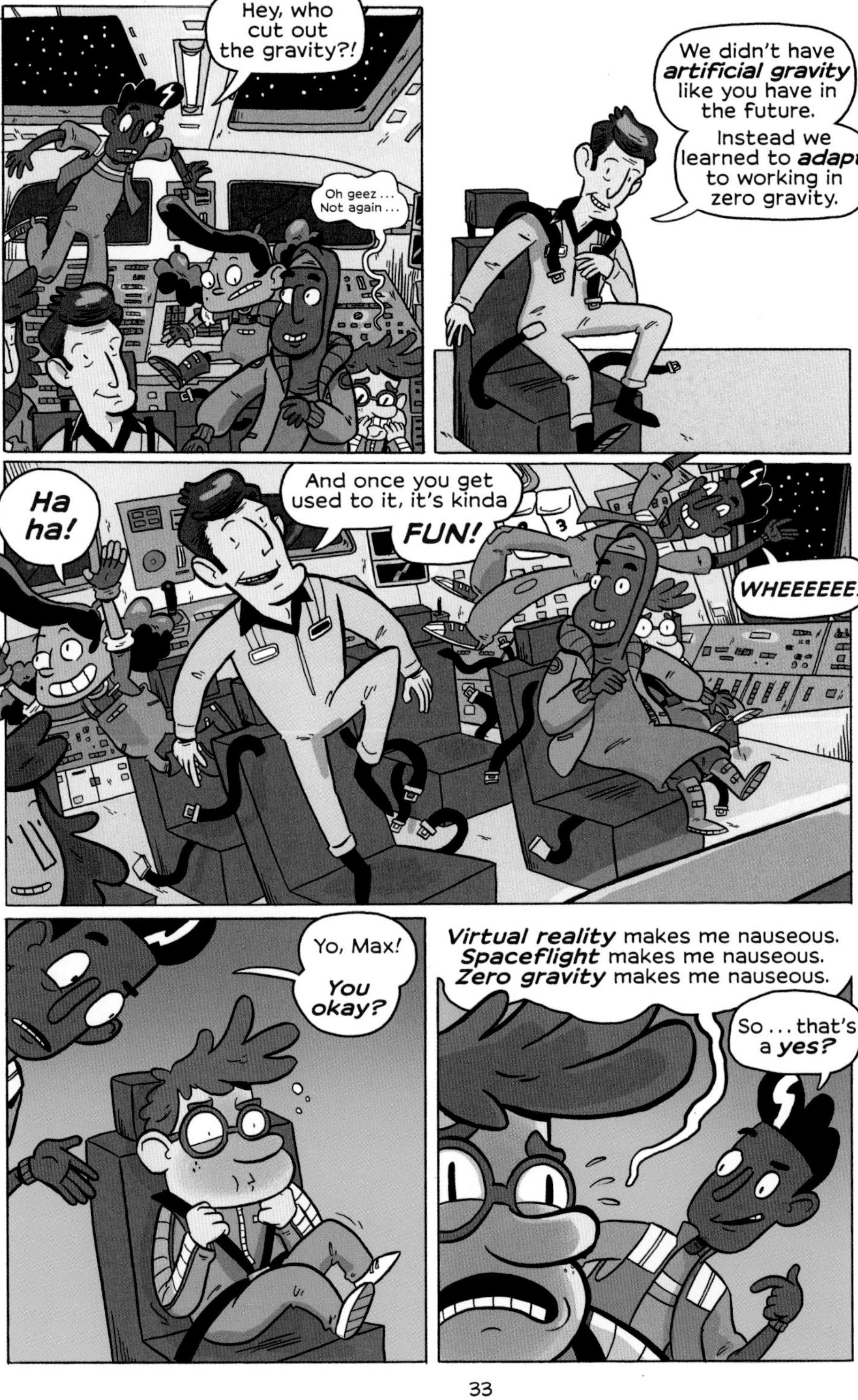
Hey, who cut out the gravity?!
Oh geez ... Not again ...
We didn't have *artificial gravity* like you have in the future.
Instead we learned to *adapt* to working in zero gravity.
Ha ha!
And once you get used to it, it's kinda *FUN!*
WHEEEEEE!
Yo, Max!
You okay?
Virtual reality makes me nauseous. *Spaceflight* makes me nauseous. *Zero gravity* makes me nauseous.
So ... that's a *yes?*

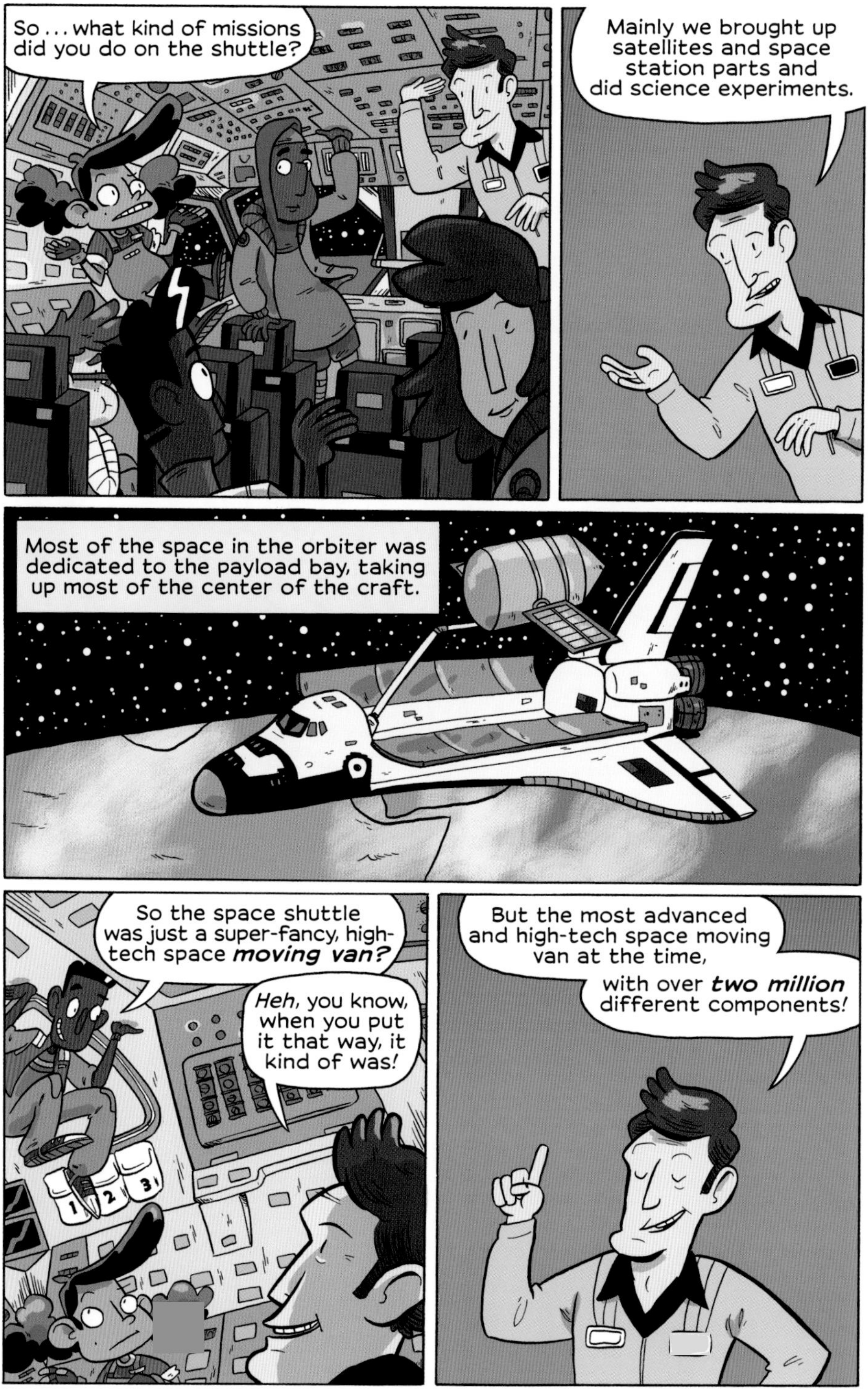
So . . . what kind of missions did you do on the shuttle?
Mainly we brought up satellites and space station parts and did science experiments.
Most of the space in the orbiter was dedicated to the payload bay, taking up most of the center of the craft.
So the space shuttle was just a super-fancy, high-tech space ***moving van?***
Heh, you know, when you put it that way, it kind of was!
1
2
3
But the most advanced and high-tech space moving van at the time,
with over ***two million*** different components!

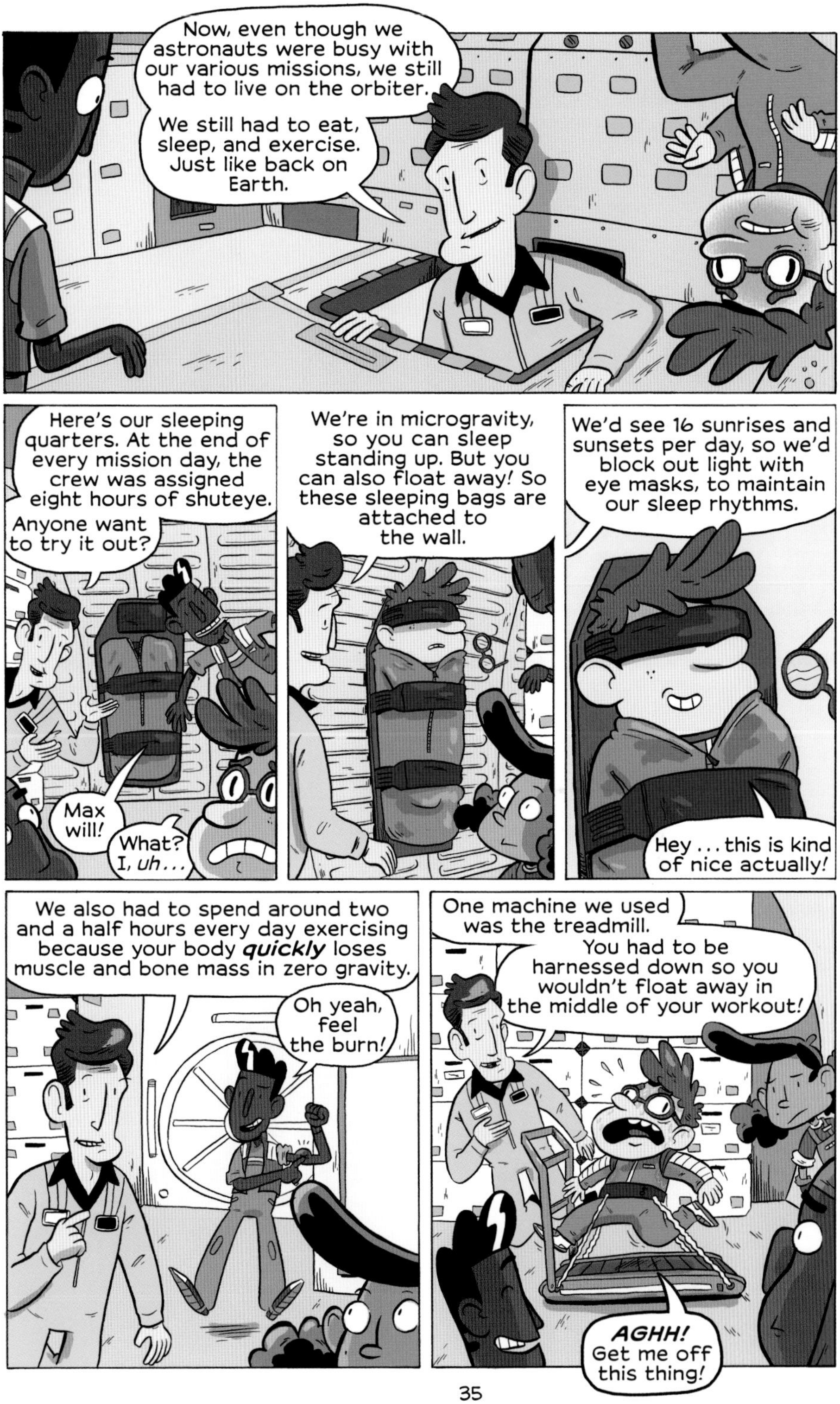
Now, even though we astronauts were busy with our various missions, we still had to live on the orbiter.
We still had to eat, sleep, and exercise. Just like back on Earth.
Here's our sleeping quarters. At the end of every mission day, the crew was assigned eight hours of shuteye.
Anyone want to try it out?
Max will!
What? I, *uh*...
We're in microgravity, so you can sleep standing up. But you can also float away! So these sleeping bags are attached to the wall.
We'd see 16 sunrises and sunsets per day, so we'd block out light with eye masks, to maintain our sleep rhythms.
Hey ... this is kind of nice actually!
We also had to spend around two and a half hours every day exercising because your body ***quickly*** loses muscle and bone mass in zero gravity.
Oh yeah, feel the burn!
One machine we used was the treadmill.
You had to be harnessed down so you wouldn't float away in the middle of your workout!
AGHH! Get me off this thing!

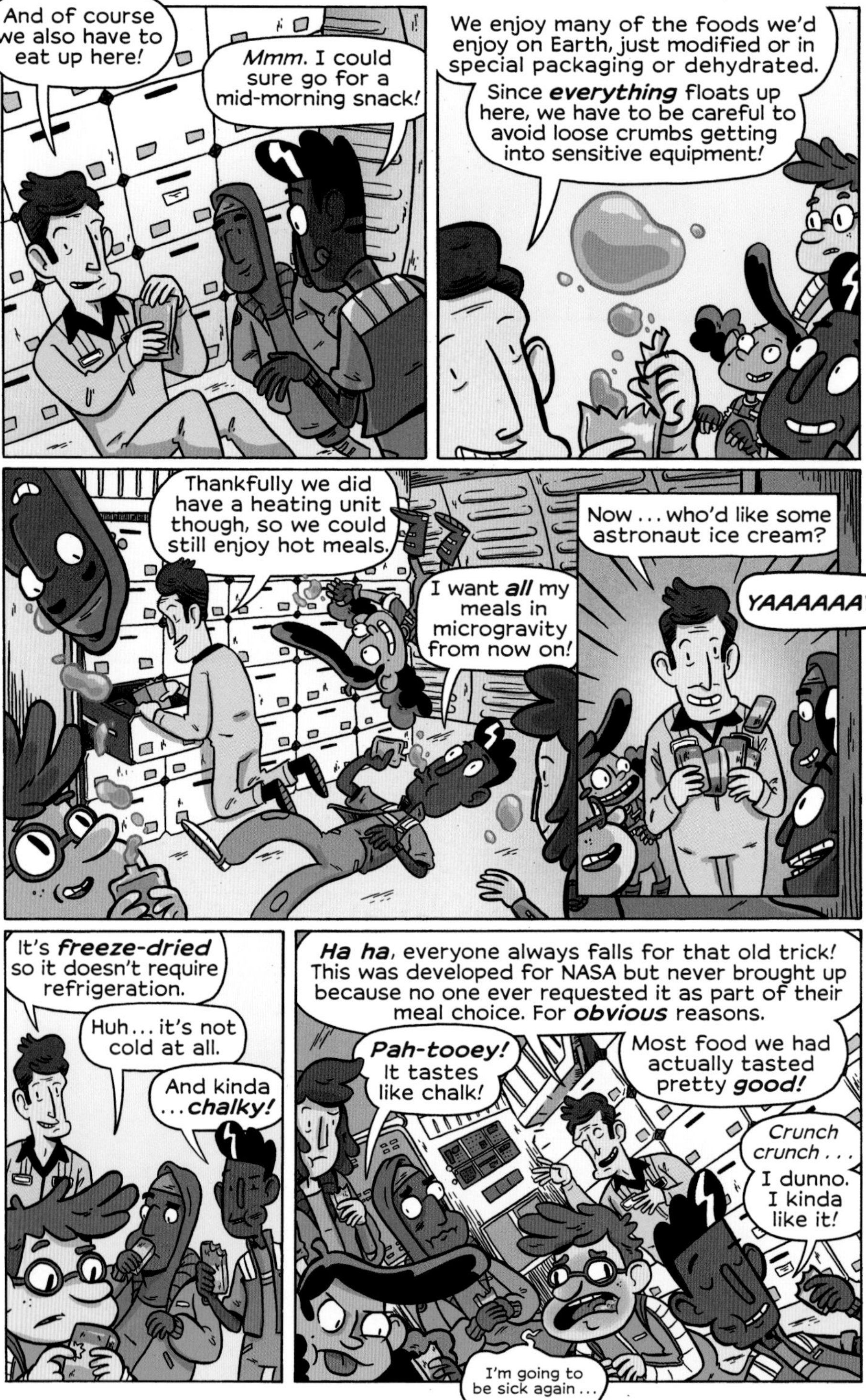
And of course we also have to eat up here!
Mmm. I could sure go for a mid-morning snack!
We enjoy many of the foods we'd enjoy on Earth, just modified or in special packaging or dehydrated.
Since ***everything*** floats up here, we have to be careful to avoid loose crumbs getting into sensitive equipment!
Thankfully we did have a heating unit though, so we could still enjoy hot meals.
I want ***all*** my meals in microgravity from now on!
Now . . . who'd like some astronaut ice cream?
YAAAAAAY!
It's ***freeze-dried*** so it doesn't require refrigeration.
Huh . . . it's not cold at all.
And kinda . . . ***chalky!***
Ha ha, everyone always falls for that old trick! This was developed for NASA but never brought up because no one ever requested it as part of their meal choice. For ***obvious*** reasons.
Pah-tooey! It tastes like chalk!
Most food we had actually tasted pretty ***good!***
Crunch crunch . . .
I dunno. I kinda like it!
I'm going to be sick again . . .

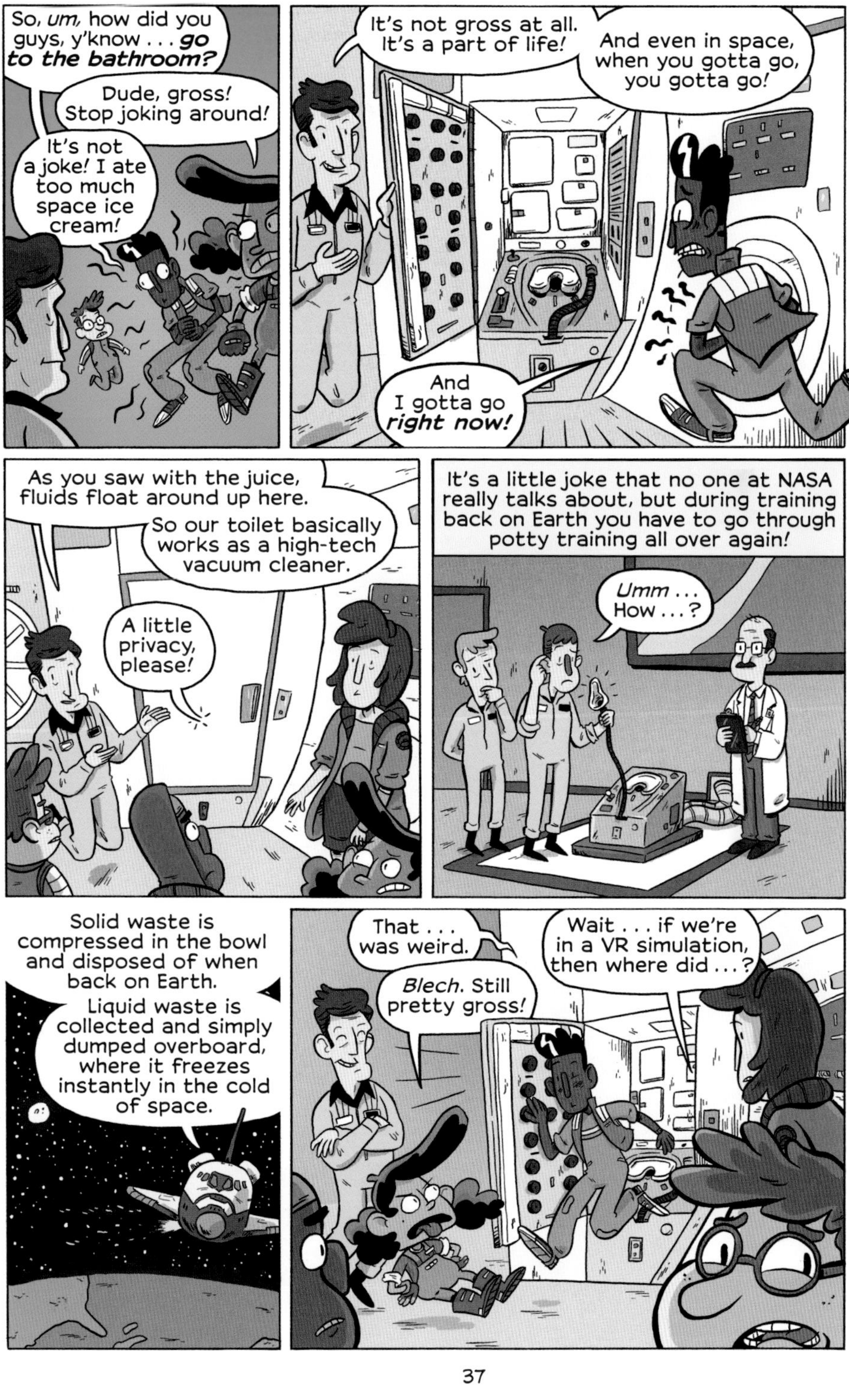
So, *um,* how did you guys, y'know . . . ***go to the bathroom?***
Dude, gross! Stop joking around!
It's not a joke! I ate too much space ice cream!
It's not gross at all. It's a part of life!
And even in space, when you gotta go, you gotta go!
And I gotta go ***right now!***
As you saw with the juice, fluids float around up here.
So our toilet basically works as a high-tech vacuum cleaner.
A little privacy, please!
It's a little joke that no one at NASA really talks about, but during training back on Earth you have to go through potty training all over again!
Umm . . . How . . . ?
Solid waste is compressed in the bowl and disposed of when back on Earth.
Liquid waste is collected and simply dumped overboard, where it freezes instantly in the cold of space.
That . . . was weird.
Blech. Still pretty gross!
Wait . . . if we're in a VR simulation, then where did . . . ?

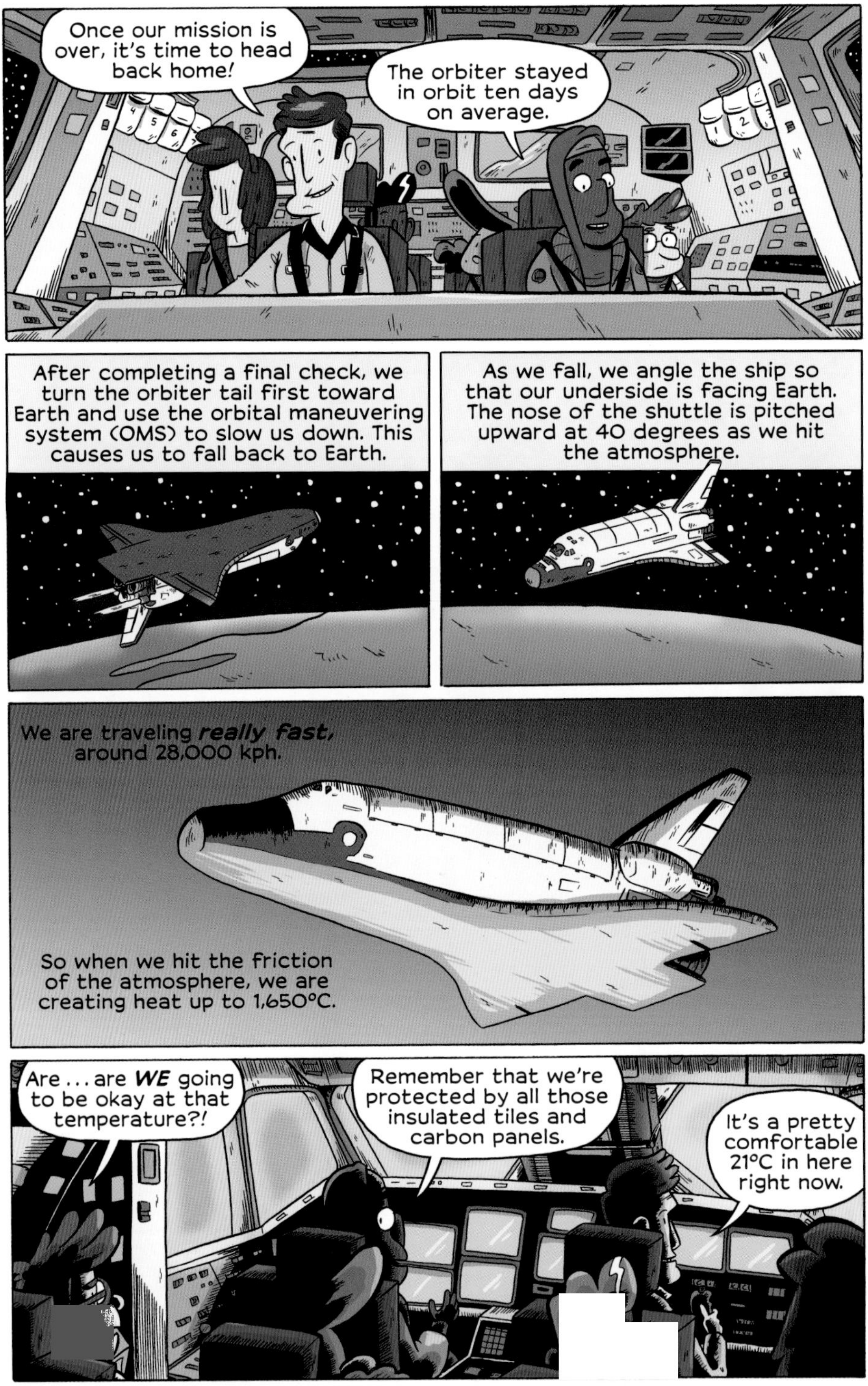
Once our mission is over, it's time to head back home!
The orbiter stayed in orbit ten days on average.
After completing a final check, we turn the orbiter tail first toward Earth and use the orbital maneuvering system (OMS) to slow us down. This causes us to fall back to Earth.
As we fall, we angle the ship so that our underside is facing Earth. The nose of the shuttle is pitched upward at 40 degrees as we hit the atmosphere.
We are traveling *really fast,* around 28,000 kph.
So when we hit the friction of the atmosphere, we are creating heat up to 1,650°C.
Are . . . are *WE* going to be okay at that temperature?!
Remember that we're protected by all those insulated tiles and carbon panels.
It's a pretty comfortable 21°C in here right now.

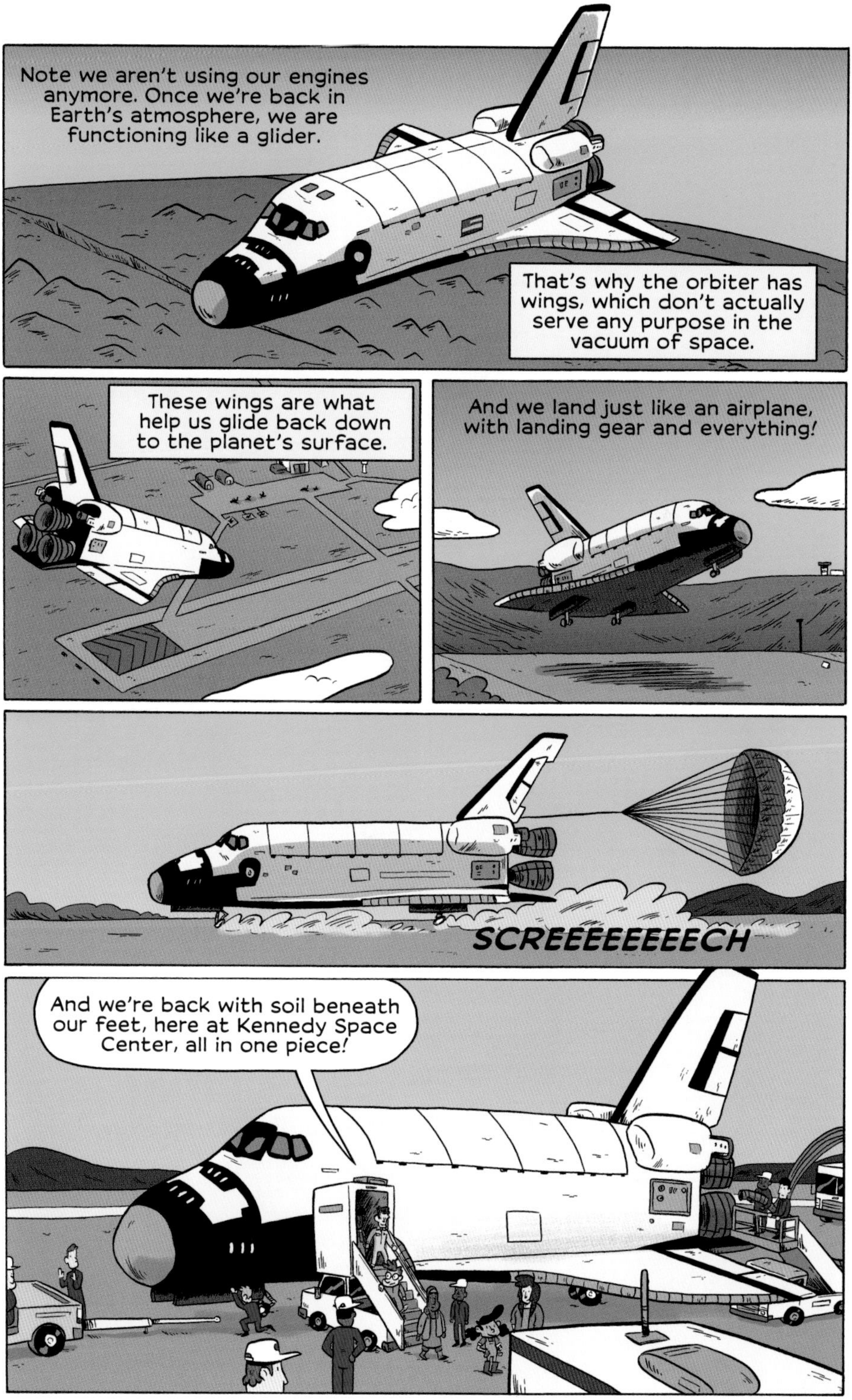
Note we aren't using our engines anymore. Once we're back in Earth's atmosphere, we are functioning like a glider.
That's why the orbiter has wings, which don't actually serve any purpose in the vacuum of space.
These wings are what help us glide back down to the planet's surface.
And we land just like an airplane, with landing gear and everything!
SCREEEEEEEEECH
And we're back with soil beneath our feet, here at Kennedy Space Center, all in one piece!

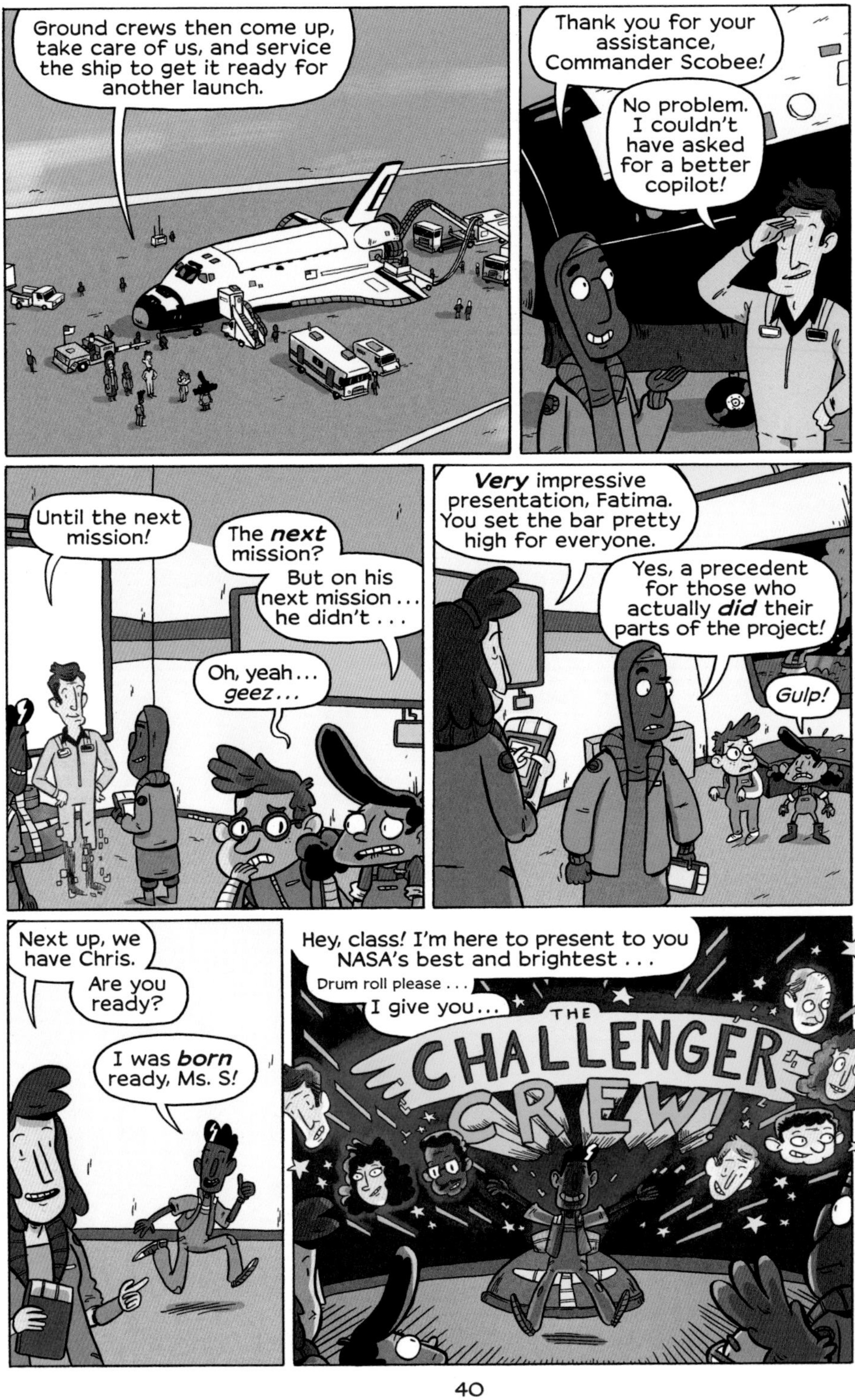
Ground crews then come up, take care of us, and service the ship to get it ready for another launch.
Thank you for your assistance, Commander Scobee!
No problem. I couldn't have asked for a better copilot!
Until the next mission!
The **next** mission?
But on his next mission . . . he didn't . . .
Oh, yeah . . . *geez . . .*
Very impressive presentation, Fatima. You set the bar pretty high for everyone.
Yes, a precedent for those who actually **did** their parts of the project!
Gulp!
Next up, we have Chris.
Are you ready?
I was **born** ready, Ms. S!
Hey, class! I'm here to present to you NASA's best and brightest . . .
Drum roll please . . .
I give you . . .
THE CHALLENGER CREW!

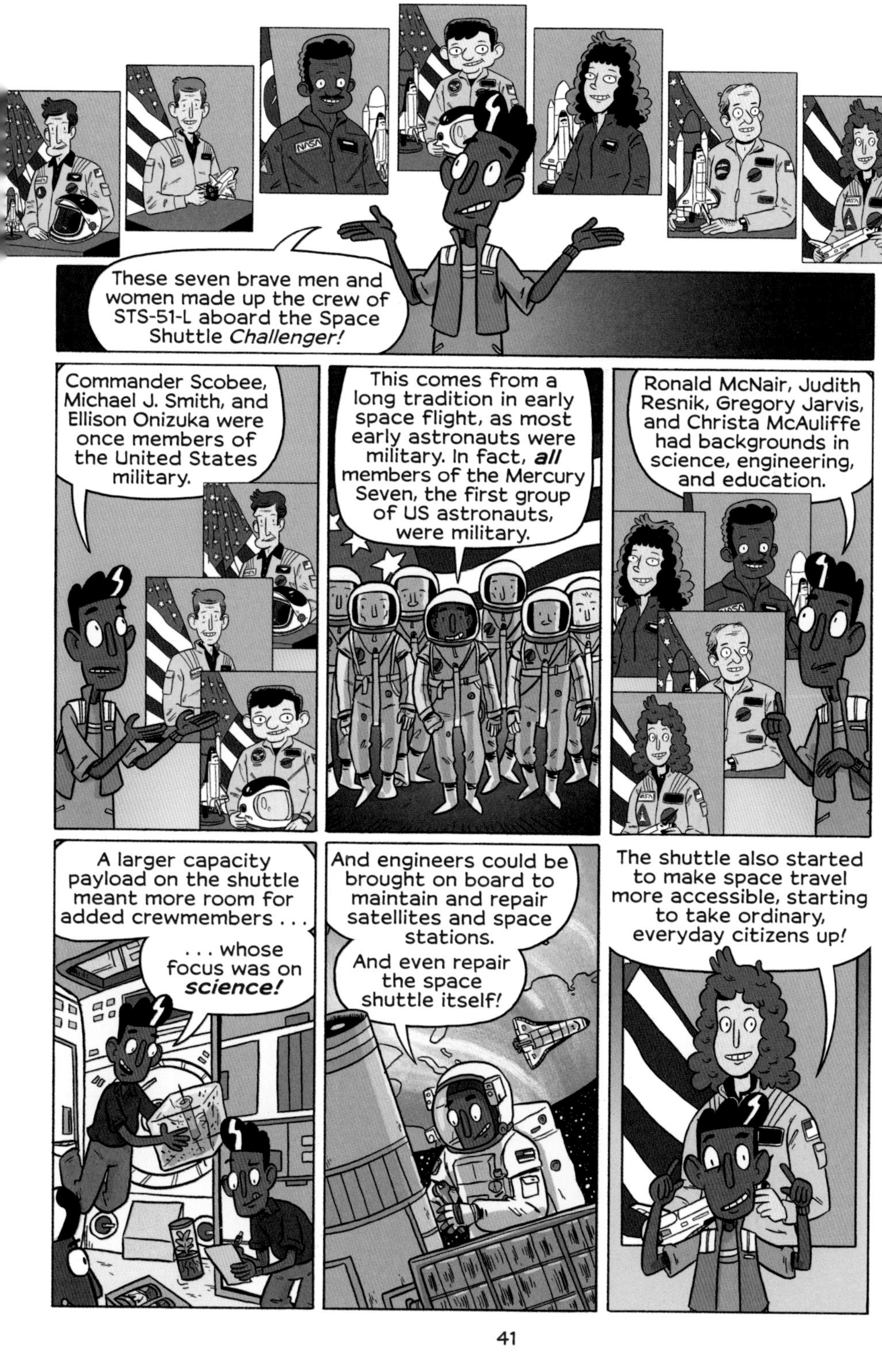
These seven brave men and women made up the crew of STS-51-L aboard the Space Shuttle *Challenger!*
Commander Scobee, Michael J. Smith, and Ellison Onizuka were once members of the United States military.
This comes from a long tradition in early space flight, as most early astronauts were military. In fact, ***all*** members of the Mercury Seven, the first group of US astronauts, were military.
Ronald McNair, Judith Resnik, Gregory Jarvis, and Christa McAuliffe had backgrounds in science, engineering, and education.
A larger capacity payload on the shuttle meant more room for added crewmembers . . .
. . . whose focus was on ***science!***
And engineers could be brought on board to maintain and repair satellites and space stations.
And even repair the space shuttle itself!
The shuttle also started to make space travel more accessible, starting to take ordinary, everyday citizens up!

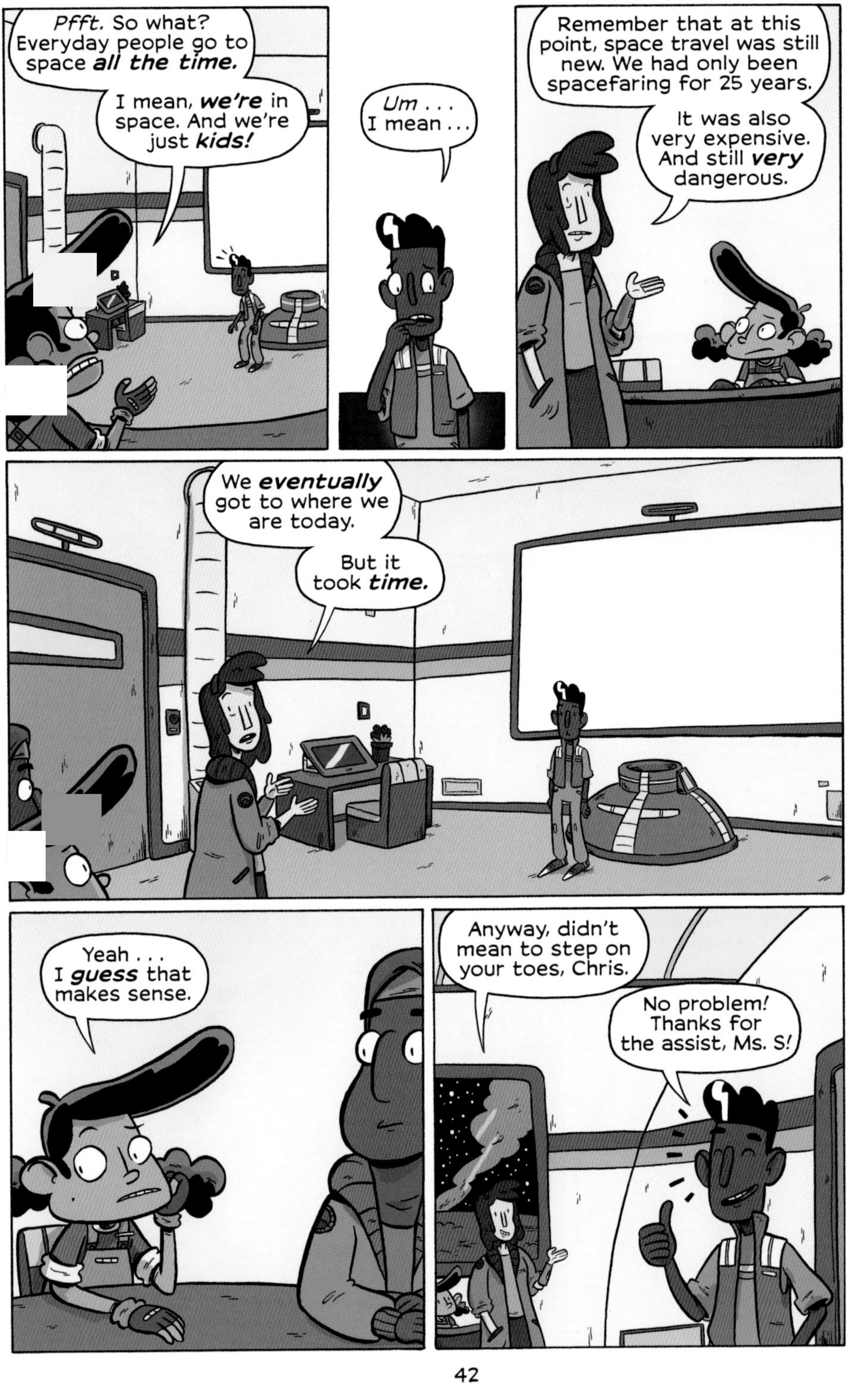
Pfft. So what? Everyday people go to space all the time.
I mean, we're in space. And we're just kids!
Um . . . I mean . . .
Remember that at this point, space travel was still new. We had only been spacefaring for 25 years.
It was also very expensive. And still very dangerous.
We eventually got to where we are today.
But it took time.
Yeah . . . I guess that makes sense.
Anyway, didn't mean to step on your toes, Chris.
No problem! Thanks for the assist, Ms. S!

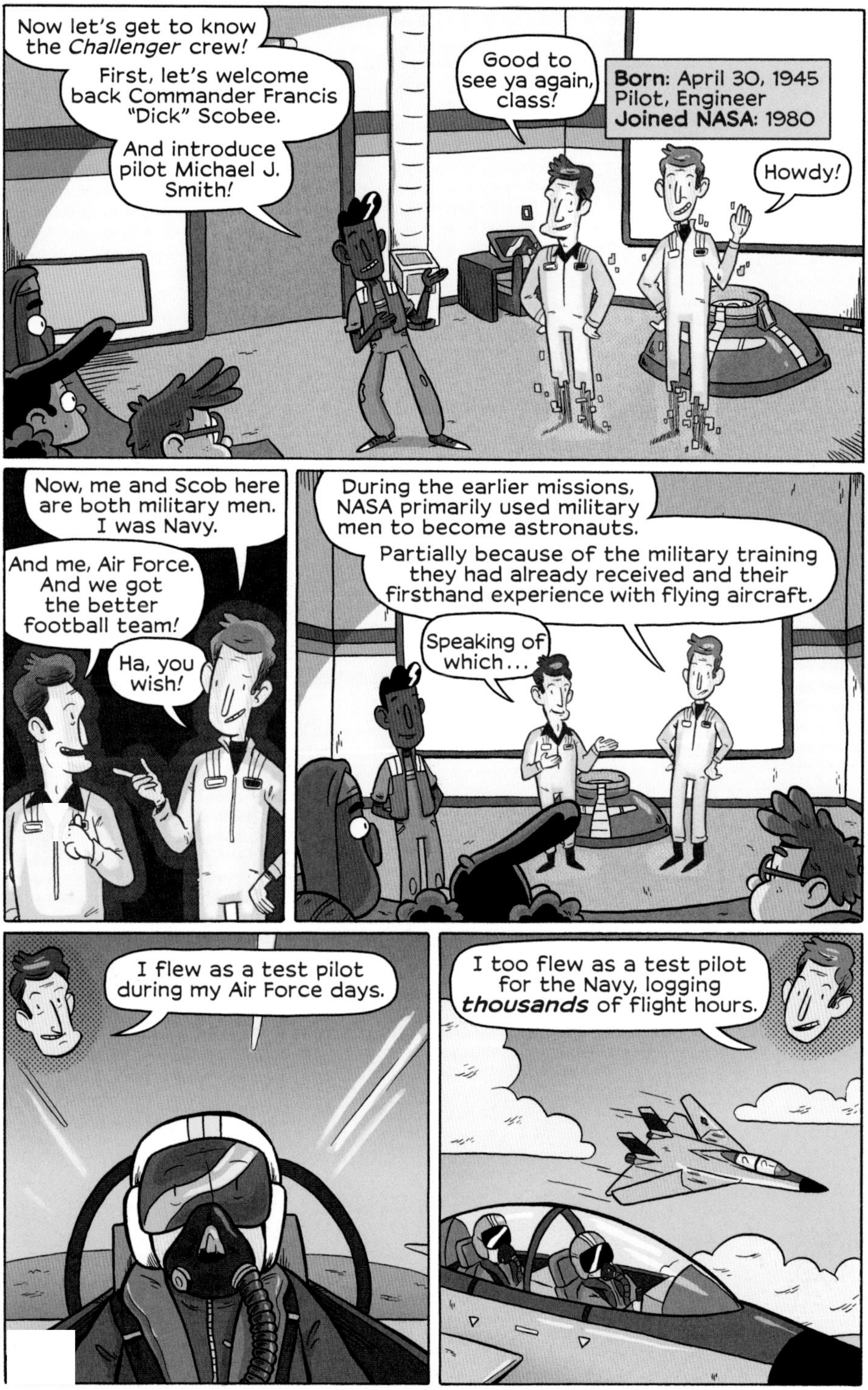
Now let's get to know the *Challenger* crew!
First, let's welcome back Commander Francis "Dick" Scobee.
And introduce pilot Michael J. Smith!
Good to see ya again, class!
Born: April 30, 1945
Pilot, Engineer
Joined NASA: 1980
Howdy!
Now, me and Scob here are both military men. I was Navy.
And me, Air Force. And we got the better football team!
Ha, you wish!
During the earlier missions, NASA primarily used military men to become astronauts.
Partially because of the military training they had already received and their firsthand experience with flying aircraft.
Speaking of which...
I flew as a test pilot during my Air Force days.
I too flew as a test pilot for the Navy, logging ***thousands*** of flight hours.

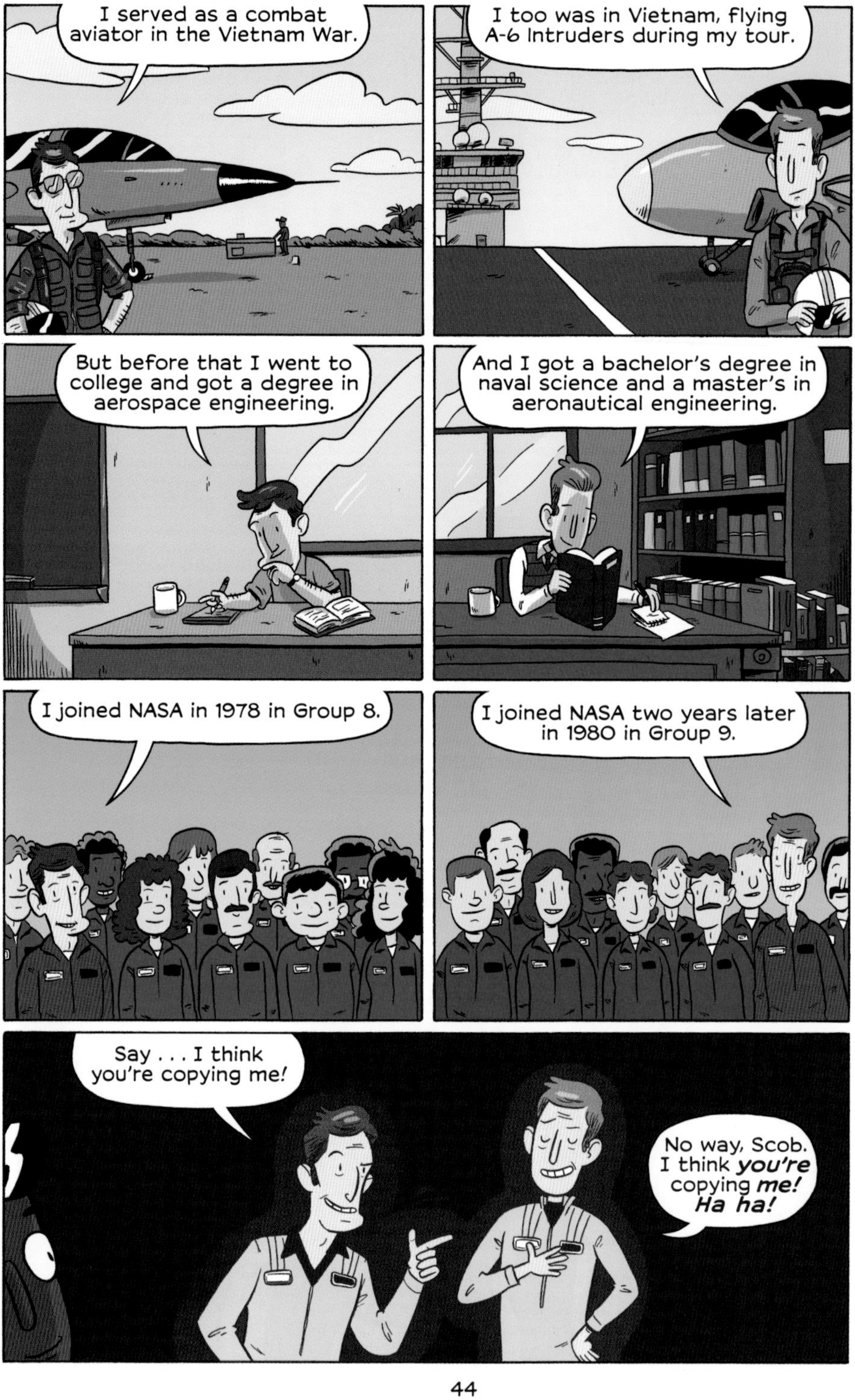
I served as a combat aviator in the Vietnam War.
I too was in Vietnam, flying A-6 Intruders during my tour.
But before that I went to college and got a degree in aerospace engineering.
And I got a bachelor's degree in naval science and a master's in aeronautical engineering.
I joined NASA in 1978 in Group 8.
I joined NASA two years later in 1980 in Group 9.
Say . . . I think you're copying me!
No way, Scob. I think *you're* copying *me!* *Ha ha!*

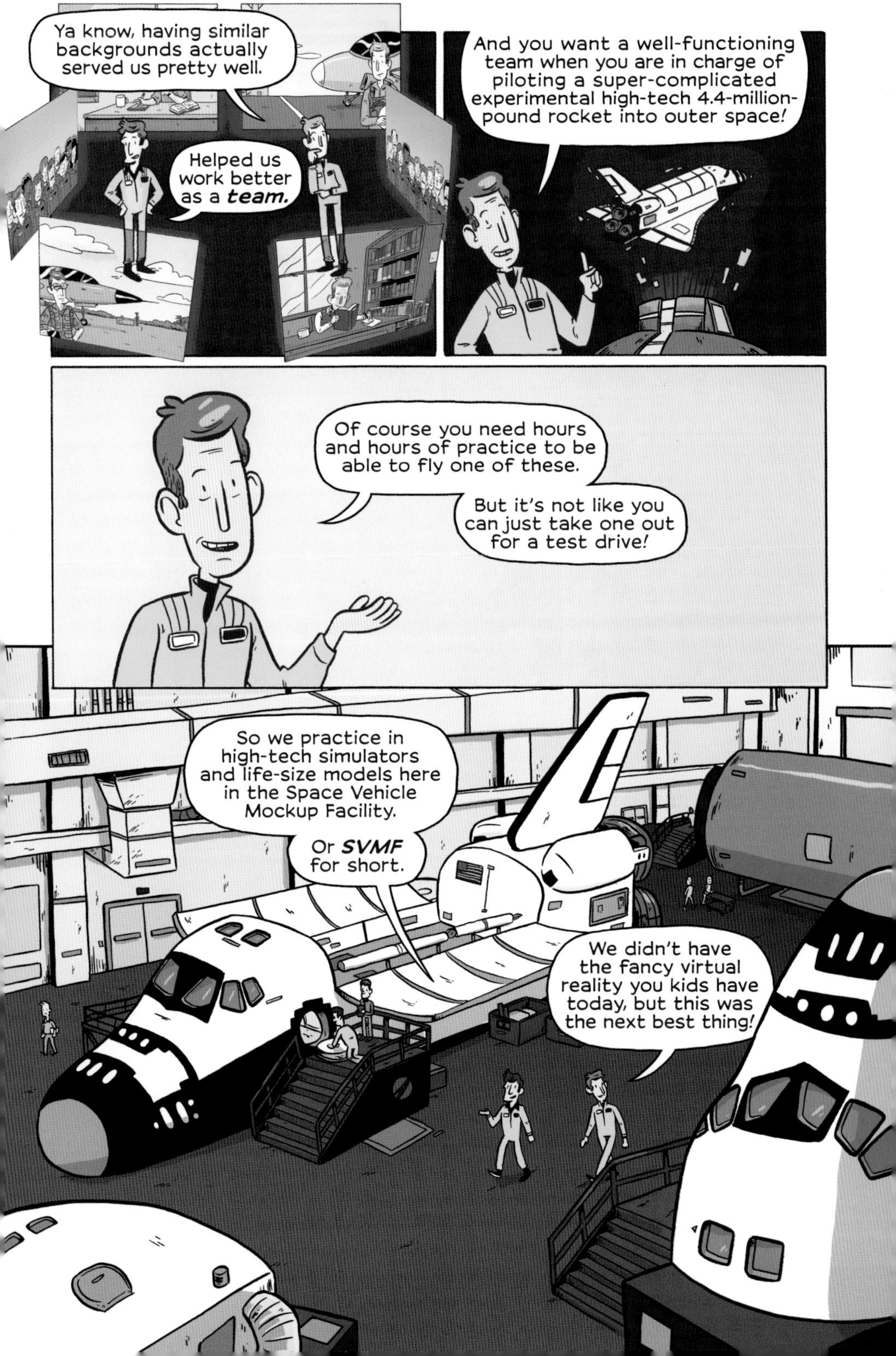
Ya know, having similar backgrounds actually served us pretty well.
Helped us work better as a ***team.***
And you want a well-functioning team when you are in charge of piloting a super-complicated experimental high-tech 4.4-million-pound rocket into outer space!
Of course you need hours and hours of practice to be able to fly one of these.
But it's not like you can just take one out for a test drive!
So we practice in high-tech simulators and life-size models here in the Space Vehicle Mockup Facility.
Or ***SVMF*** for short.
We didn't have the fancy virtual reality you kids have today, but this was the next best thing!

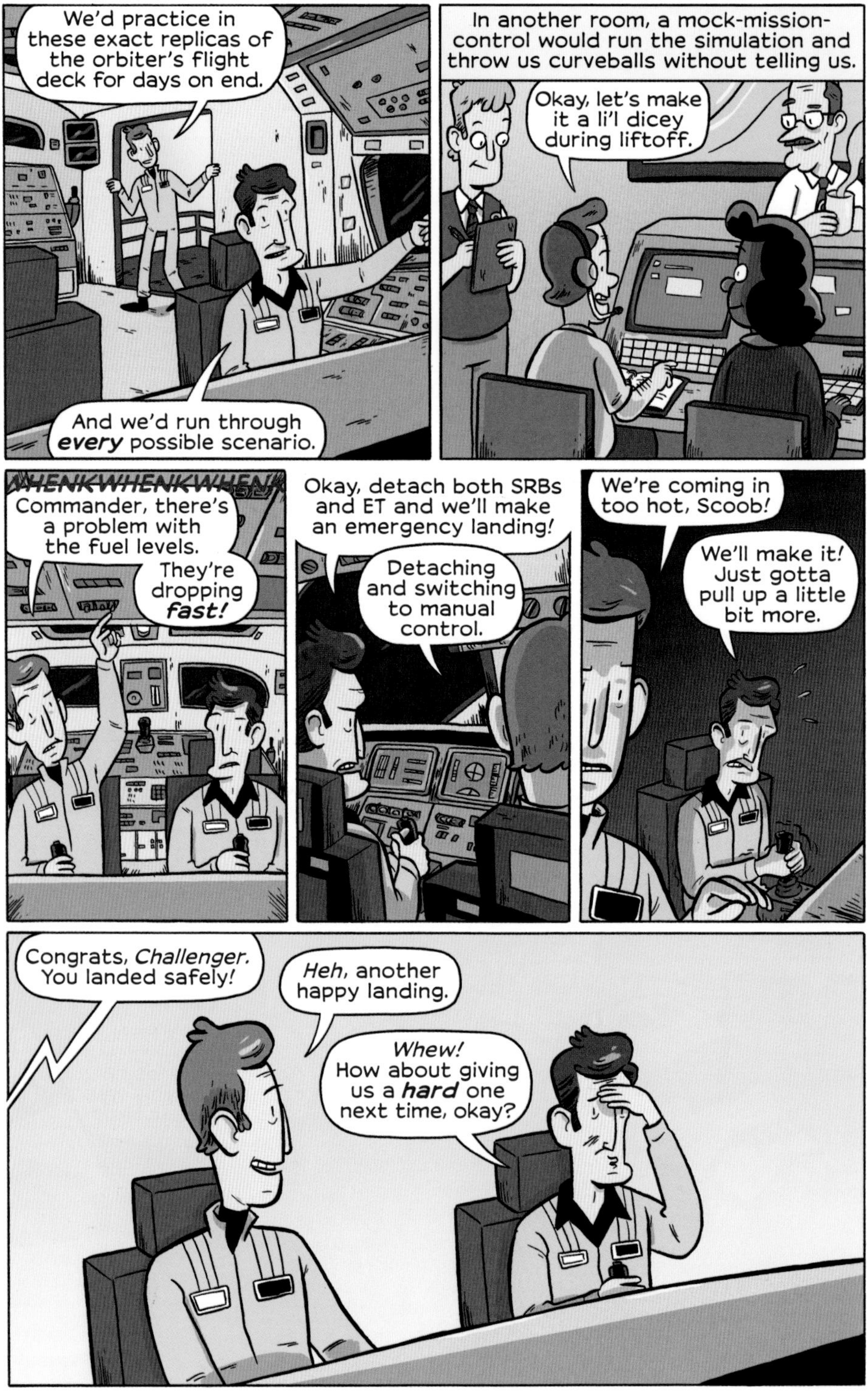
We'd practice in these exact replicas of the orbiter's flight deck for days on end.
And we'd run through ***every*** possible scenario.
In another room, a mock-mission-control would run the simulation and throw us curveballs without telling us.
Okay, let's make it a li'l dicey during liftoff.
WHENKWHENKWHENK
Commander, there's a problem with the fuel levels.
They're dropping ***fast!***
Okay, detach both SRBs and ET and we'll make an emergency landing!
Detaching and switching to manual control.
We're coming in too hot, Scoob!
We'll make it! Just gotta pull up a little bit more.
Congrats, *Challenger.* You landed safely!
Heh, another happy landing.
Whew! How about giving us a ***hard*** one next time, okay?

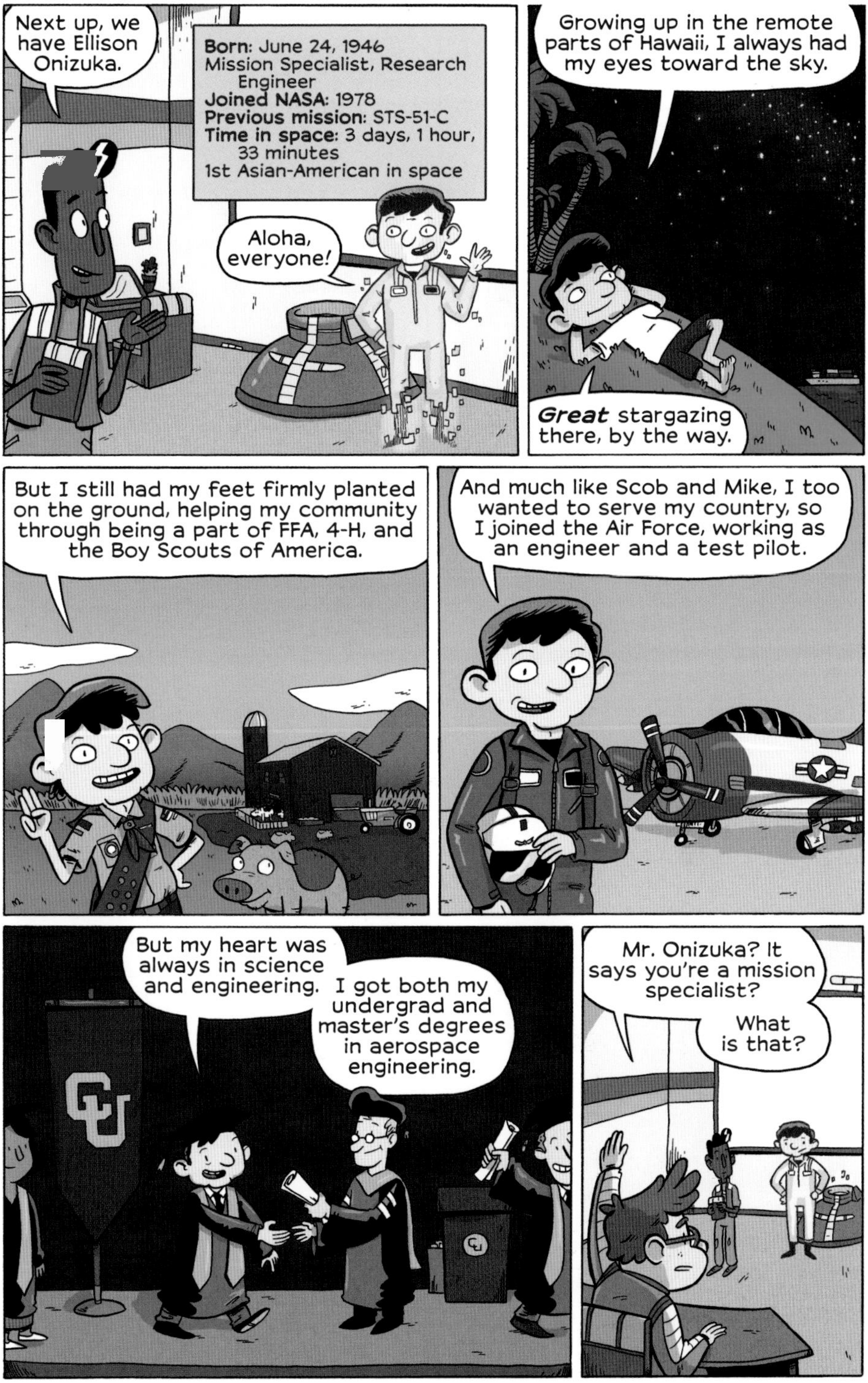
Next up, we have Ellison Onizuka.
Born: June 24, 1946
Mission Specialist, Research Engineer
Joined NASA: 1978
Previous mission: STS-51-C
Time in space: 3 days, 1 hour, 33 minutes
1st Asian-American in space
Aloha, everyone!
Growing up in the remote parts of Hawaii, I always had my eyes toward the sky.
Great stargazing there, by the way.
But I still had my feet firmly planted on the ground, helping my community through being a part of FFA, 4-H, and the Boy Scouts of America.
And much like Scob and Mike, I too wanted to serve my country, so I joined the Air Force, working as an engineer and a test pilot.
But my heart was always in science and engineering.
I got both my undergrad and master's degrees in aerospace engineering.
CU
Mr. Onizuka? It says you're a mission specialist?
What is that?

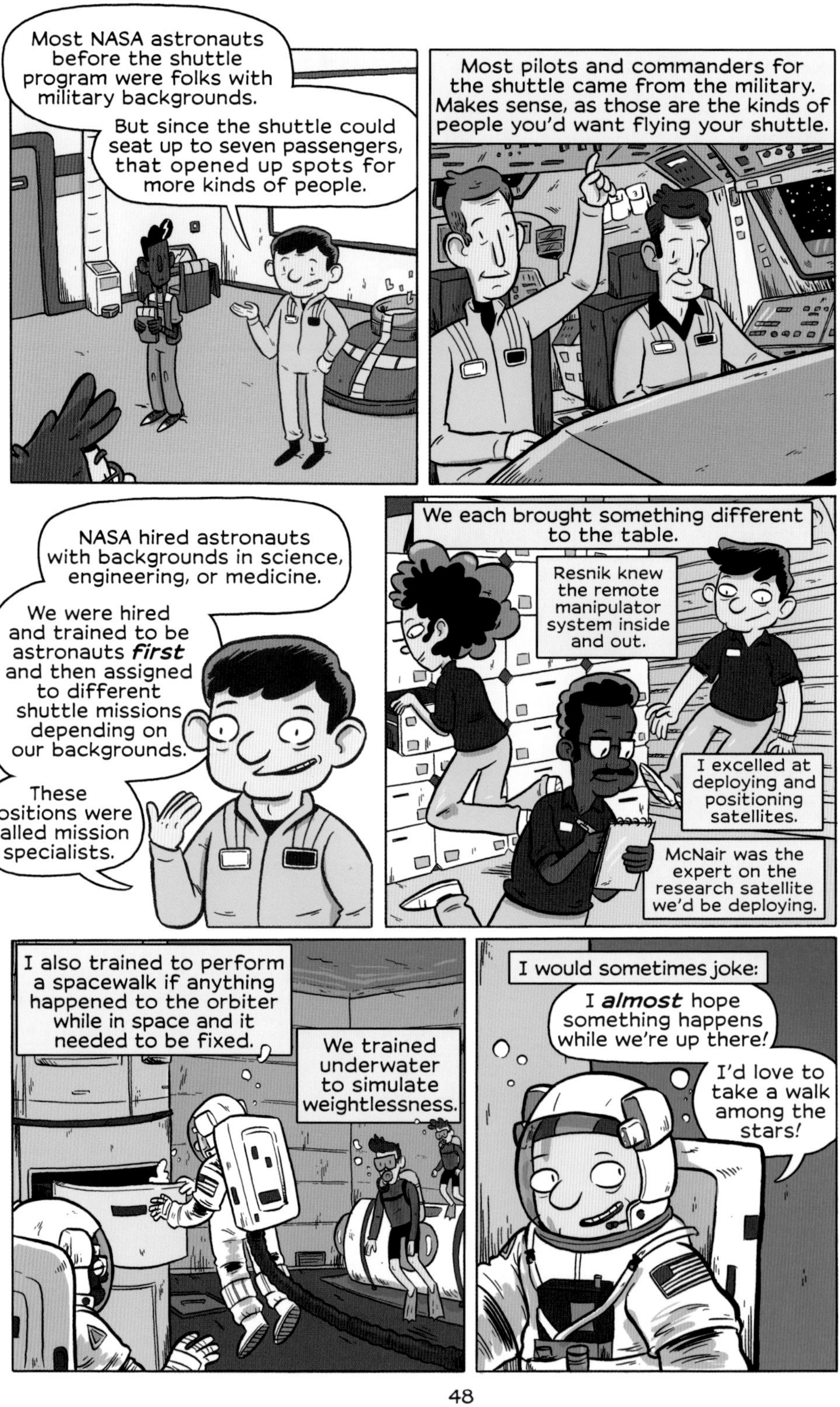
Most NASA astronauts before the shuttle program were folks with military backgrounds.
But since the shuttle could seat up to seven passengers, that opened up spots for more kinds of people.
Most pilots and commanders for the shuttle came from the military. Makes sense, as those are the kinds of people you'd want flying your shuttle.
NASA hired astronauts with backgrounds in science, engineering, or medicine.
We were hired and trained to be astronauts *first* and then assigned to different shuttle missions depending on our backgrounds.
These positions were called mission specialists.
We each brought something different to the table.
Resnik knew the remote manipulator system inside and out.
I excelled at deploying and positioning satellites.
McNair was the expert on the research satellite we'd be deploying.
I also trained to perform a spacewalk if anything happened to the orbiter while in space and it needed to be fixed.
We trained underwater to simulate weightlessness.
I would sometimes joke:
I *almost* hope something happens while we're up there!
I'd love to take a walk among the stars!

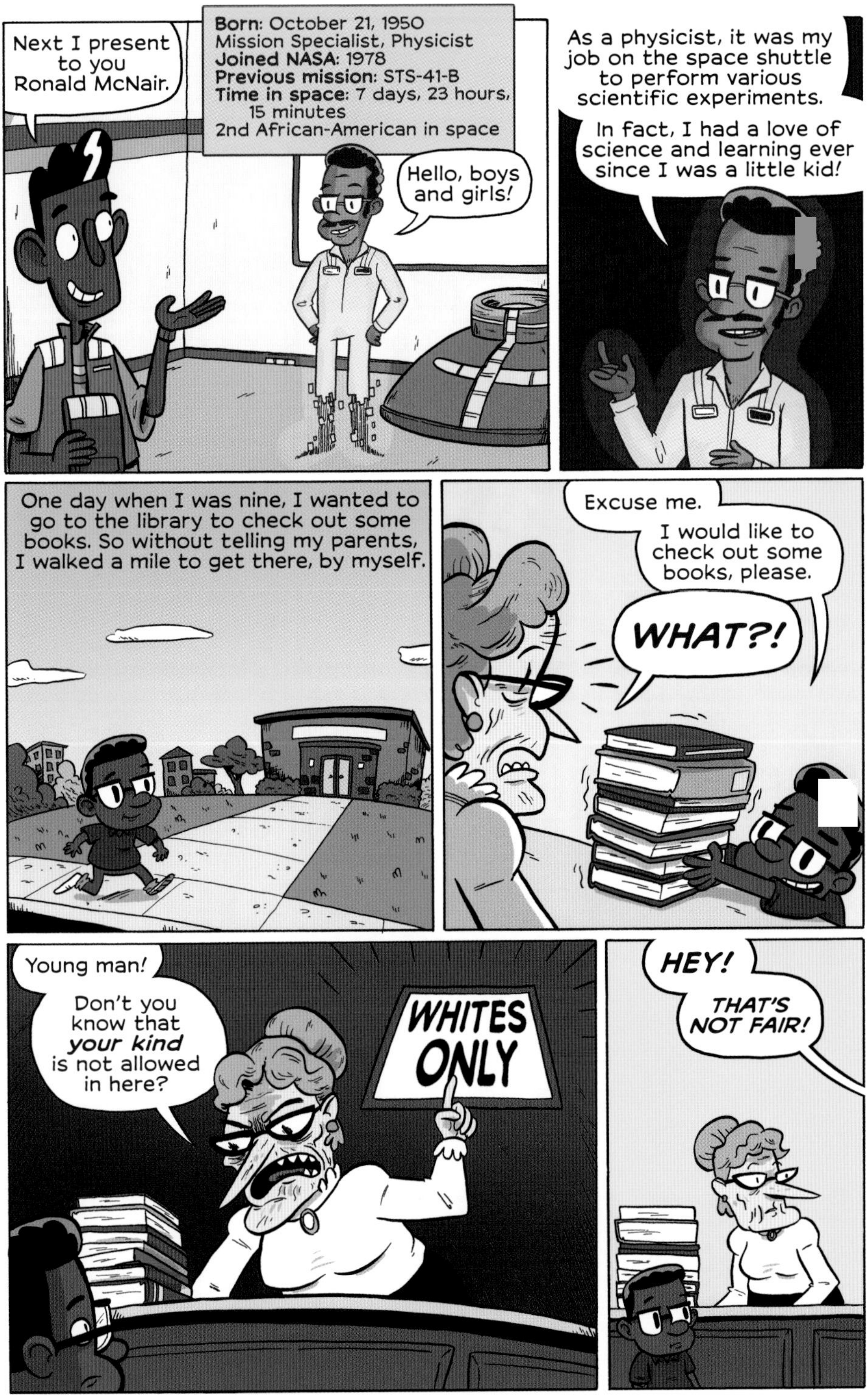
Next I present to you Ronald McNair.
Born: October 21, 1950
Mission Specialist, Physicist
Joined NASA: 1978
Previous mission: STS-41-B
Time in space: 7 days, 23 hours, 15 minutes
2nd African-American in space
Hello, boys and girls!
As a physicist, it was my job on the space shuttle to perform various scientific experiments.
In fact, I had a love of science and learning ever since I was a little kid!
One day when I was nine, I wanted to go to the library to check out some books. So without telling my parents, I walked a mile to get there, by myself.
Excuse me.
I would like to check out some books, please.
WHAT?!
Young man!
Don't you know that your kind is not allowed in here?
WHITES ONLY
HEY!
THAT'S NOT FAIR!

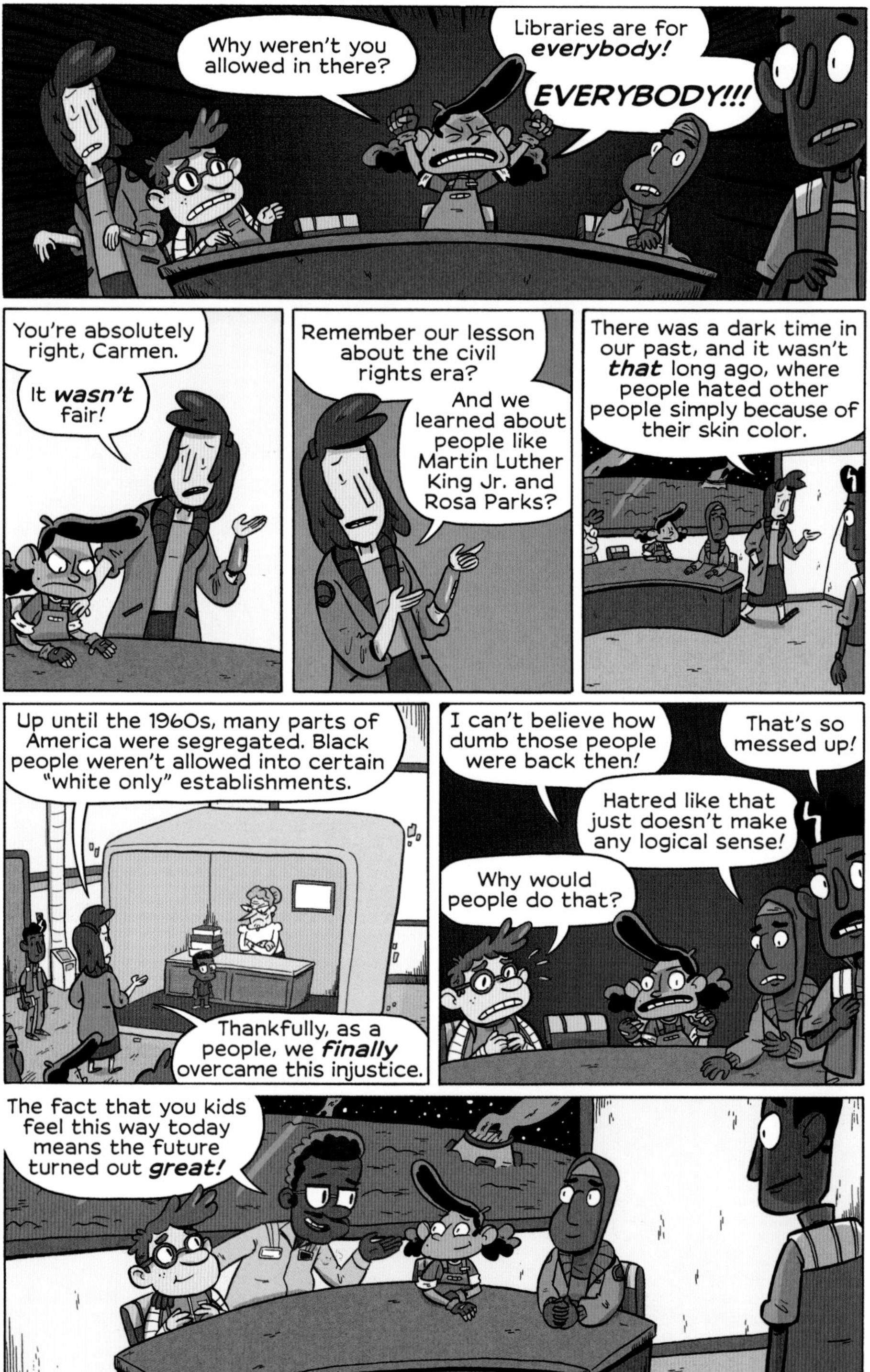

Why weren't you allowed in there?
Libraries are for *everybody!*
EVERYBODY!!!
You're absolutely right, Carmen.
It *wasn't* fair!
Remember our lesson about the civil rights era?
And we learned about people like Martin Luther King Jr. and Rosa Parks?
There was a dark time in our past, and it wasn't *that* long ago, where people hated other people simply because of their skin color.
Up until the 1960s, many parts of America were segregated. Black people weren't allowed into certain "white only" establishments.
Thankfully, as a people, we *finally* overcame this injustice.
I can't believe how dumb those people were back then!
That's so messed up!
Hatred like that just doesn't make any logical sense!
Why would people do that?
The fact that you kids feel this way today means the future turned out *great!*

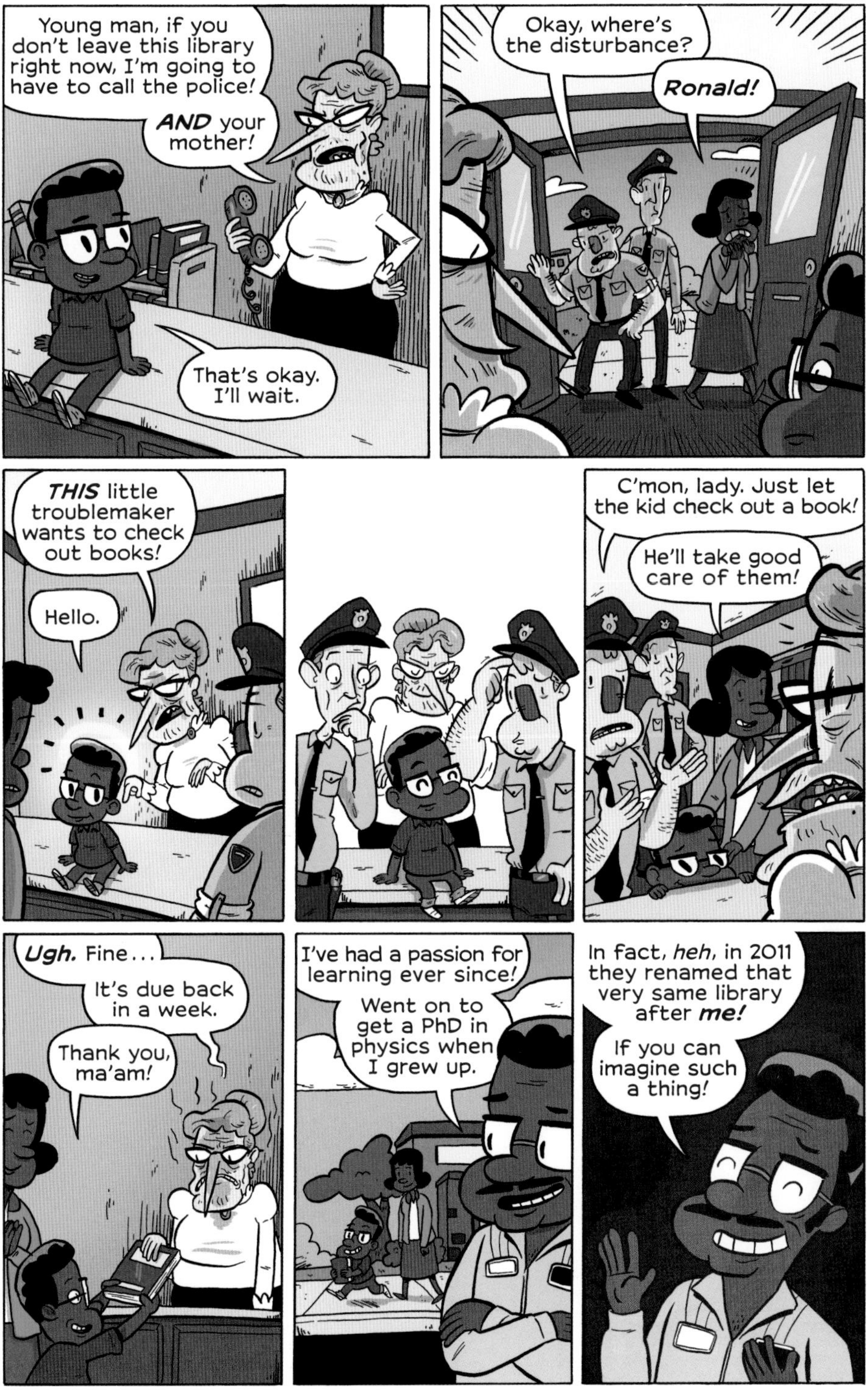
Young man, if you don't leave this library right now, I'm going to have to call the police!
AND your mother!
That's okay. I'll wait.
Okay, where's the disturbance?
Ronald!
THIS little troublemaker wants to check out books!
Hello.
C'mon, lady. Just let the kid check out a book!
He'll take good care of them!
Ugh. Fine...
It's due back in a week.
Thank you, ma'am!
I've had a passion for learning ever since!
Went on to get a PhD in physics when I grew up.
In fact, *heh,* in 2011 they renamed that very same library after ***me!***
If you can imagine such a thing!

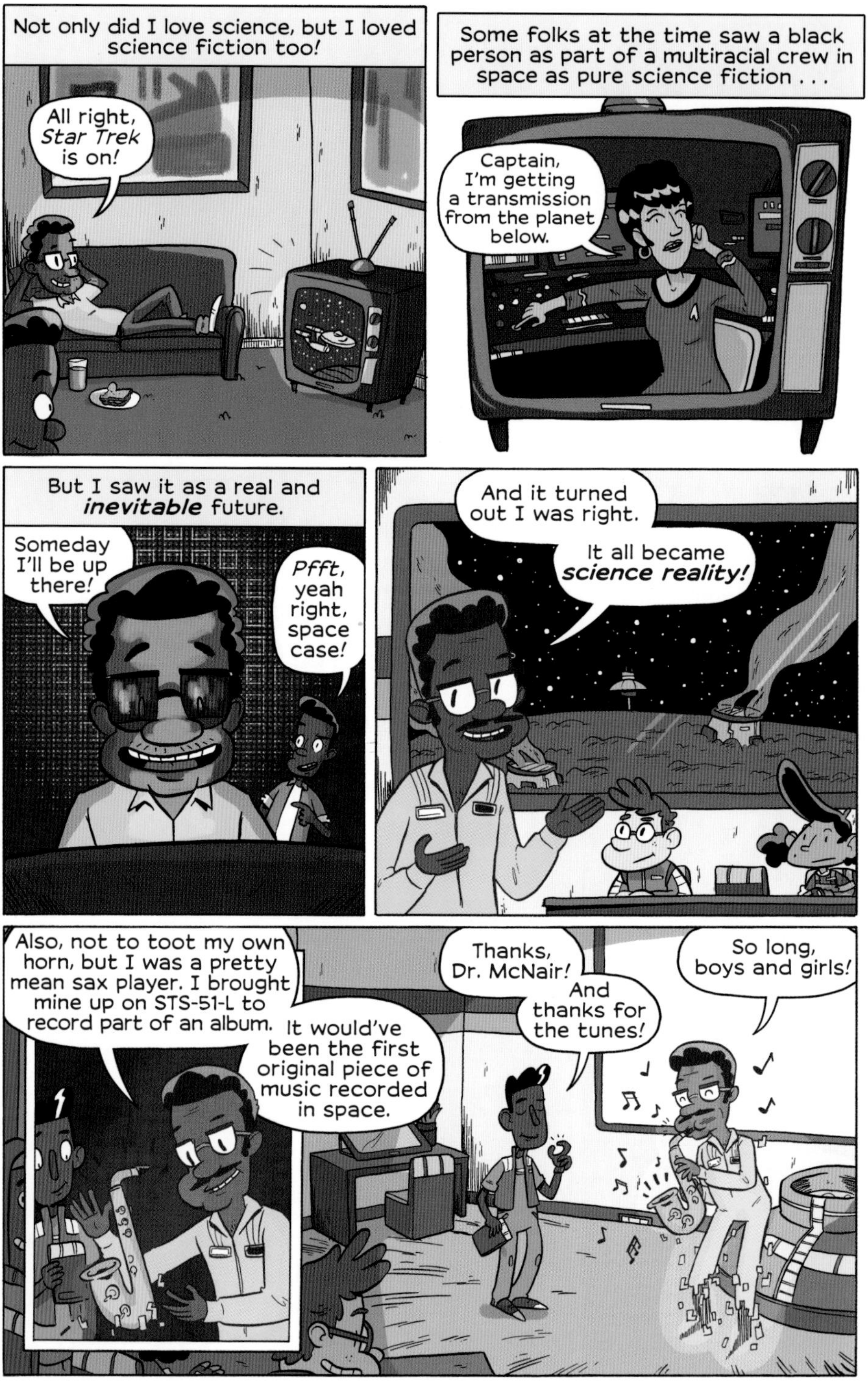

Not only did I love science, but I loved science fiction too!
All right, Star Trek is on!
Some folks at the time saw a black person as part of a multiracial crew in space as pure science fiction . . .
Captain, I'm getting a transmission from the planet below.
But I saw it as a real and inevitable future.
Someday I'll be up there!
Pfft, yeah right, space case!
And it turned out I was right.
It all became science reality!
Also, not to toot my own horn, but I was a pretty mean sax player. I brought mine up on STS-51-L to record part of an album.
It would've been the first original piece of music recorded in space.
Thanks, Dr. McNair!
And thanks for the tunes!
So long, boys and girls!

Next, let's meet Judith Resnik.

Hi, class! Great to be here!

Born: April 5, 1949
Mission Specialist, Engineer
Joined NASA: 1978
Previous mission: STS-41-D
Time in space: 6 days, 56 minutes
2nd American woman in space, 4th woman overall, 1st Jewish woman, 1st Jewish-American

Look at all those famous firsts!

...ys
56 minutes
2nd American woman in space, 4th woman overall, 1st Jewish woman, 1st Jewish-American

Huh, that's quite a few!

NASA would select potential astronauts in large groups every few years. In 1978, I was part of Astronaut Group 8. This group was the first group to include women and minorities.

35 E 1978

My crewmates McNair, Onizuka, and Scobee were also part of this group.

Nichelle Nichols, the actress from *Star Trek*, was employed by NASA as an official ambassador to reach out and encourage women and people of color to apply. And it worked!

Science is not a boy's game, it's not a girl's game. It's **everyone's** game.

It's about where we are and where we're **going**.

All six of us women from Group 8 had backgrounds in science and went up into space at least once in our careers.

Shannon Lucid
Biochemist
1st US woman on a long-duration space station mission

Sally Ride
Physicist
1st US woman in space

Anna Fisher
Chemist

Rhea Seddon
Physician

Kathryn Sullivan
Geologist
1st US woman to spacewalk

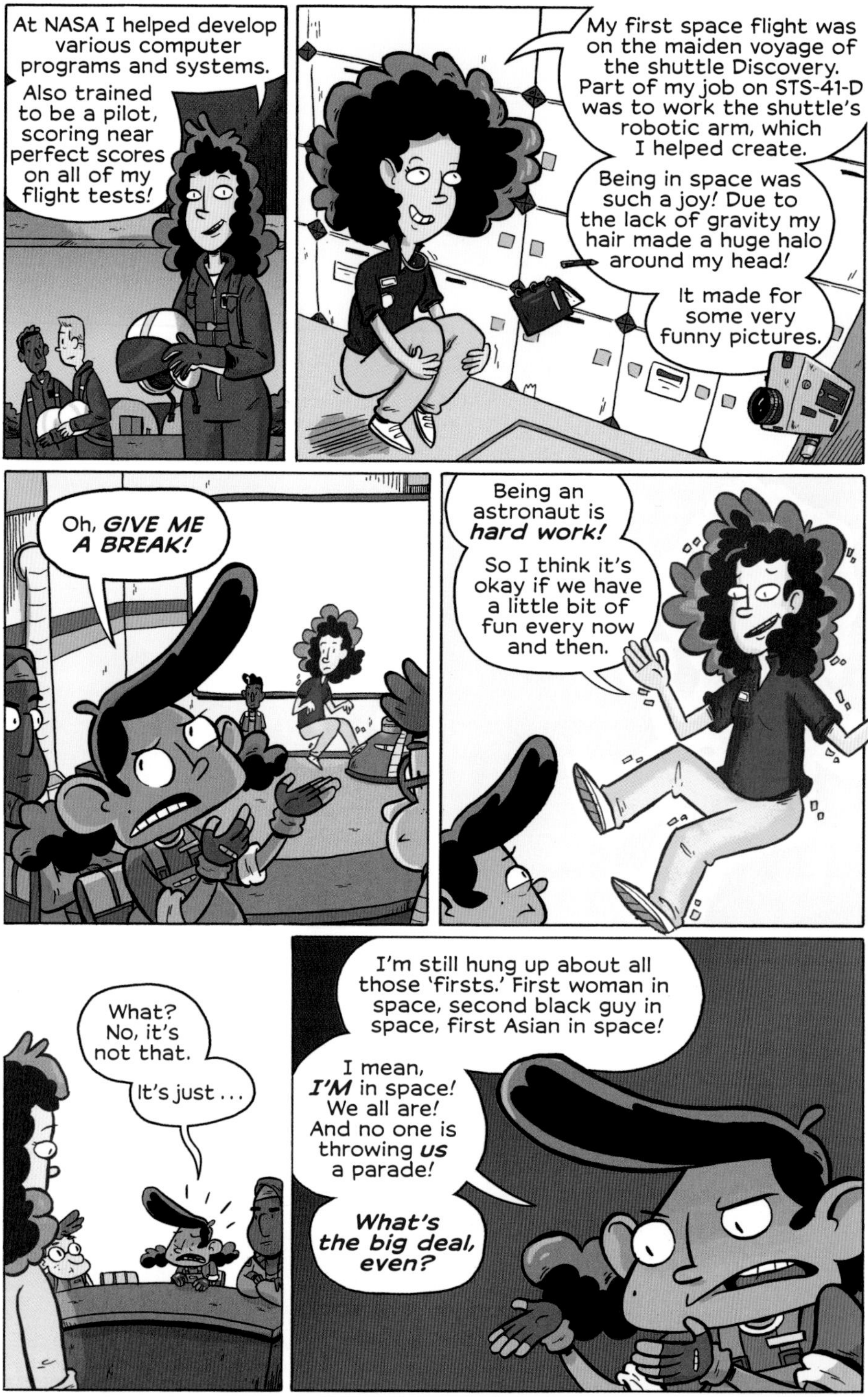
At NASA I helped develop various computer programs and systems.
Also trained to be a pilot, scoring near perfect scores on all of my flight tests!
My first space flight was on the maiden voyage of the shuttle Discovery. Part of my job on STS-41-D was to work the shuttle's robotic arm, which I helped create.
Being in space was such a joy! Due to the lack of gravity my hair made a huge halo around my head!
It made for some very funny pictures.
Oh, *GIVE ME A BREAK!*
Being an astronaut is ***hard work!***
So I think it's okay if we have a little bit of fun every now and then.
What? No, it's not that.
It's just . . .
I'm still hung up about all those 'firsts.' First woman in space, second black guy in space, first Asian in space!
I mean, ***I'M*** in space! We all are! And no one is throwing ***us*** a parade!
What's the big deal, even?

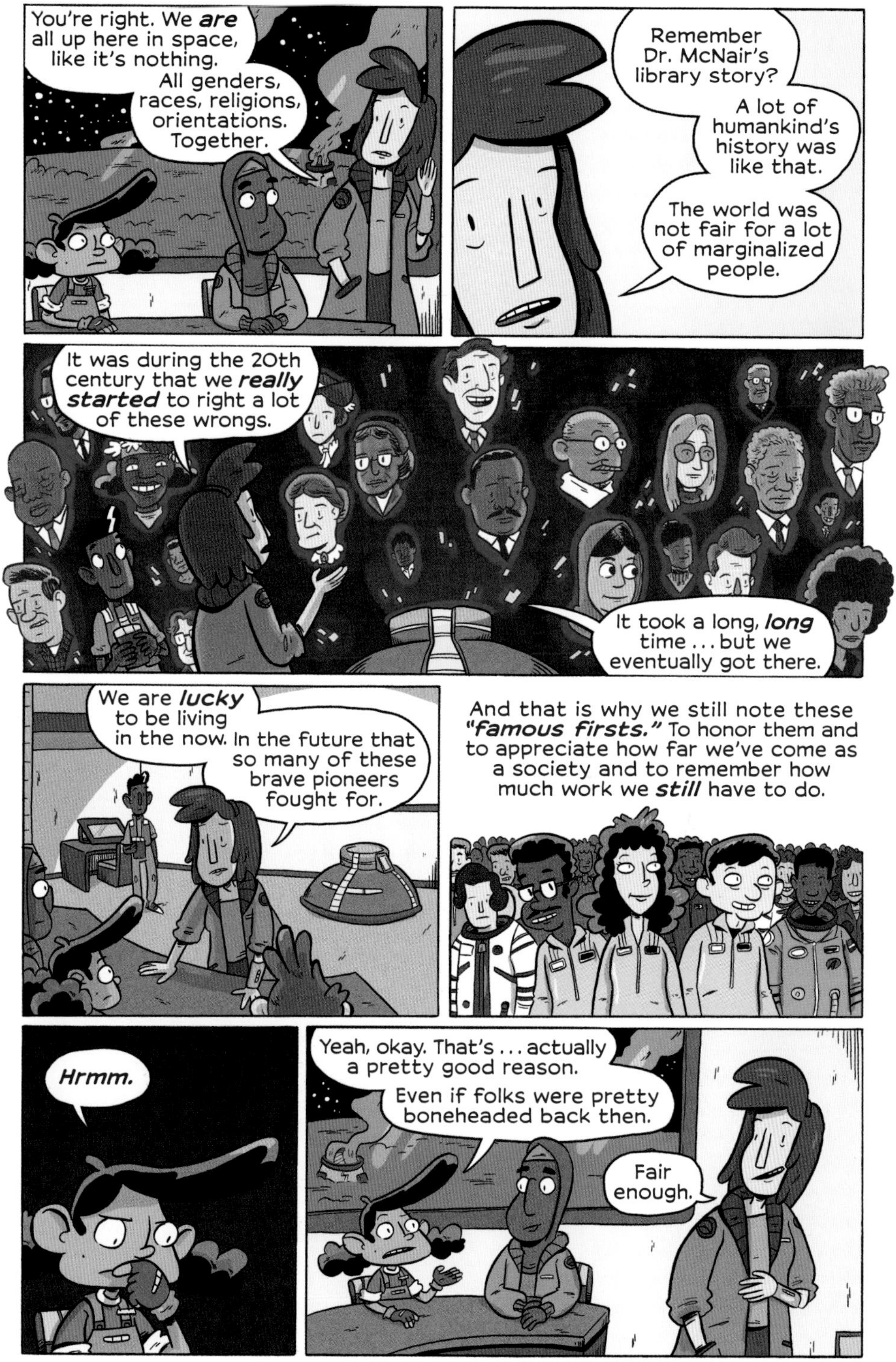
You're right. We *are* all up here in space, like it's nothing.
All genders, races, religions, orientations. Together.
Remember Dr. McNair's library story?
A lot of humankind's history was like that.
The world was not fair for a lot of marginalized people.
It was during the 20th century that we *really started* to right a lot of these wrongs.
It took a long, *long* time . . . but we eventually got there.
We are *lucky* to be living in the now.
In the future that so many of these brave pioneers fought for.
And that is why we still note these *"famous firsts."* To honor them and to appreciate how far we've come as a society and to remember how much work we *still* have to do.
Hrmm.
Yeah, okay. That's . . . actually a pretty good reason.
Even if folks were pretty boneheaded back then.
Fair enough.

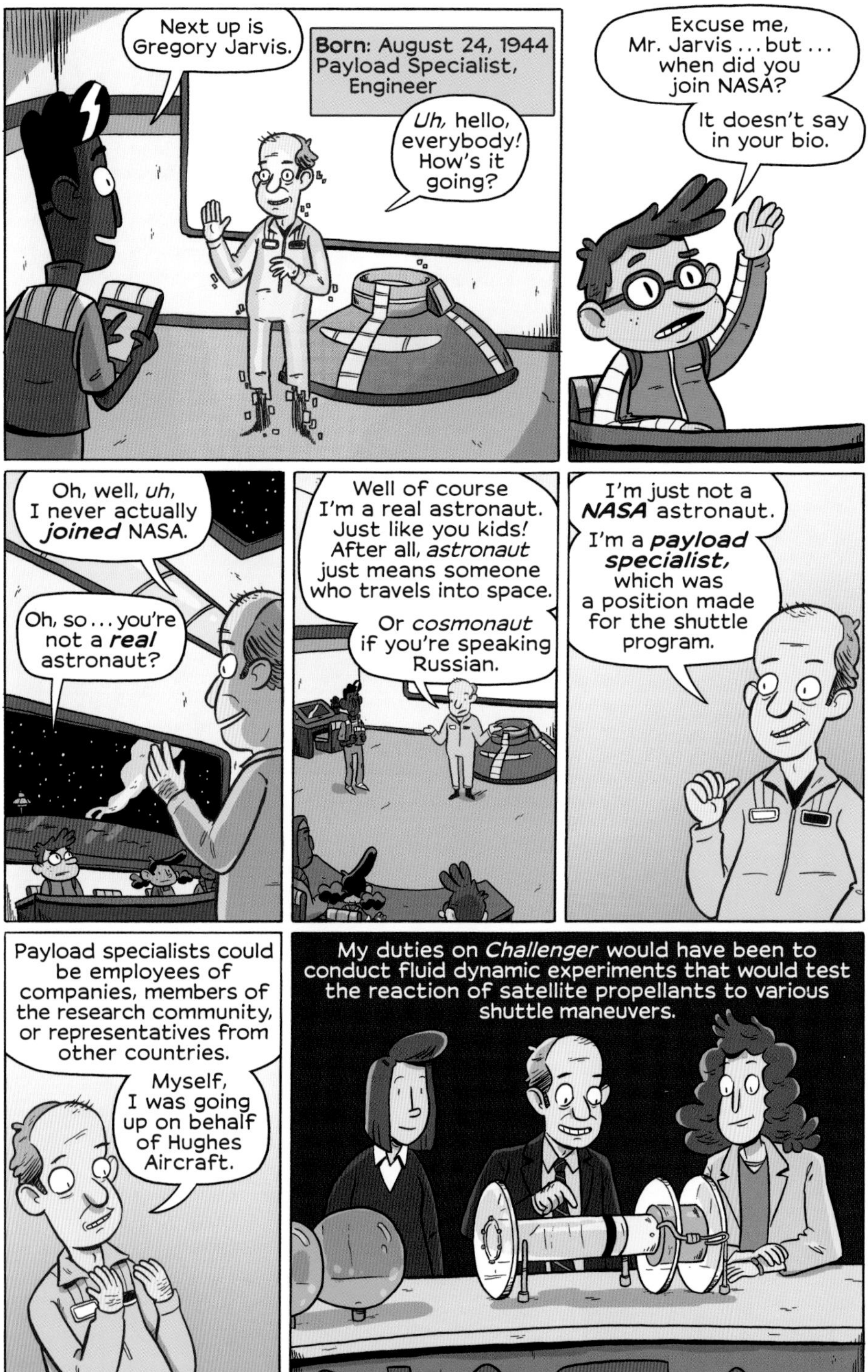
Next up is Gregory Jarvis.
Born: August 24, 1944
Payload Specialist, Engineer
Uh, hello, everybody! How's it going?
Excuse me, Mr. Jarvis . . . but . . . when did you join NASA?
It doesn't say in your bio.
Oh, well, uh, I never actually joined NASA.
Oh, so . . . you're not a real astronaut?
Well of course I'm a real astronaut. Just like you kids! After all, astronaut just means someone who travels into space.
Or cosmonaut if you're speaking Russian.
I'm just not a NASA astronaut.
I'm a payload specialist, which was a position made for the shuttle program.
Payload specialists could be employees of companies, members of the research community, or representatives from other countries.
Myself, I was going up on behalf of Hughes Aircraft.
My duties on Challenger would have been to conduct fluid dynamic experiments that would test the reaction of satellite propellants to various shuttle maneuvers.

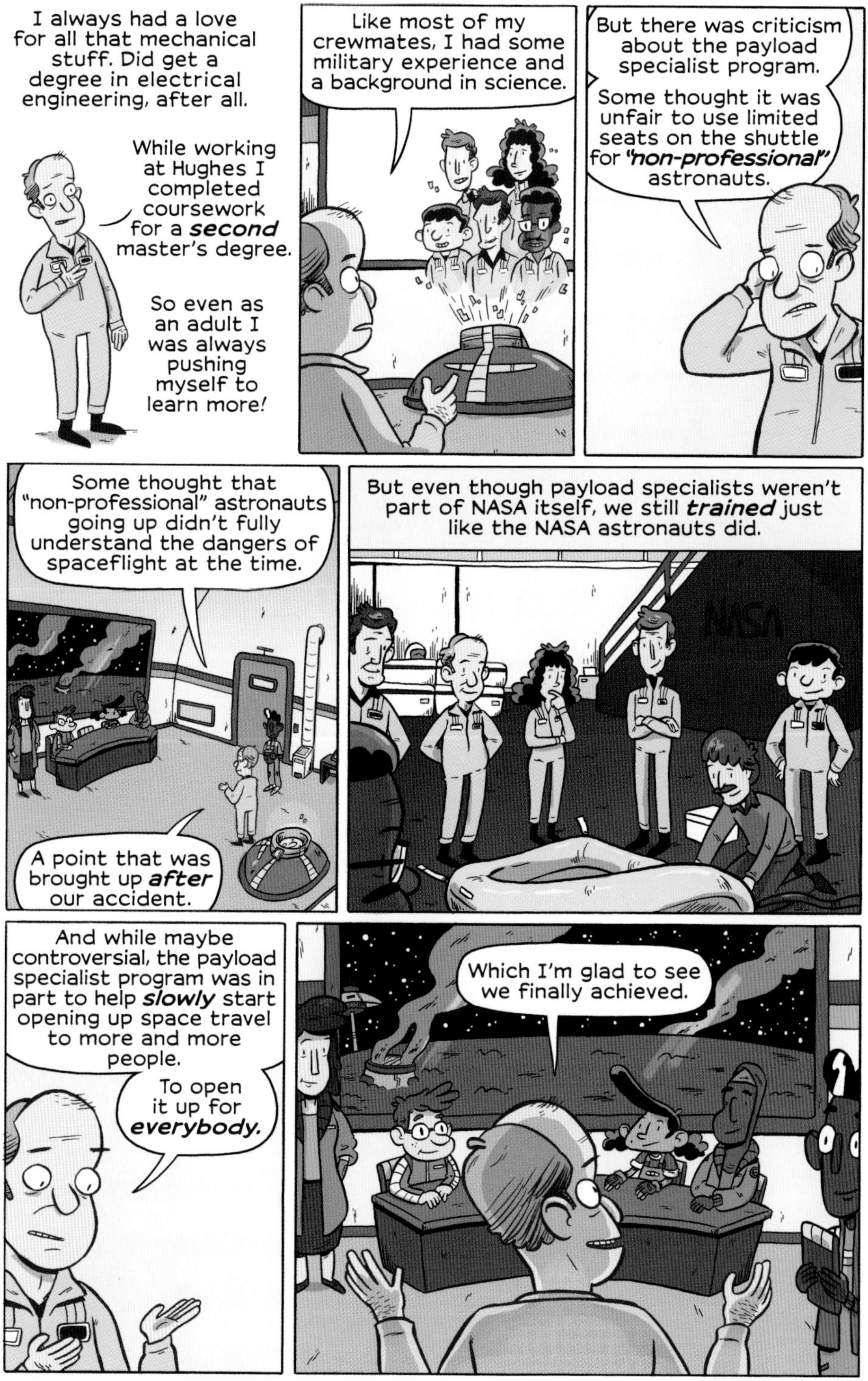

I always had a love for all that mechanical stuff. Did get a degree in electrical engineering, after all.
While working at Hughes I completed coursework for a **second** master's degree.
So even as an adult I was always pushing myself to learn more!
Like most of my crewmates, I had some military experience and a background in science.
But there was criticism about the payload specialist program.
Some thought it was unfair to use limited seats on the shuttle for ***"non-professional"*** astronauts.
Some thought that "non-professional" astronauts going up didn't fully understand the dangers of spaceflight at the time.
A point that was brought up **after** our accident.
But even though payload specialists weren't part of NASA itself, we still **trained** just like the NASA astronauts did.
NASA
And while maybe controversial, the payload specialist program was in part to help **slowly** start opening up space travel to more and more people.
To open it up for **everybody.**
Which I'm glad to see we finally achieved.

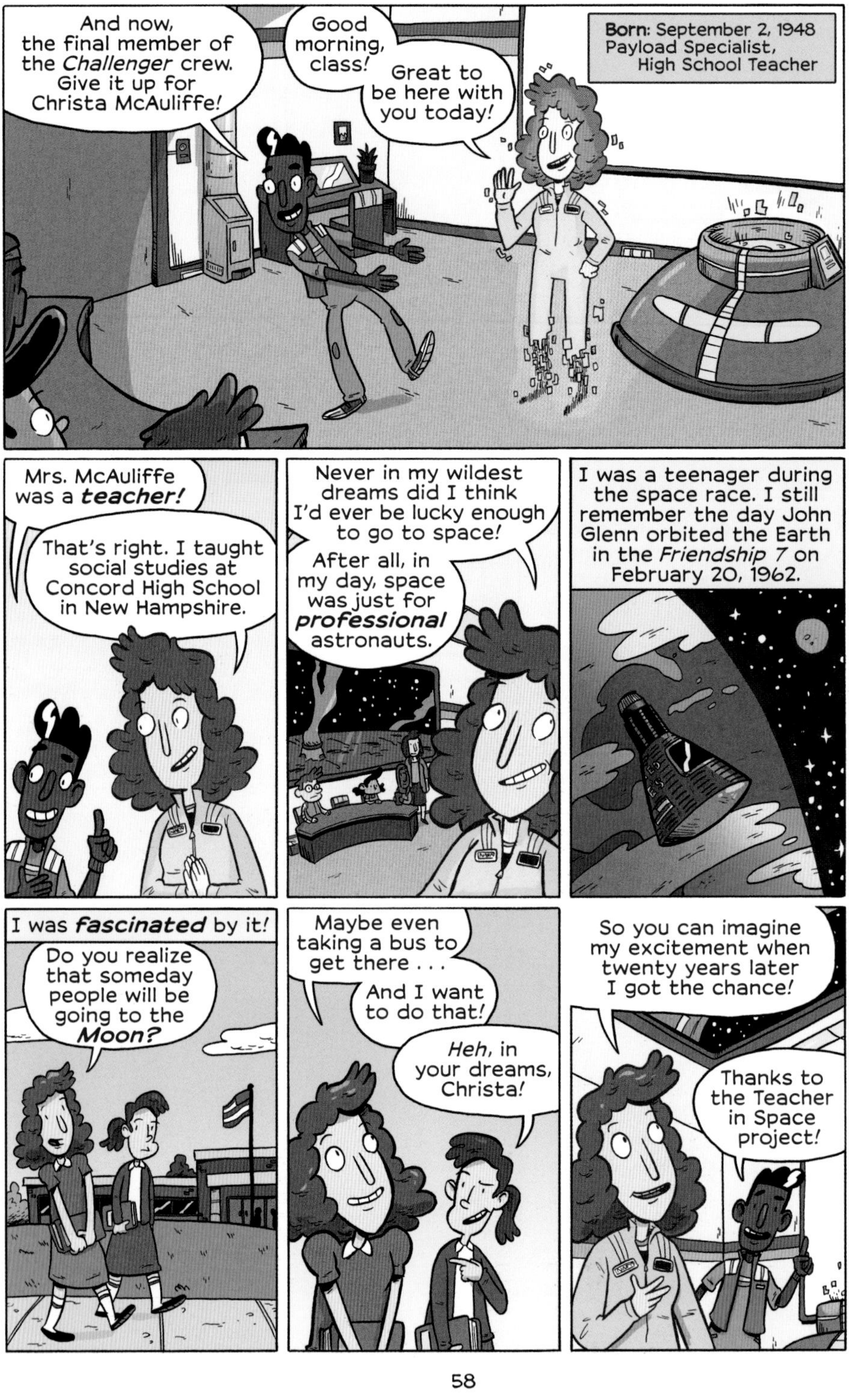
And now, the final member of the *Challenger* crew. Give it up for Christa McAuliffe!
Good morning, class!
Great to be here with you today!
Born: September 2, 1948 Payload Specialist, High School Teacher
Mrs. McAuliffe was a ***teacher!***
That's right. I taught social studies at Concord High School in New Hampshire.
Never in my wildest dreams did I think I'd ever be lucky enough to go to space!
After all, in my day, space was just for ***professional*** astronauts.
I was a teenager during the space race. I still remember the day John Glenn orbited the Earth in the *Friendship 7* on February 20, 1962.
I was ***fascinated*** by it!
Do you realize that someday people will be going to the ***Moon?***
Maybe even taking a bus to get there . . .
And I want to do that!
Heh, in your dreams, Christa!
So you can imagine my excitement when twenty years later I got the chance!
Thanks to the Teacher in Space project!

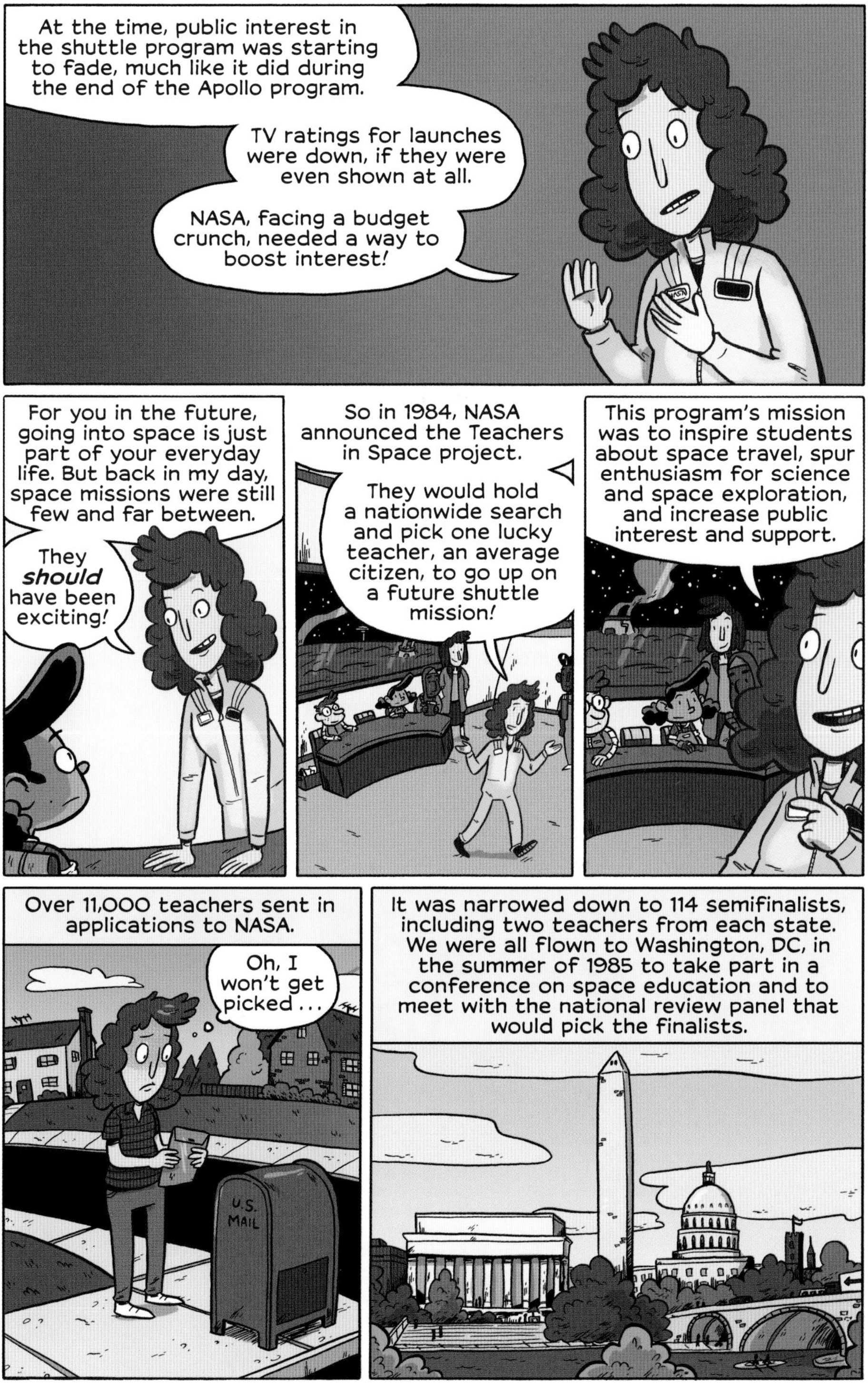
At the time, public interest in the shuttle program was starting to fade, much like it did during the end of the Apollo program.
TV ratings for launches were down, if they were even shown at all.
NASA, facing a budget crunch, needed a way to boost interest!
NASA
For you in the future, going into space is just part of your everyday life. But back in my day, space missions were still few and far between.
They *should* have been exciting!
So in 1984, NASA announced the Teachers in Space project.
They would hold a nationwide search and pick one lucky teacher, an average citizen, to go up on a future shuttle mission!
This program's mission was to inspire students about space travel, spur enthusiasm for science and space exploration, and increase public interest and support.
Over 11,000 teachers sent in applications to NASA.
Oh, I won't get picked . . .
U.S. MAIL
It was narrowed down to 114 semifinalists, including two teachers from each state. We were all flown to Washington, DC, in the summer of 1985 to take part in a conference on space education and to meet with the national review panel that would pick the finalists.

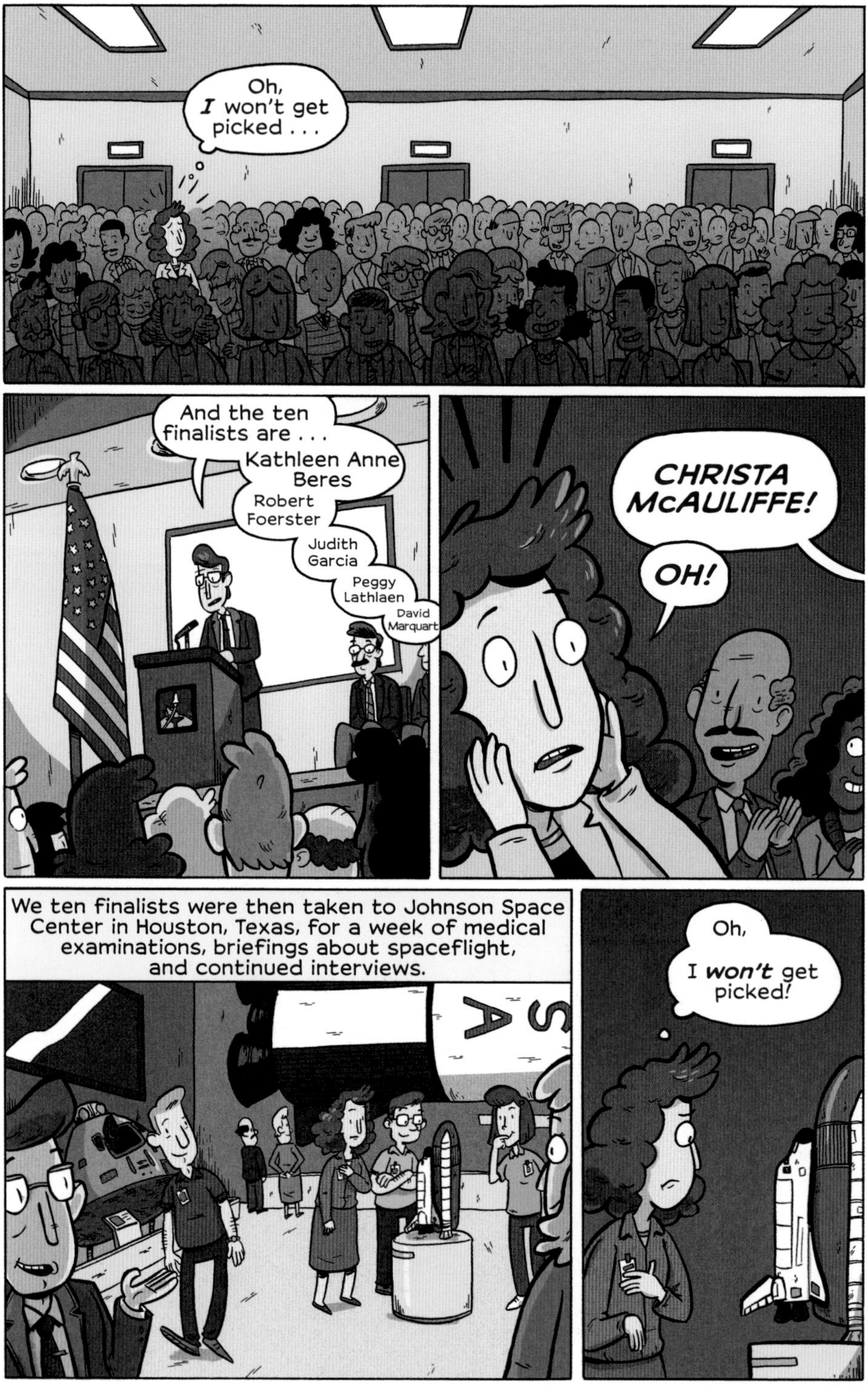
Oh, *I* won't get picked . . .
And the ten finalists are . . .
Kathleen Anne Beres
Robert Foerster
Judith Garcia
Peggy Lathlaen
David Marquart
CHRISTA McAULIFFE!
OH!
We ten finalists were then taken to Johnson Space Center in Houston, Texas, for a week of medical examinations, briefings about spaceflight, and continued interviews.
SA
Oh, I *won't* get picked!

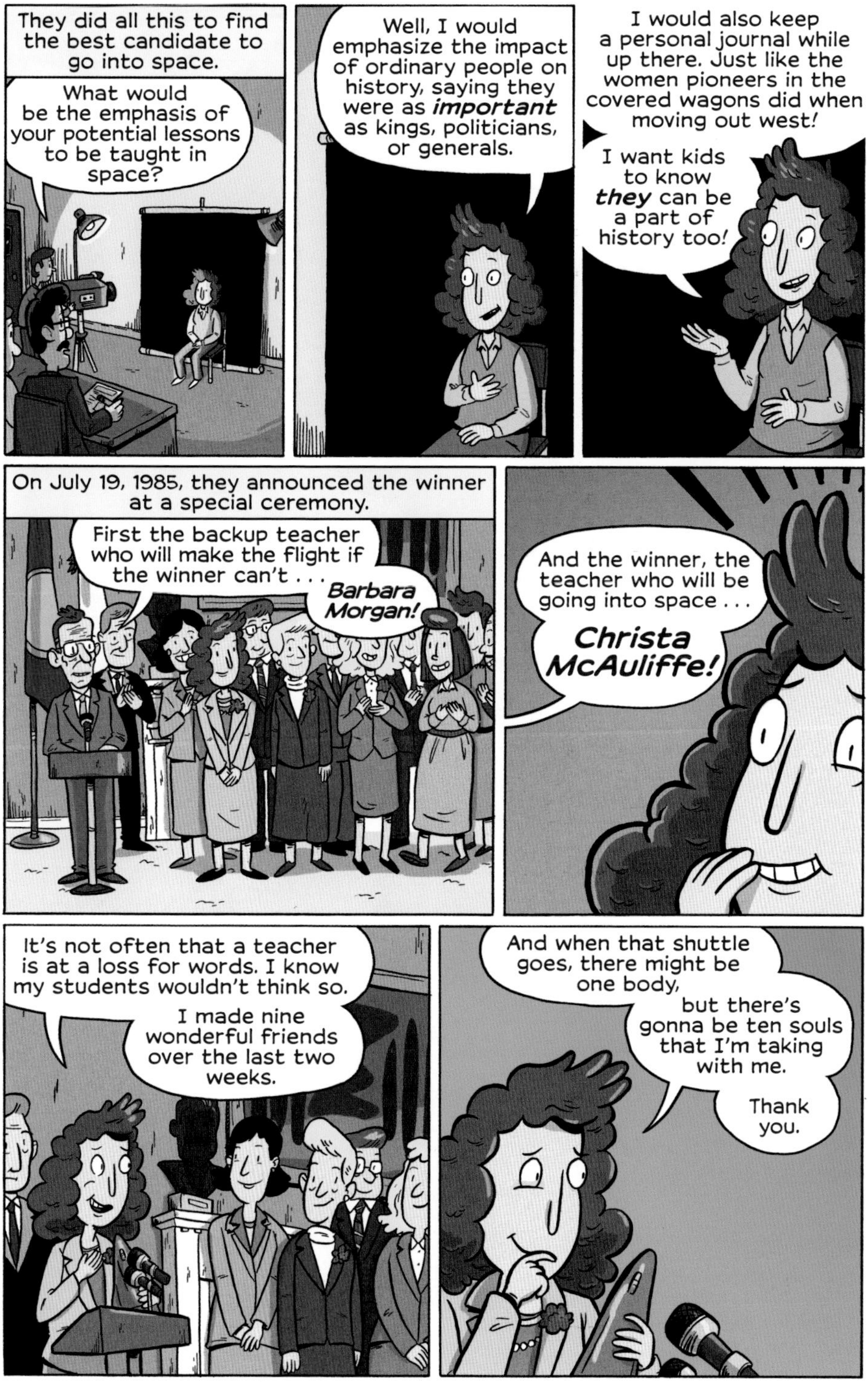
They did all this to find the best candidate to go into space.
What would be the emphasis of your potential lessons to be taught in space?
Well, I would emphasize the impact of ordinary people on history, saying they were as *important* as kings, politicians, or generals.
I would also keep a personal journal while up there. Just like the women pioneers in the covered wagons did when moving out west!
I want kids to know *they* can be a part of history too!
On July 19, 1985, they announced the winner at a special ceremony.
First the backup teacher who will make the flight if the winner can't . . .
Barbara Morgan!
And the winner, the teacher who will be going into space . . .
Christa McAuliffe!
It's not often that a teacher is at a loss for words. I know my students wouldn't think so.
I made nine wonderful friends over the last two weeks.
And when that shuttle goes, there might be one body,
but there's gonna be ten souls that I'm taking with me.
Thank you.

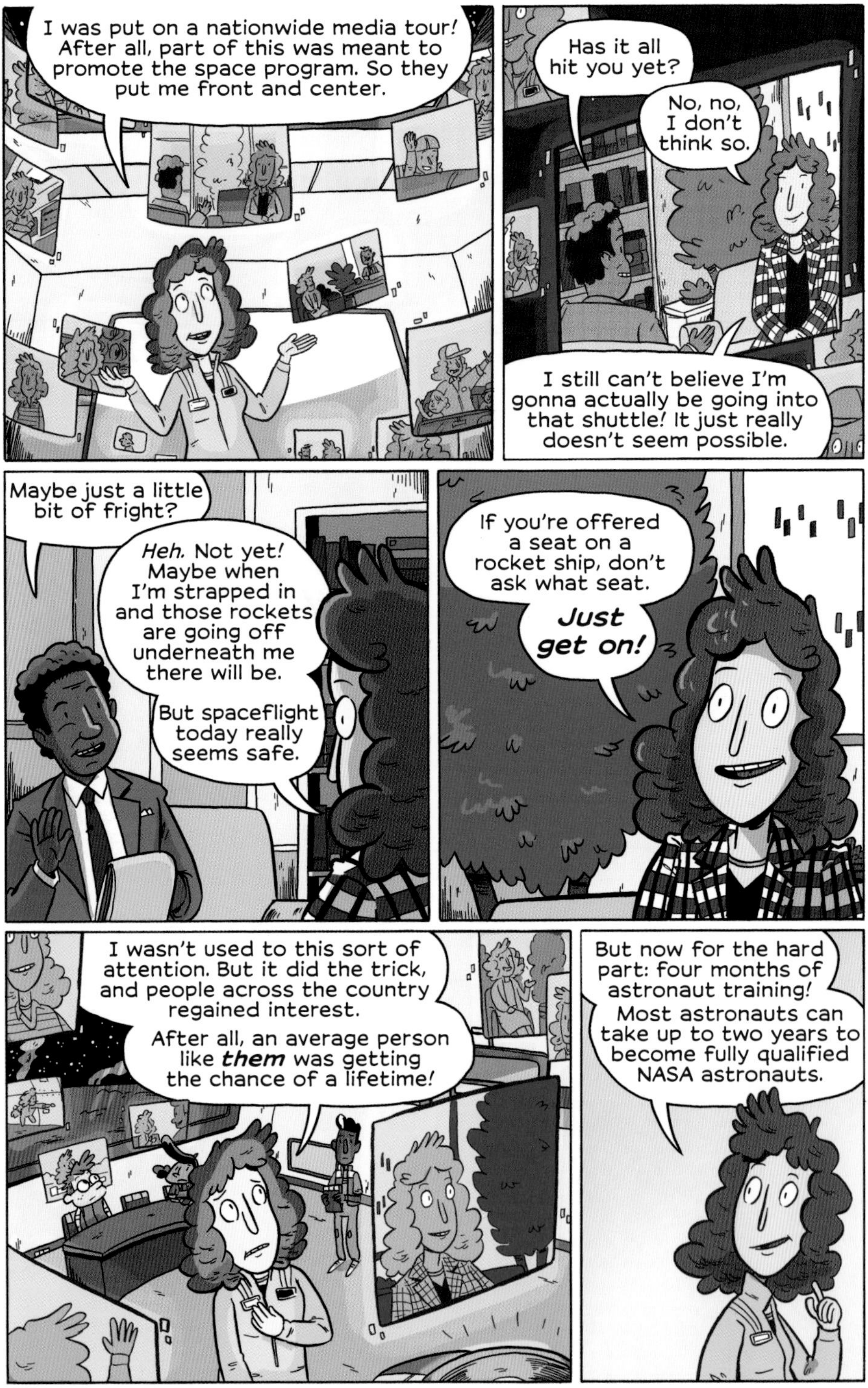
I was put on a nationwide media tour! After all, part of this was meant to promote the space program. So they put me front and center.
Has it all hit you yet?
No, no, I don't think so.
I still can't believe I'm gonna actually be going into that shuttle! It just really doesn't seem possible.
Maybe just a little bit of fright?
Heh. Not yet! Maybe when I'm strapped in and those rockets are going off underneath me there will be.
But spaceflight today really seems safe.
If you're offered a seat on a rocket ship, don't ask what seat.
Just get on!
I wasn't used to this sort of attention. But it did the trick, and people across the country regained interest.
After all, an average person like ***them*** was getting the chance of a lifetime!
But now for the hard part: four months of astronaut training!
Most astronauts can take up to two years to become fully qualified NASA astronauts.

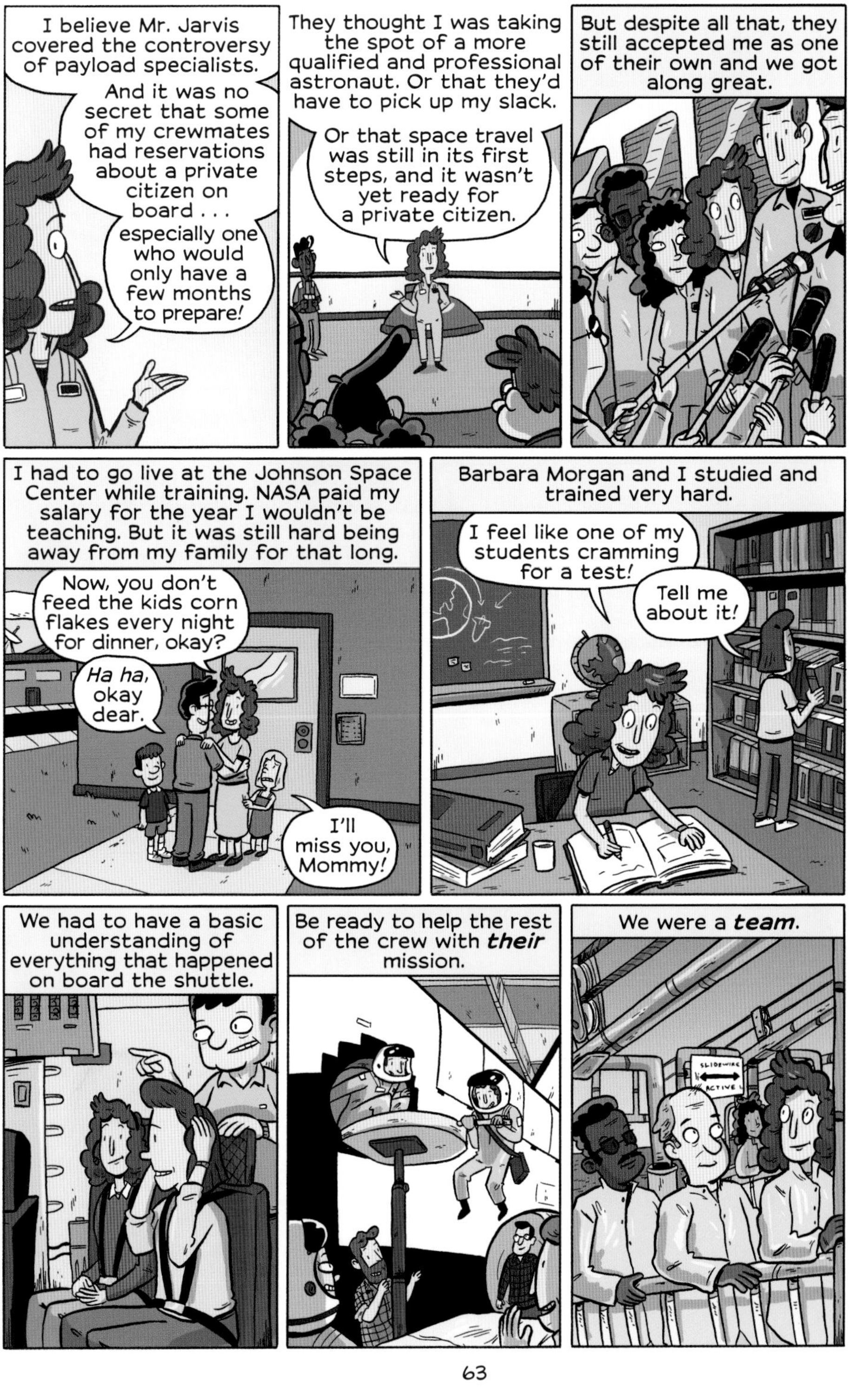
I believe Mr. Jarvis covered the controversy of payload specialists.
And it was no secret that some of my crewmates had reservations about a private citizen on board . . .
especially one who would only have a few months to prepare!
They thought I was taking the spot of a more qualified and professional astronaut. Or that they'd have to pick up my slack.
Or that space travel was still in its first steps, and it wasn't yet ready for a private citizen.
But despite all that, they still accepted me as one of their own and we got along great.
I had to go live at the Johnson Space Center while training. NASA paid my salary for the year I wouldn't be teaching. But it was still hard being away from my family for that long.
Now, you don't feed the kids corn flakes every night for dinner, okay?
Ha ha, okay dear.
I'll miss you, Mommy!
Barbara Morgan and I studied and trained very hard.
I feel like one of my students cramming for a test!
Tell me about it!
We had to have a basic understanding of everything that happened on board the shuttle.
Be ready to help the rest of the crew with ***their*** mission.
We were a ***team***.
SLIDEWIRE
ACTIVE

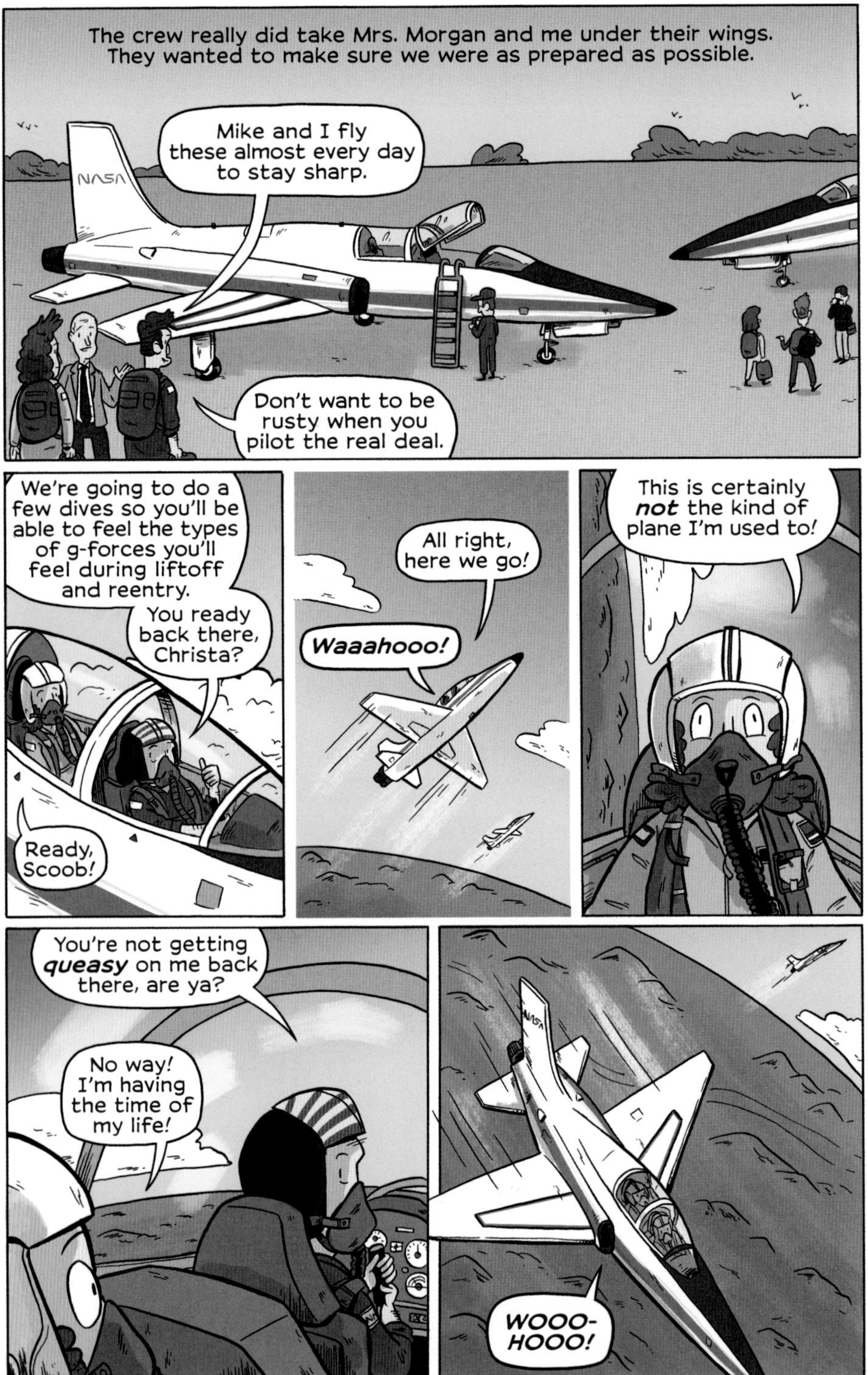
The crew really did take Mrs. Morgan and me under their wings. They wanted to make sure we were as prepared as possible.
NASA
Mike and I fly these almost every day to stay sharp.
Don't want to be rusty when you pilot the real deal.
We're going to do a few dives so you'll be able to feel the types of g-forces you'll feel during liftoff and reentry.
You ready back there, Christa?
Ready, Scoob!
All right, here we go!
Waaahooo!
This is certainly not the kind of plane I'm used to!
You're not getting queasy on me back there, are ya?
No way! I'm having the time of my life!
NASA
WOOO-HOOO!

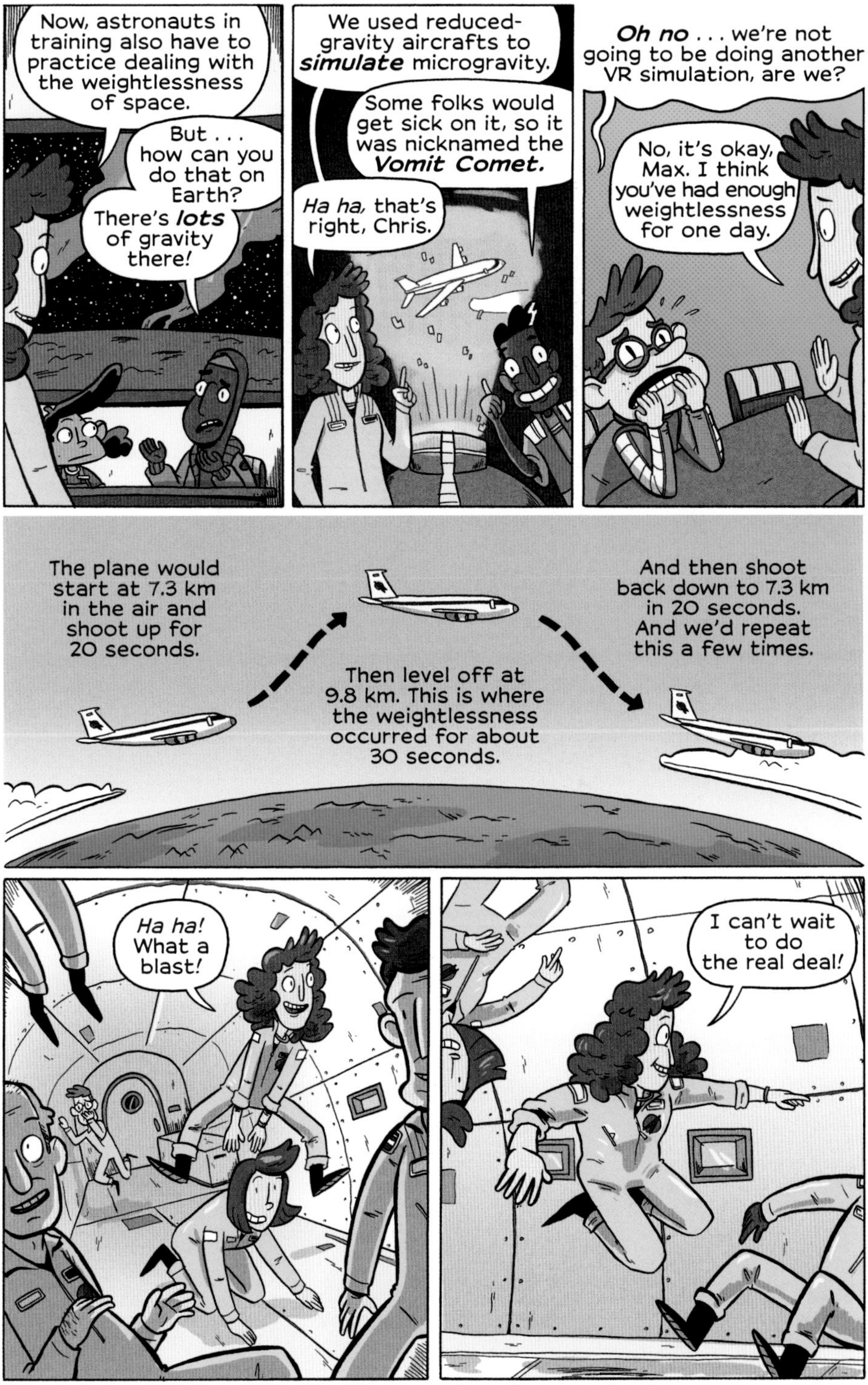
Now, astronauts in training also have to practice dealing with the weightlessness of space.
But . . . how can you do that on Earth?
There's *lots* of gravity there!
We used reduced-gravity aircrafts to *simulate* microgravity.
Some folks would get sick on it, so it was nicknamed the *Vomit Comet.*
Ha ha, that's right, Chris.
Oh no . . . we're not going to be doing another VR simulation, are we?
No, it's okay, Max. I think you've had enough weightlessness for one day.
The plane would start at 7.3 km in the air and shoot up for 20 seconds.
Then level off at 9.8 km. This is where the weightlessness occurred for about 30 seconds.
And then shoot back down to 7.3 km in 20 seconds. And we'd repeat this a few times.
Ha ha! What a blast!
I can't wait to do the real deal!

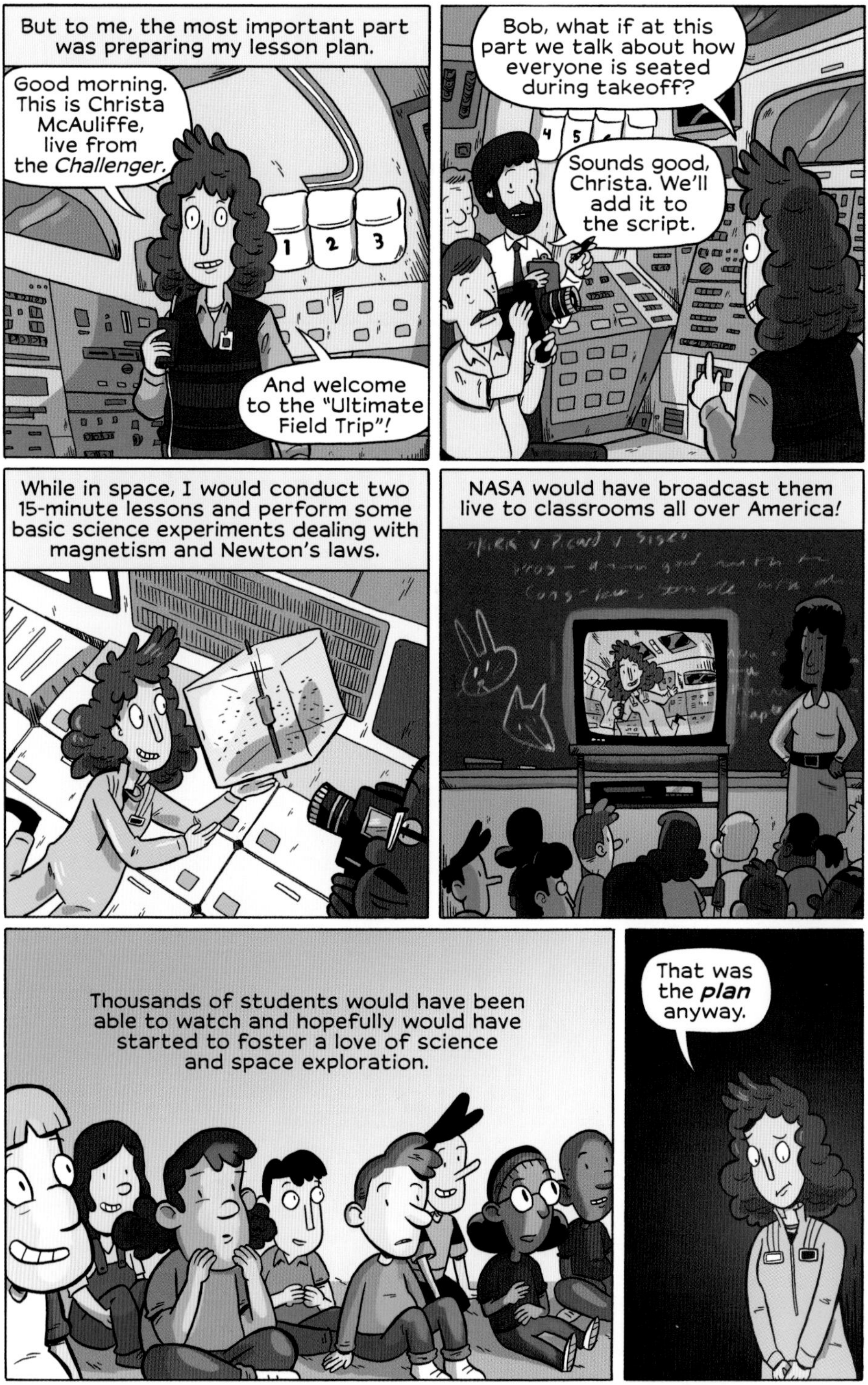
But to me, the most important part was preparing my lesson plan.
Good morning. This is Christa McAuliffe, live from the *Challenger*.
And welcome to the "Ultimate Field Trip"!
Bob, what if at this part we talk about how everyone is seated during takeoff?
Sounds good, Christa. We'll add it to the script.
While in space, I would conduct two 15-minute lessons and perform some basic science experiments dealing with magnetism and Newton's laws.
NASA would have broadcast them live to classrooms all over America!
Thousands of students would have been able to watch and hopefully would have started to foster a love of science and space exploration.
That was the ***plan*** anyway.

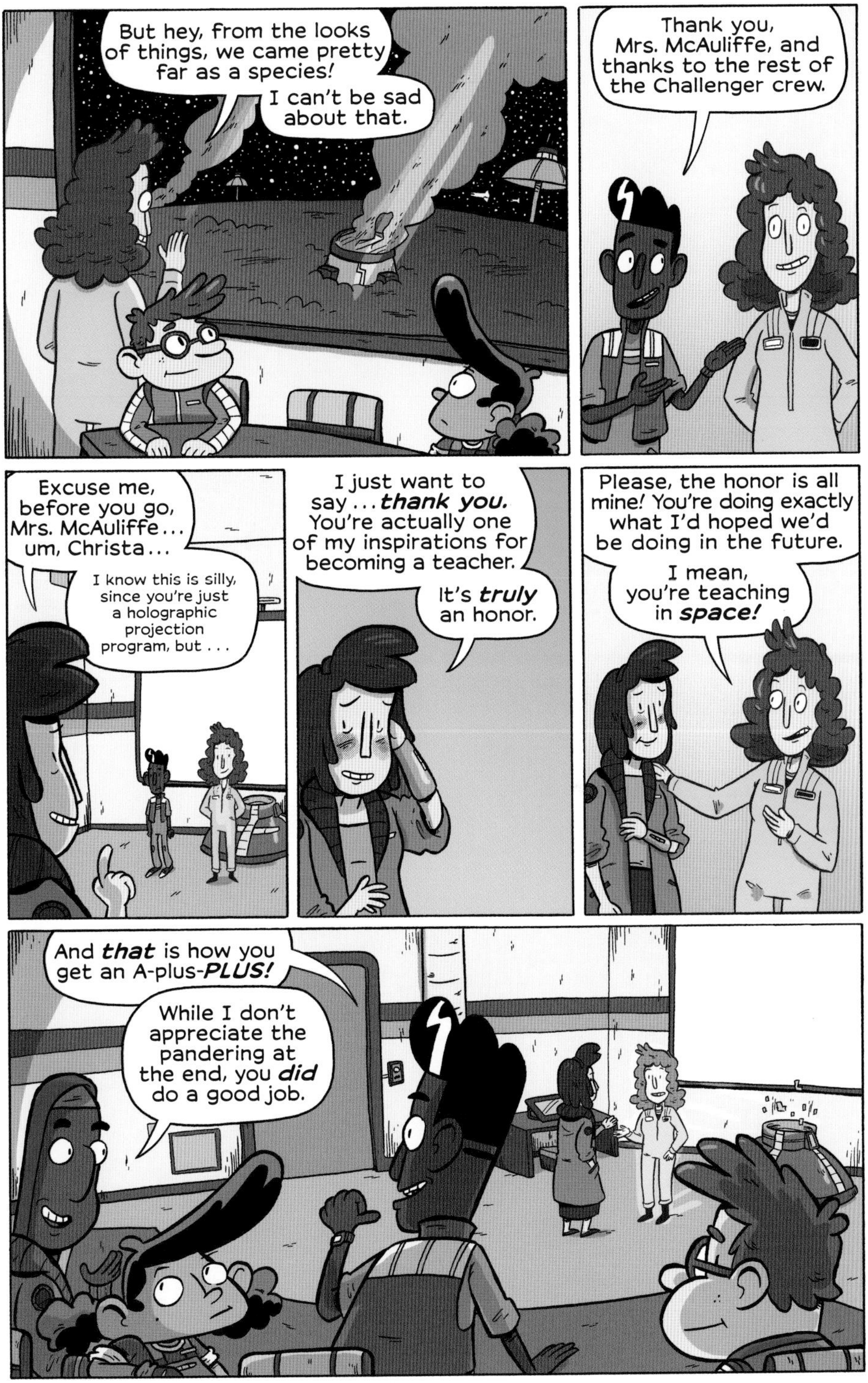
But hey, from the looks of things, we came pretty far as a species!
I can't be sad about that.
Thank you, Mrs. McAuliffe, and thanks to the rest of the Challenger crew.
Excuse me, before you go, Mrs. McAuliffe . . . um, Christa . . .
I know this is silly, since you're just a holographic projection program, but . . .
I just want to say . . . *thank you.* You're actually one of my inspirations for becoming a teacher.
It's *truly* an honor.
Please, the honor is all mine! You're doing exactly what I'd hoped we'd be doing in the future.
I mean, you're teaching in *space!*
And *that* is how you get an A-plus-*PLUS!*
While I don't appreciate the pandering at the end, you *did* do a good job.

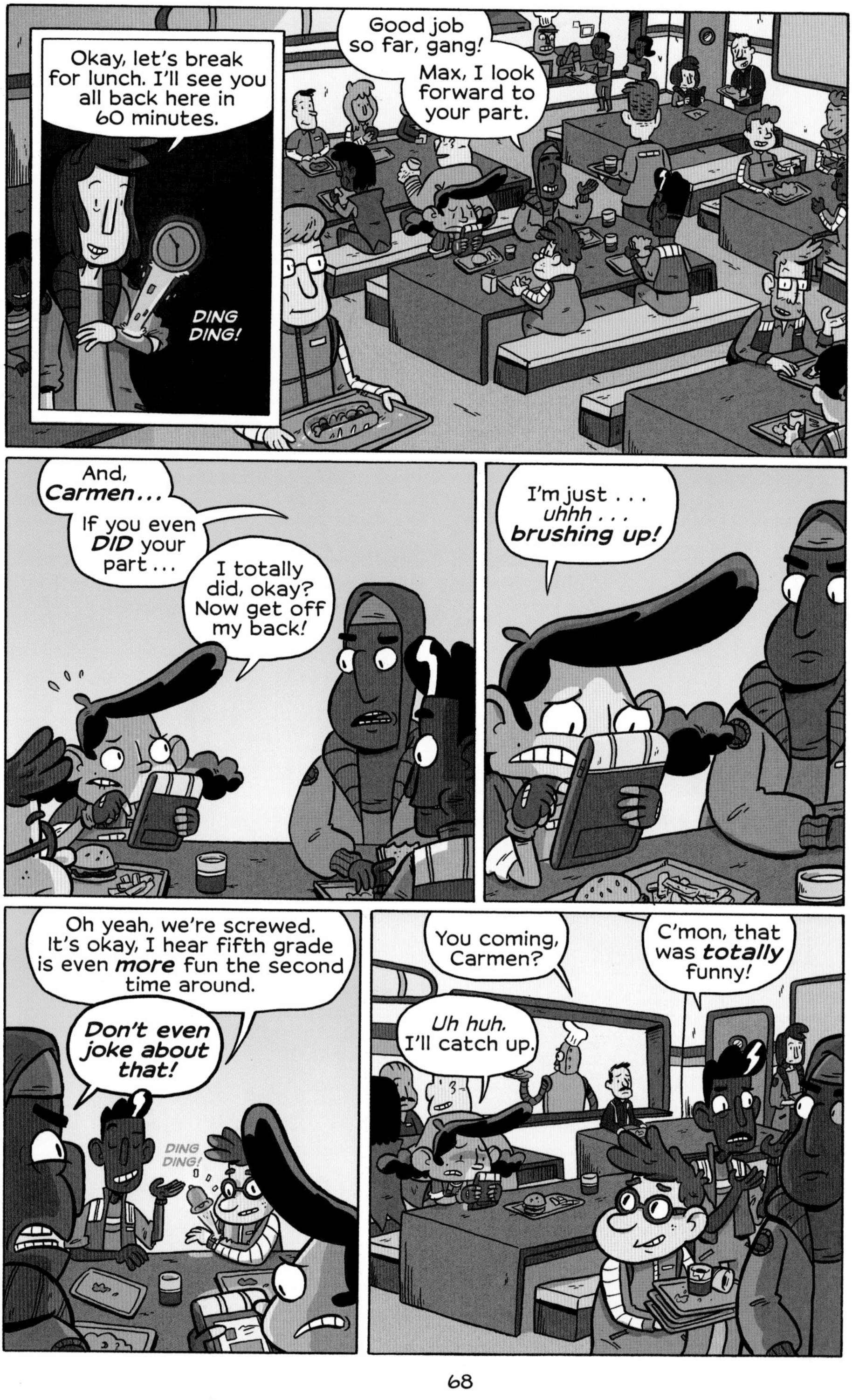
Okay, let's break for lunch. I'll see you all back here in 60 minutes.
DING DING!
Good job so far, gang!
Max, I look forward to your part.
And, Carmen...
If you even DID your part...
I totally did, okay? Now get off my back!
I'm just . . . uhhh . . . brushing up!
Oh yeah, we're screwed. It's okay, I hear fifth grade is even more fun the second time around.
Don't even joke about that!
DING DING!
You coming, Carmen?
Uh huh. I'll catch up.
C'mon, that was totally funny!

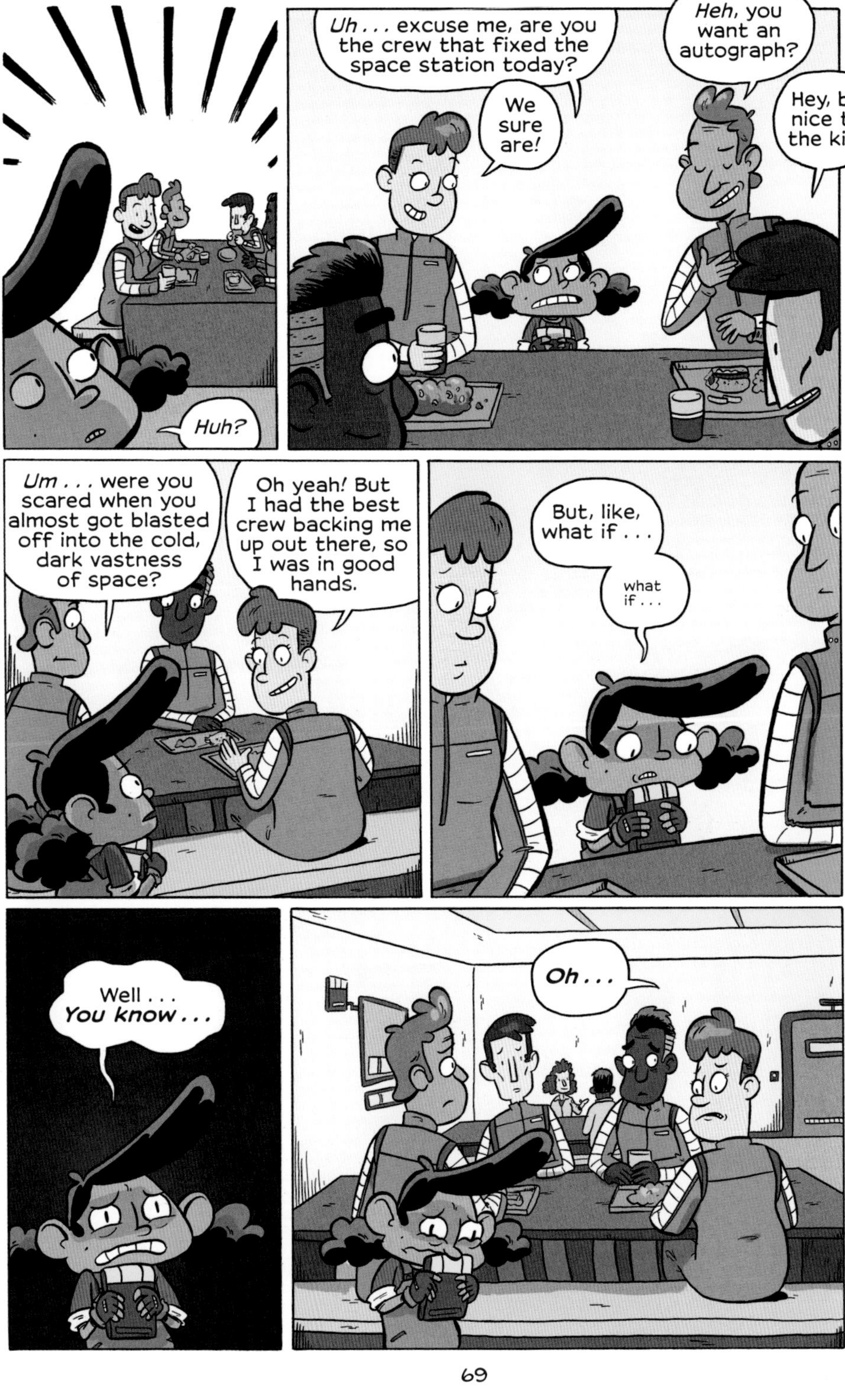

Huh?
Uh . . . excuse me, are you the crew that fixed the space station today?
We sure are!
Heh, you want an autograph?
Hey, be nice to the kid!
Um . . . were you scared when you almost got blasted off into the cold, dark vastness of space?
Oh yeah! But I had the best crew backing me up out there, so I was in good hands.
But, like, what if . . .
what if . . .
Well . . . You know . . .
Oh . . .

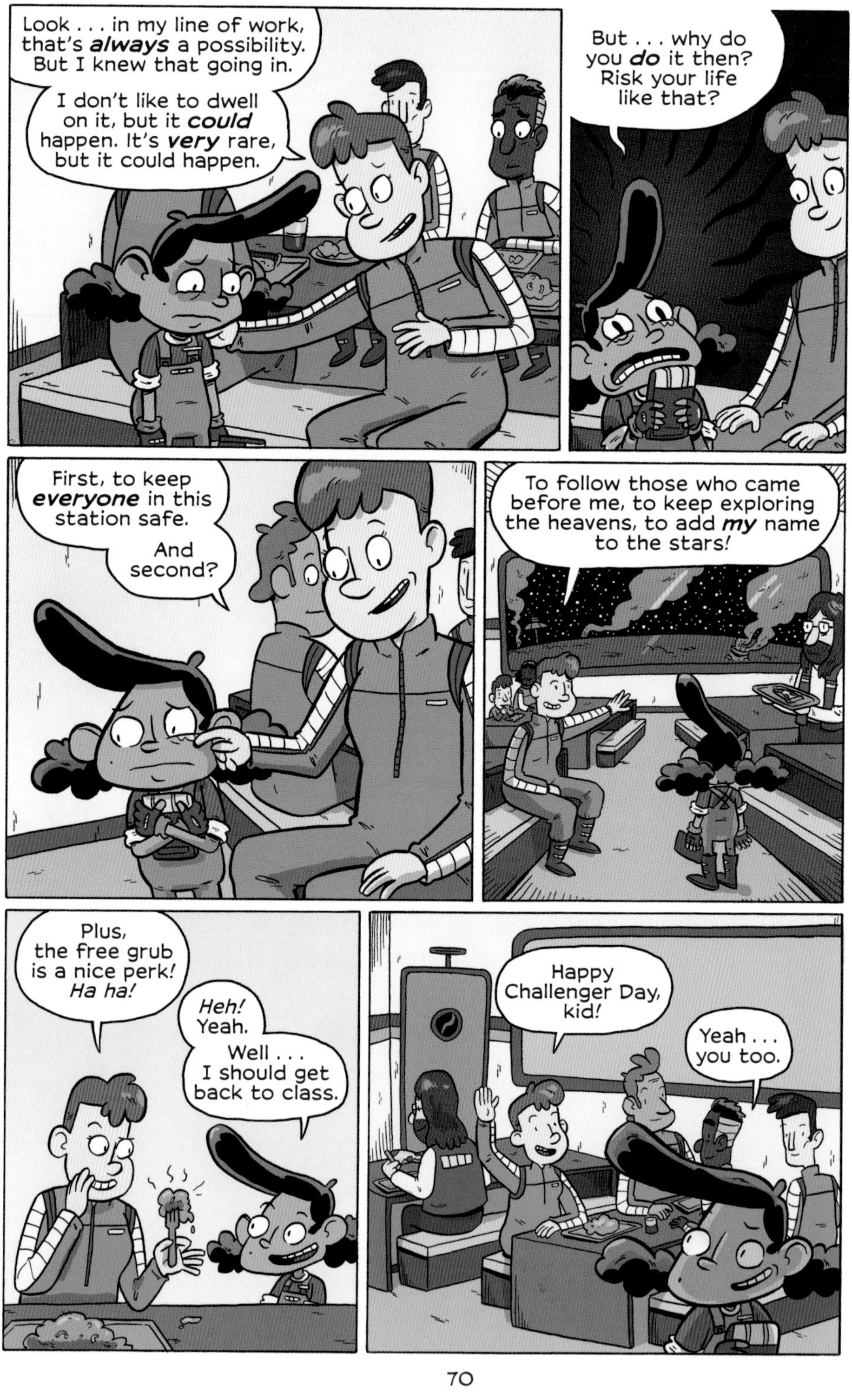
Look . . . in my line of work, that's ***always*** a possibility. But I knew that going in.
I don't like to dwell on it, but it ***could*** happen. It's ***very*** rare, but it could happen.
But . . . why do you ***do*** it then? Risk your life like that?
First, to keep ***everyone*** in this station safe.
And second?
To follow those who came before me, to keep exploring the heavens, to add ***my*** name to the stars*!*
Plus, the free grub is a nice perk*!* *Ha ha!*
Heh! Yeah.
Well . . . I should get back to class.
Happy Challenger Day, kid*!*
Yeah . . . you too.

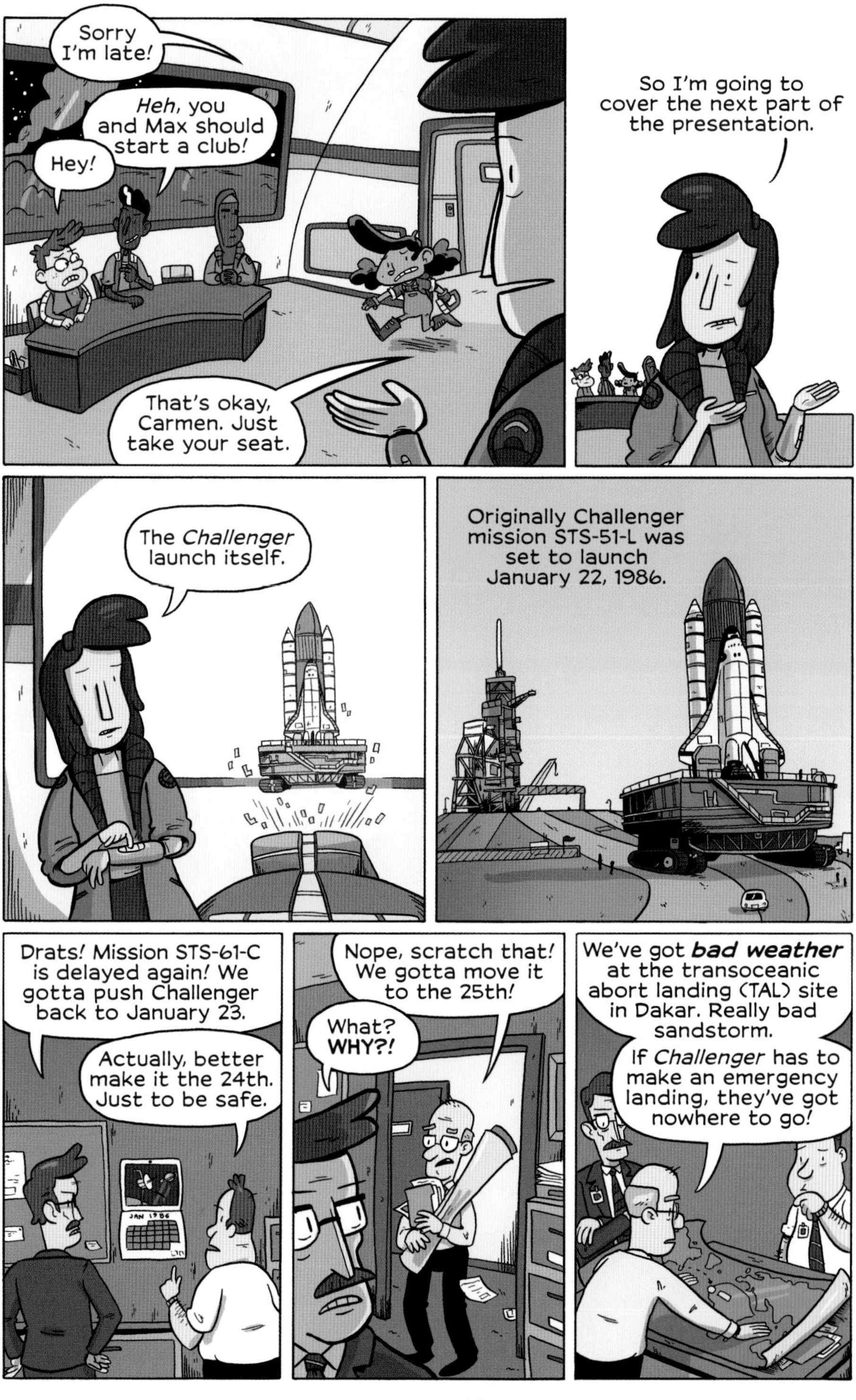
Sorry I'm late!
Heh, you and Max should start a club!
Hey!
That's okay, Carmen. Just take your seat.
So I'm going to cover the next part of the presentation.
The *Challenger* launch itself.
Originally Challenger mission STS-51-L was set to launch January 22, 1986.
Drats! Mission STS-61-C is delayed again! We gotta push Challenger back to January 23.
Actually, better make it the 24th. Just to be safe.
Nope, scratch that! We gotta move it to the 25th!
What? **WHY?!**
We've got ***bad weather*** at the transoceanic abort landing (TAL) site in Dakar. Really bad sandstorm.
If *Challenger* has to make an emergency landing, they've got nowhere to go!

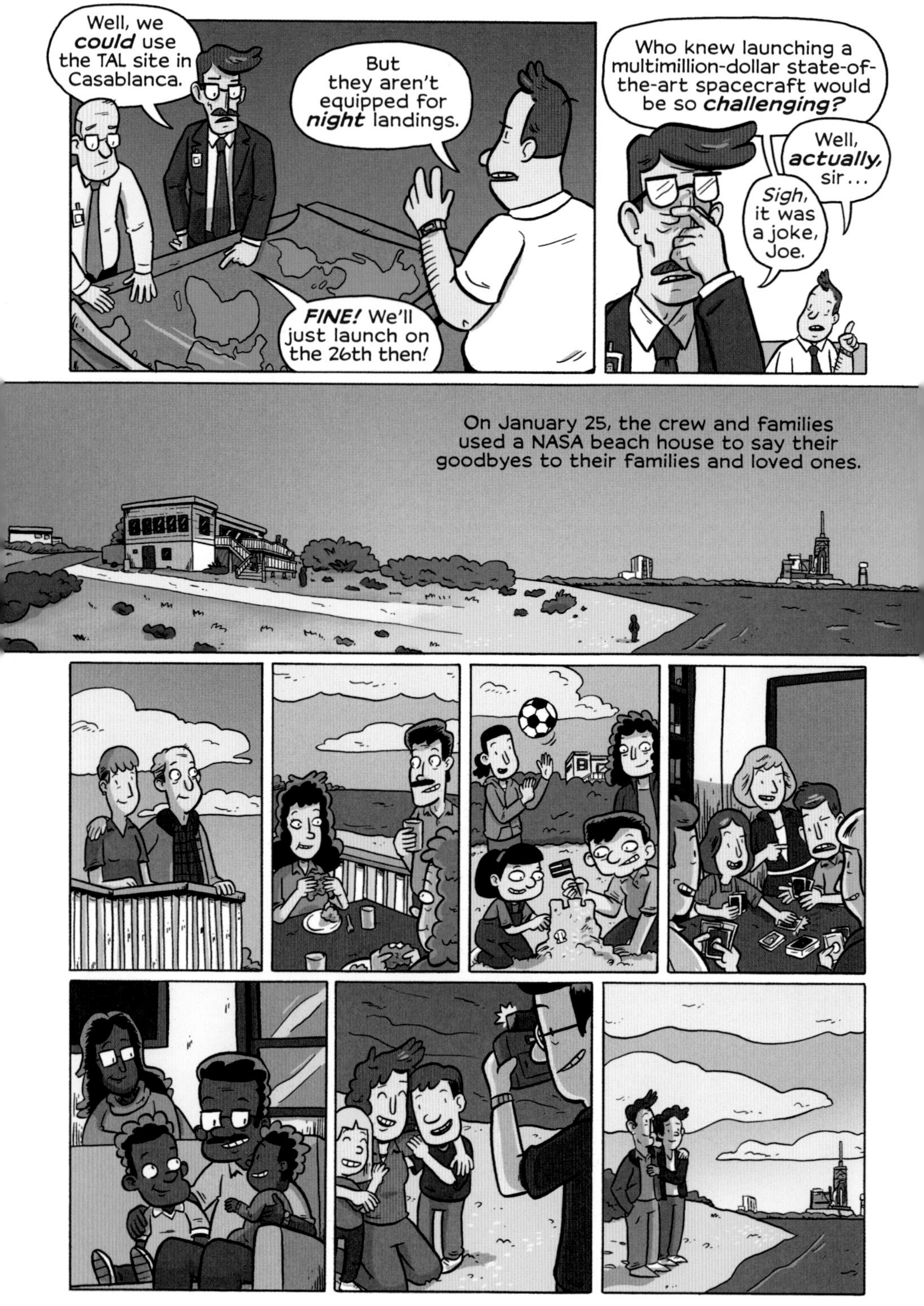
Well, we *could* use the TAL site in Casablanca.
But they aren't equipped for *night* landings.
FINE! We'll just launch on the 26th then!
Who knew launching a multimillion-dollar state-of-the-art spacecraft would be so *challenging?*
Well, *actually,* sir...
Sigh, it was a joke, Joe.
On January 25, the crew and families used a NASA beach house to say their goodbyes to their families and loved ones.

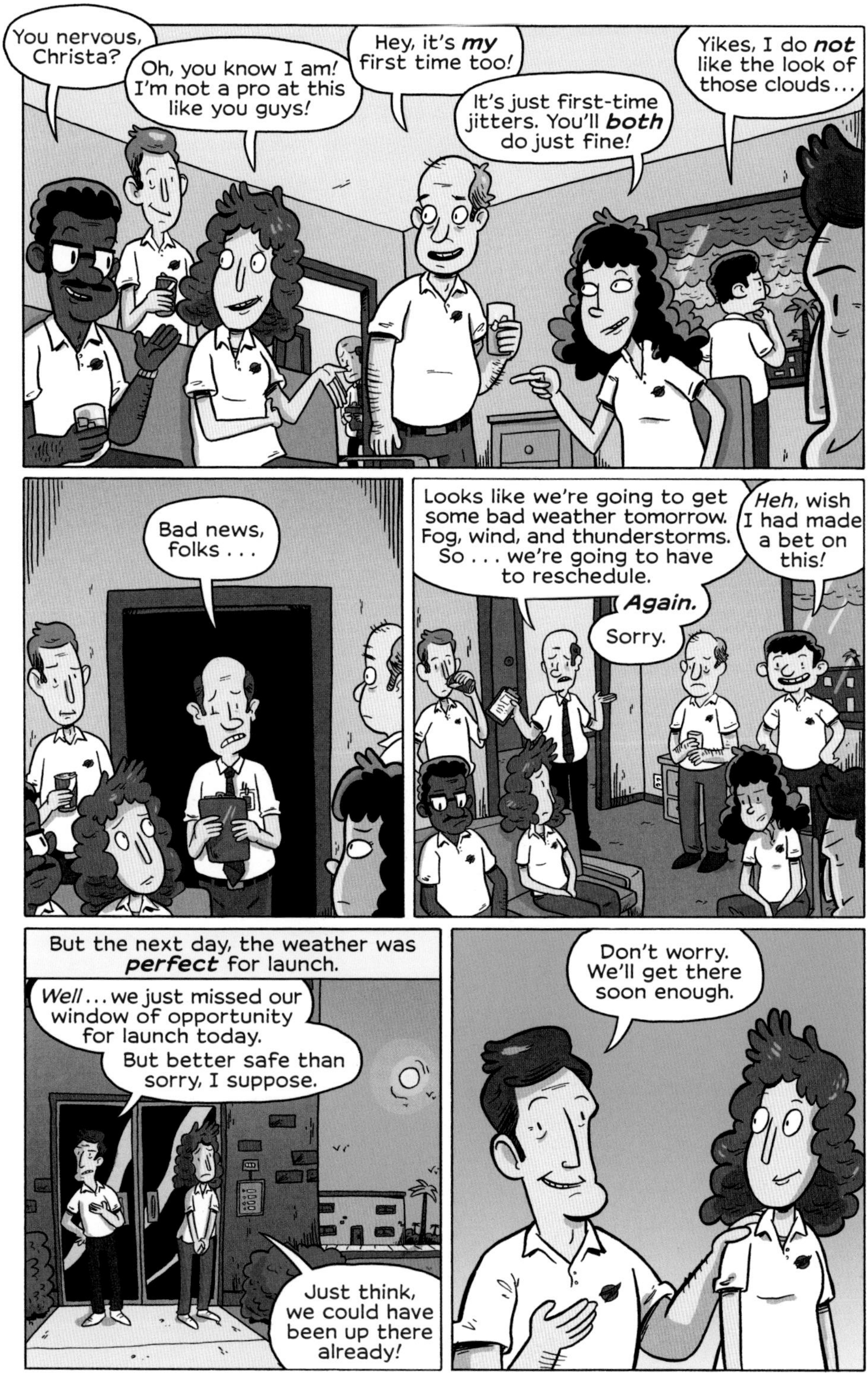
You nervous, Christa?
Oh, you know I am! I'm not a pro at this like you guys!
Hey, it's *my* first time too!
It's just first-time jitters. You'll ***both*** do just fine!
Yikes, I do ***not*** like the look of those clouds...
Bad news, folks . . .
Looks like we're going to get some bad weather tomorrow. Fog, wind, and thunderstorms. So . . . we're going to have to reschedule.
Again.
Sorry.
Heh, wish I had made a bet on this!
But the next day, the weather was ***perfect*** for launch.
Well... we just missed our window of opportunity for launch today.
But better safe than sorry, I suppose.
Just think, we could have been up there already!
Don't worry. We'll get there soon enough.

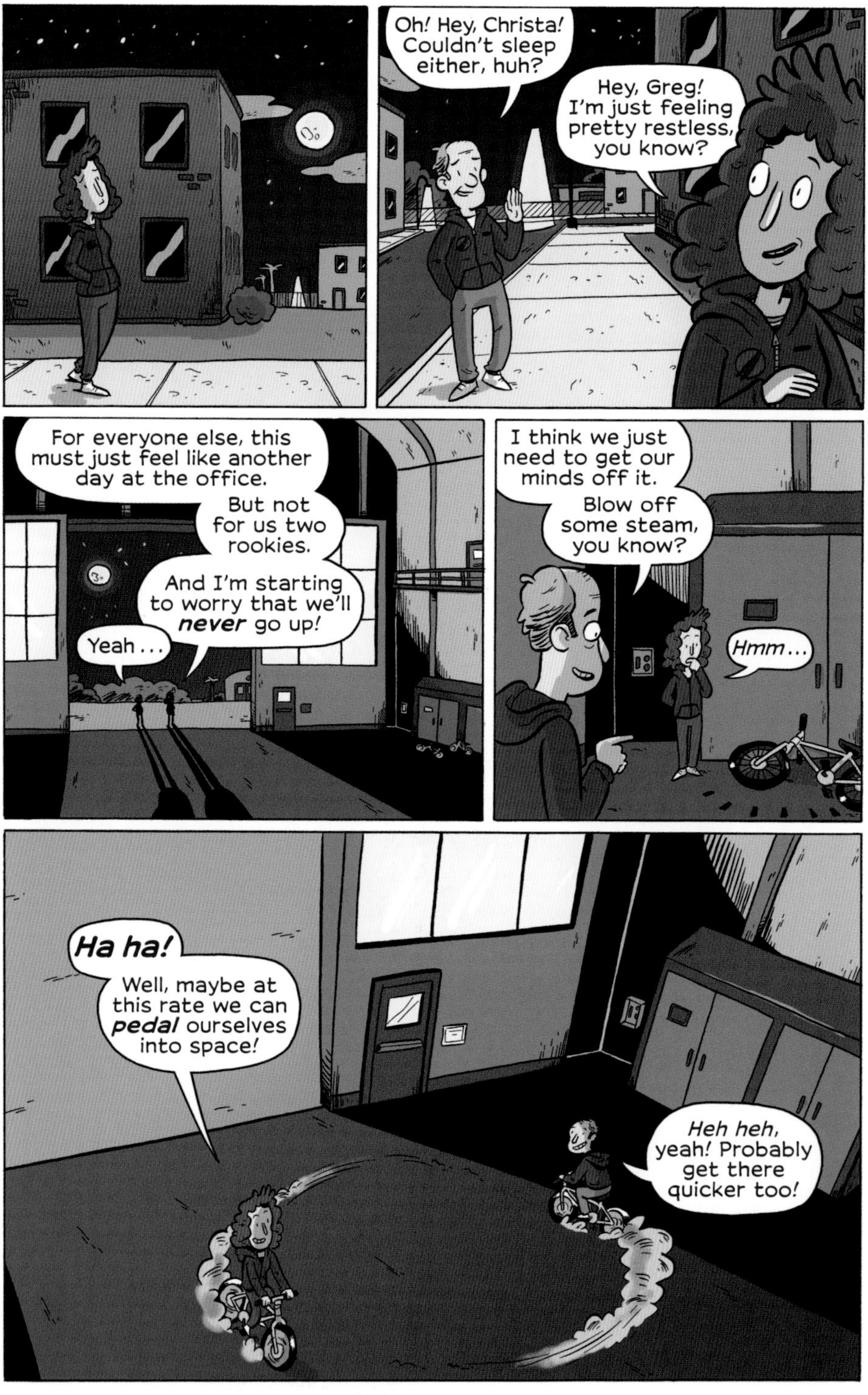
Oh! Hey, Christa! Couldn't sleep either, huh?
Hey, Greg! I'm just feeling pretty restless, you know?
For everyone else, this must just feel like another day at the office.
But not for us two rookies.
And I'm starting to worry that we'll *never* go up!
Yeah...
I think we just need to get our minds off it.
Blow off some steam, you know?
Hmm...
Ha ha!
Well, maybe at this rate we can *pedal* ourselves into space!
Heh heh, yeah! Probably get there quicker too!

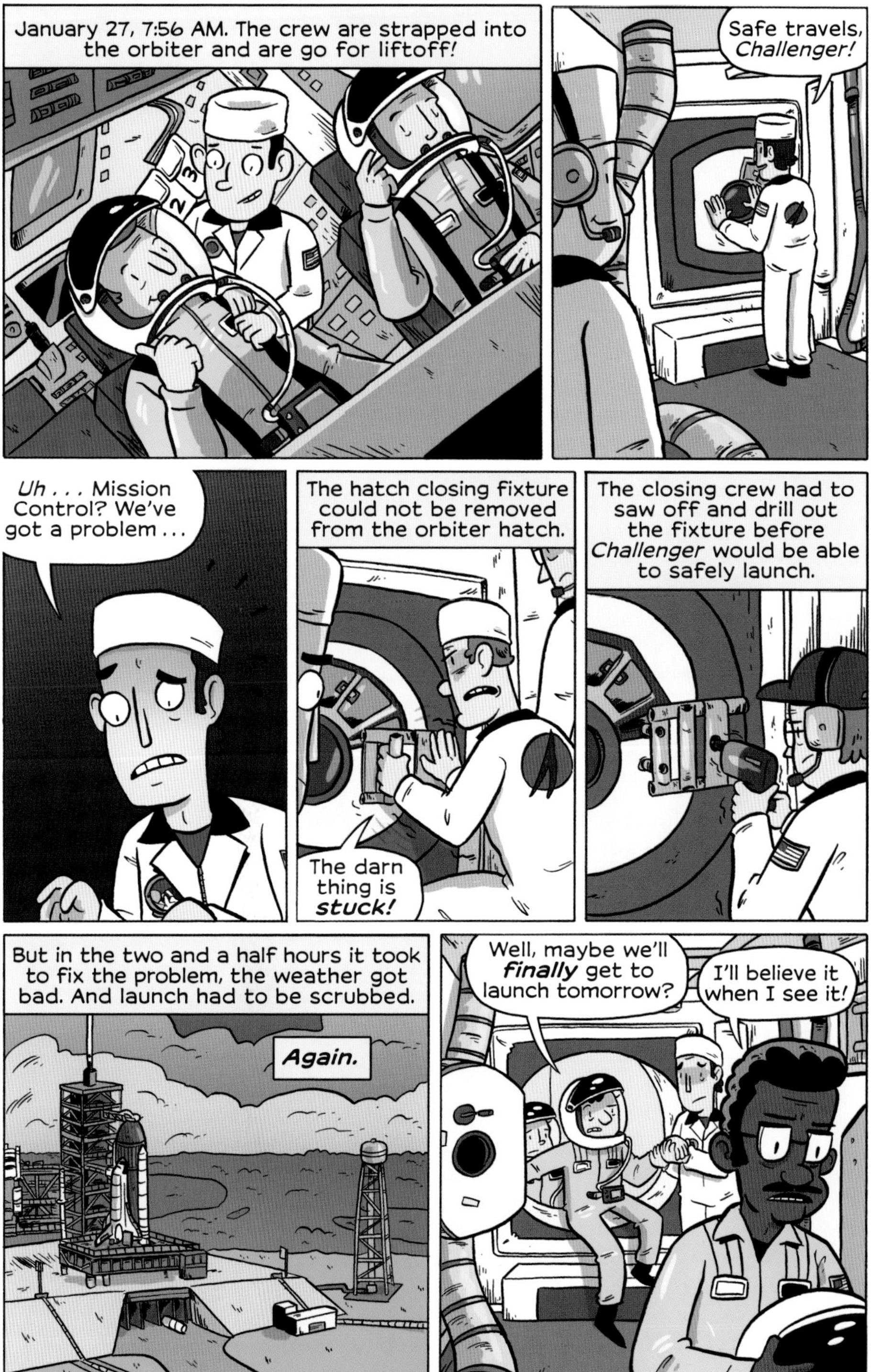
January 27, 7:56 AM. The crew are strapped into the orbiter and are go for liftoff!
Safe travels, *Challenger!*
Uh . . . Mission Control? We've got a problem . . .
The hatch closing fixture could not be removed from the orbiter hatch.
The darn thing is ***stuck!***
The closing crew had to saw off and drill out the fixture before *Challenger* would be able to safely launch.
But in the two and a half hours it took to fix the problem, the weather got bad. And launch had to be scrubbed.
Again.
Well, maybe we'll ***finally*** get to launch tomorrow?
I'll believe it when I see it!

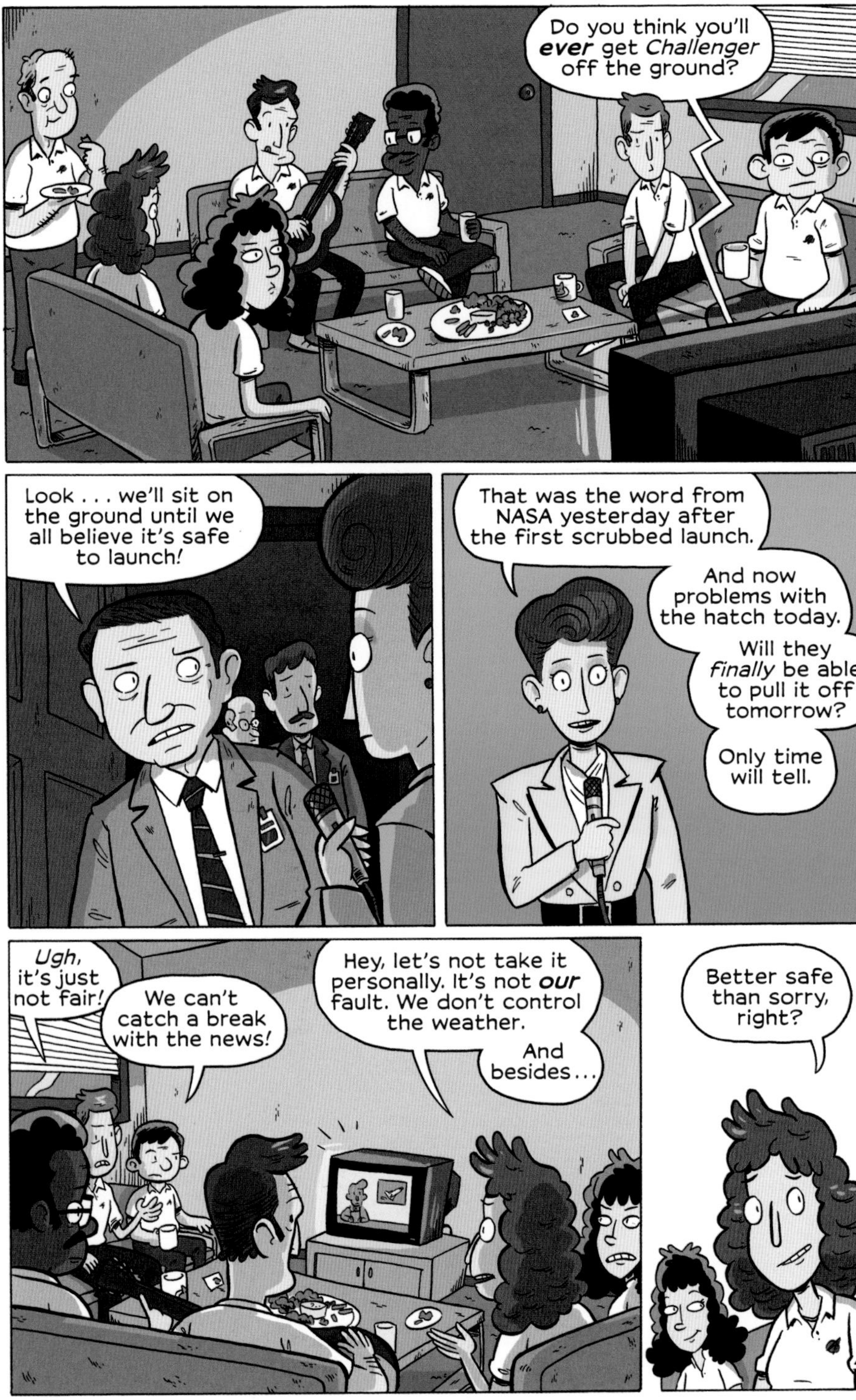
Do you think you'll *ever* get *Challenger* off the ground?
Look . . . we'll sit on the ground until we all believe it's safe to launch!
That was the word from NASA yesterday after the first scrubbed launch.
And now problems with the hatch today.
Will they *finally* be able to pull it off tomorrow?
Only time will tell.
Ugh, it's just not fair!
We can't catch a break with the news!
Hey, let's not take it personally. It's not *our* fault. We don't control the weather.
And besides . . .
Better safe than sorry, right?

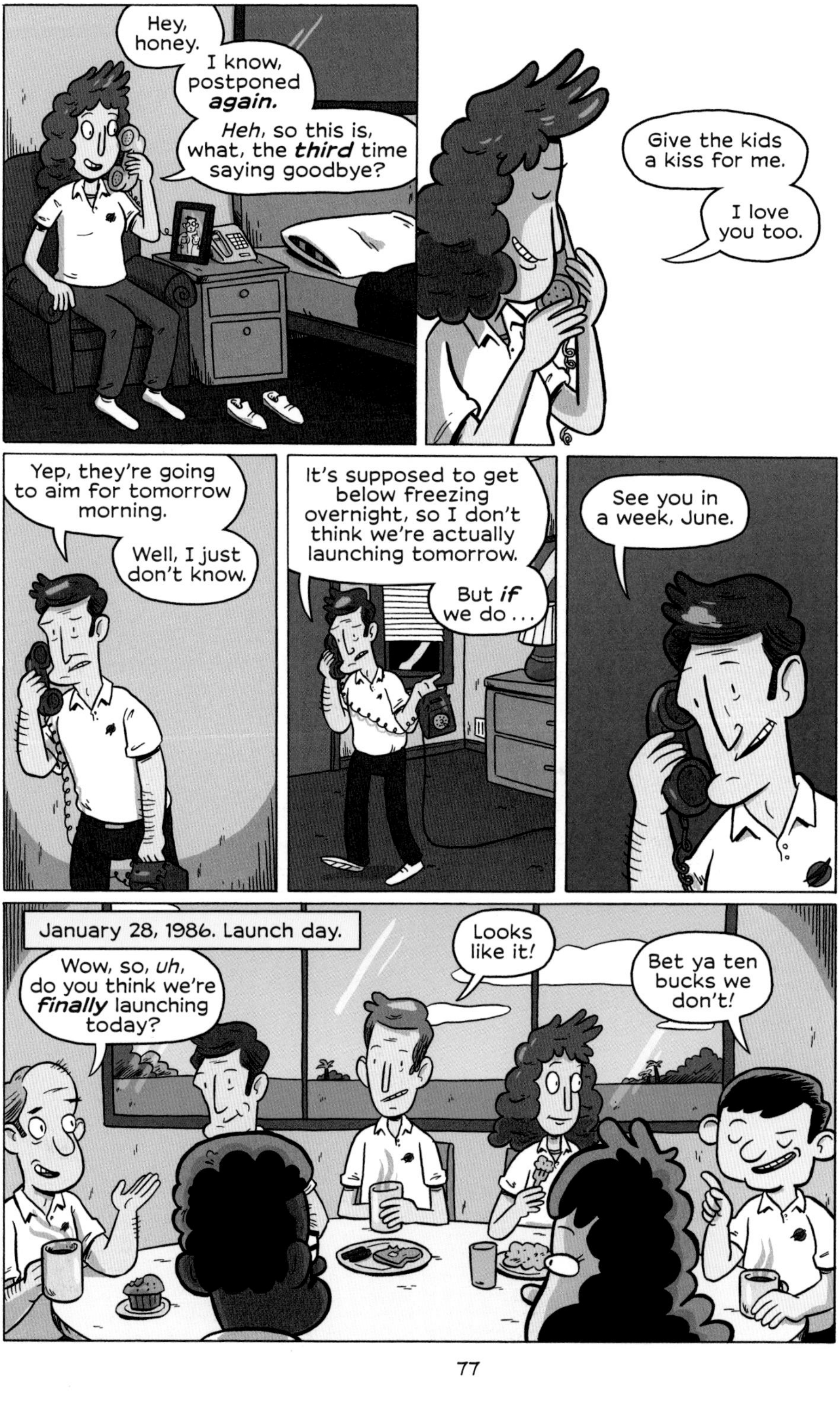
Hey, honey.
I know, postponed **again.**
Heh, so this is, what, the ***third*** time saying goodbye?
Give the kids a kiss for me.
I love you too.
Yep, they're going to aim for tomorrow morning.
Well, I just don't know.
It's supposed to get below freezing overnight, so I don't think we're actually launching tomorrow.
But *if* we do . . .
See you in a week, June.
January 28, 1986. Launch day.
Wow, so, *uh*, do you think we're ***finally*** launching today?
Looks like it!
Bet ya ten bucks we don't!

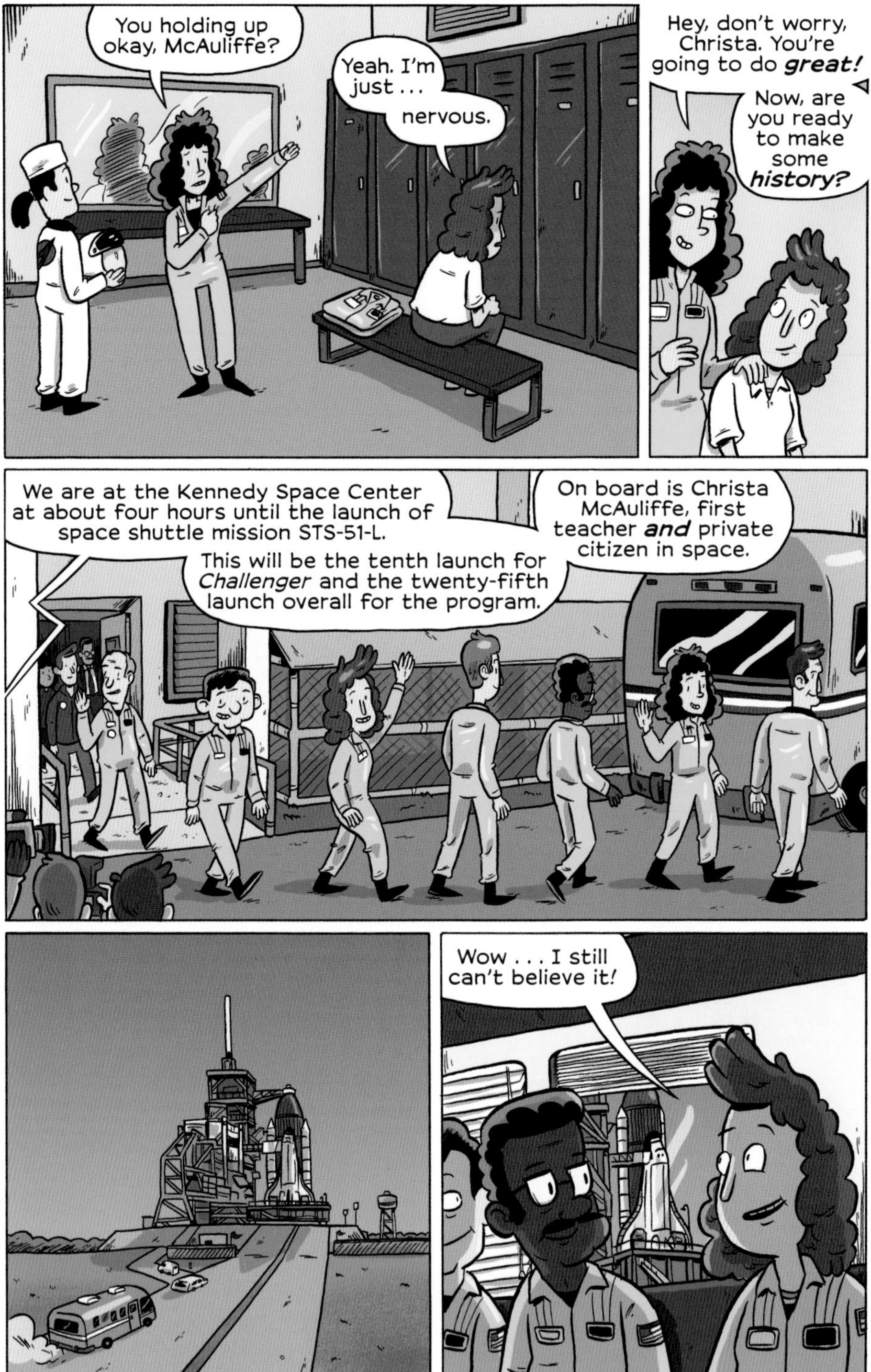
You holding up okay, McAuliffe?
Yeah. I'm just . . .
nervous.
Hey, don't worry, Christa. You're going to do *great!*
Now, are you ready to make some *history?*
We are at the Kennedy Space Center at about four hours until the launch of space shuttle mission STS-51-L.
This will be the tenth launch for *Challenger* and the twenty-fifth launch overall for the program.
On board is Christa McAuliffe, first teacher *and* private citizen in space.
Wow . . . I still can't believe it!

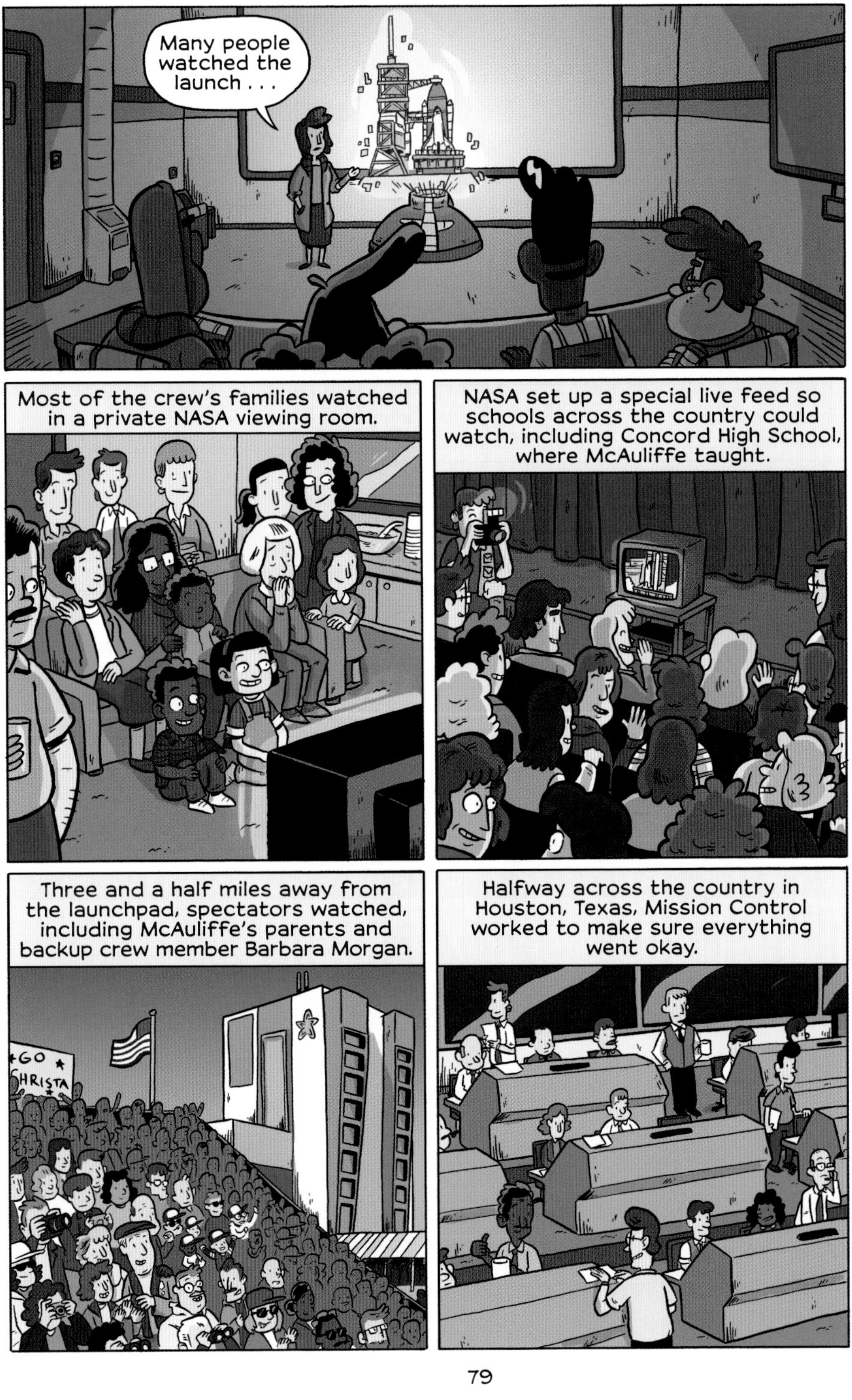
Many people watched the launch . . .
Most of the crew's families watched in a private NASA viewing room.
NASA set up a special live feed so schools across the country could watch, including Concord High School, where McAuliffe taught.
Three and a half miles away from the launchpad, spectators watched, including McAuliffe's parents and backup crew member Barbara Morgan.
GO CHRISTA
Halfway across the country in Houston, Texas, Mission Control worked to make sure everything went okay.

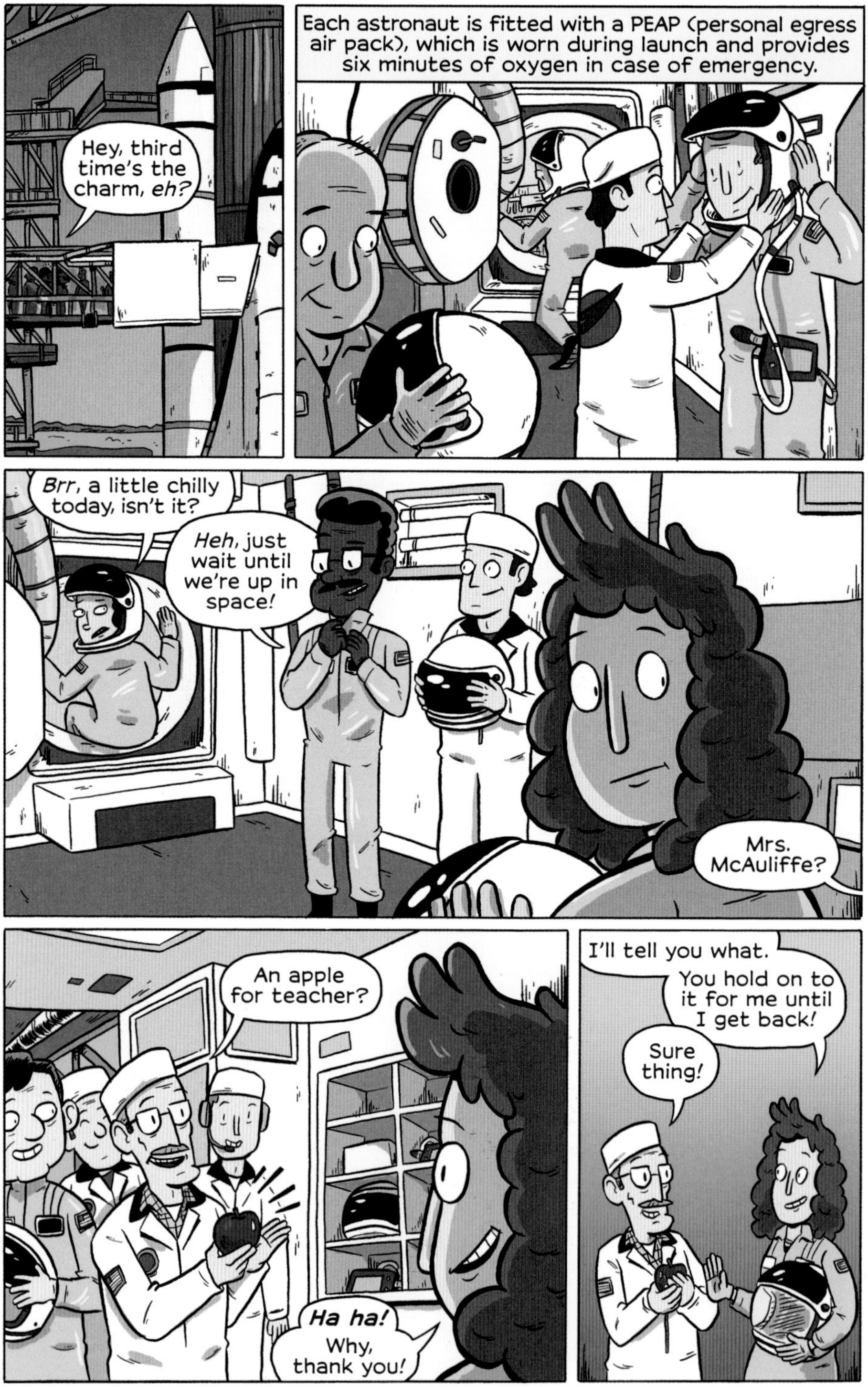

Hey, third time's the charm, *eh?*
Each astronaut is fitted with a PEAP (personal egress air pack), which is worn during launch and provides six minutes of oxygen in case of emergency.
Brr, a little chilly today, isn't it?
Heh, just wait until we're up in space!
Mrs. McAuliffe?
An apple for teacher?
Ha ha! Why, thank you!
I'll tell you what.
You hold on to it for me until I get back!
Sure thing!

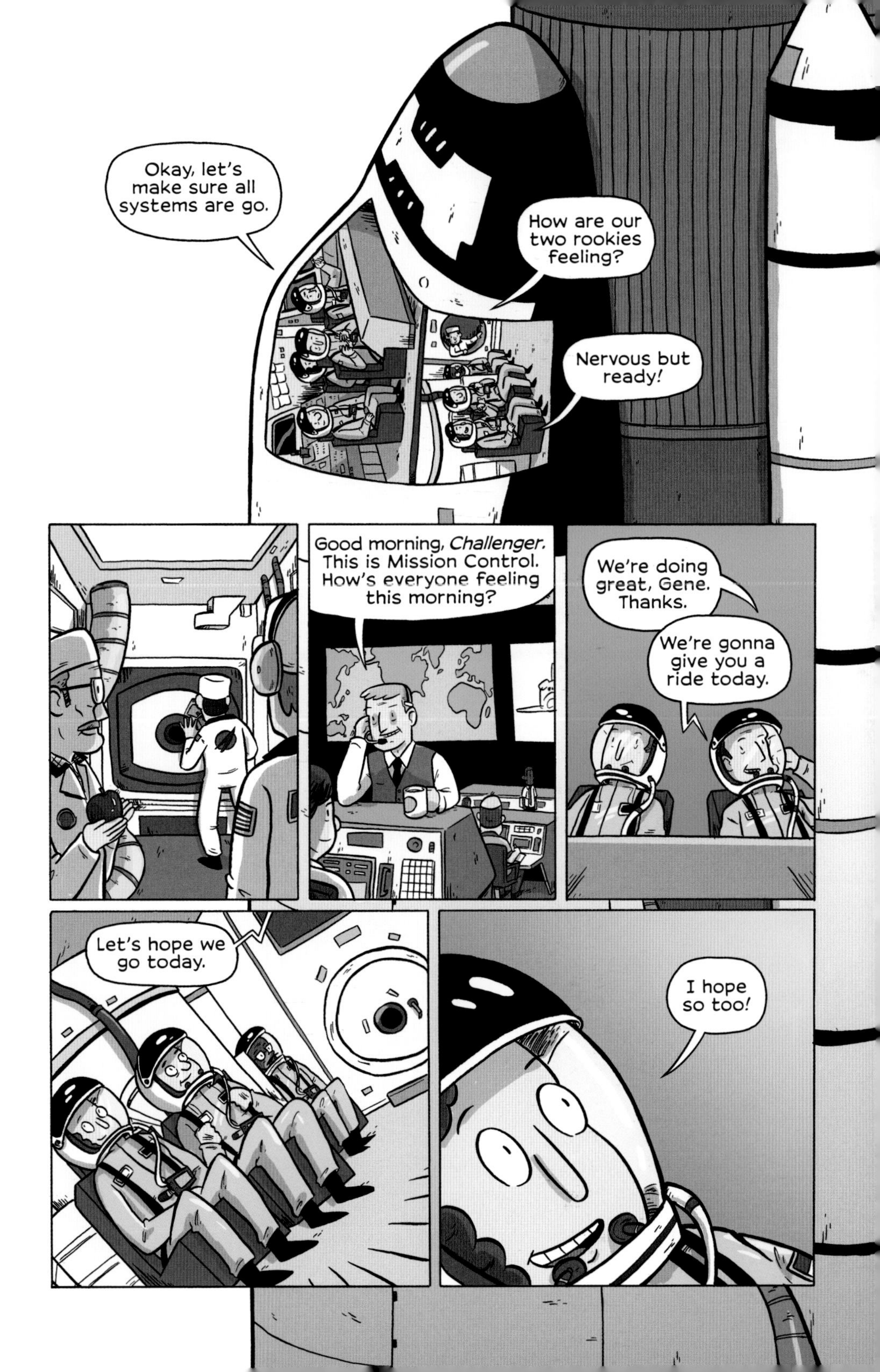
Okay, let's make sure all systems are go.
How are our two rookies feeling?
Nervous but ready!
Good morning, *Challenger*. This is Mission Control. How's everyone feeling this morning?
We're doing great, Gene. Thanks.
We're gonna give you a ride today.
Let's hope we go today.
I hope so too!

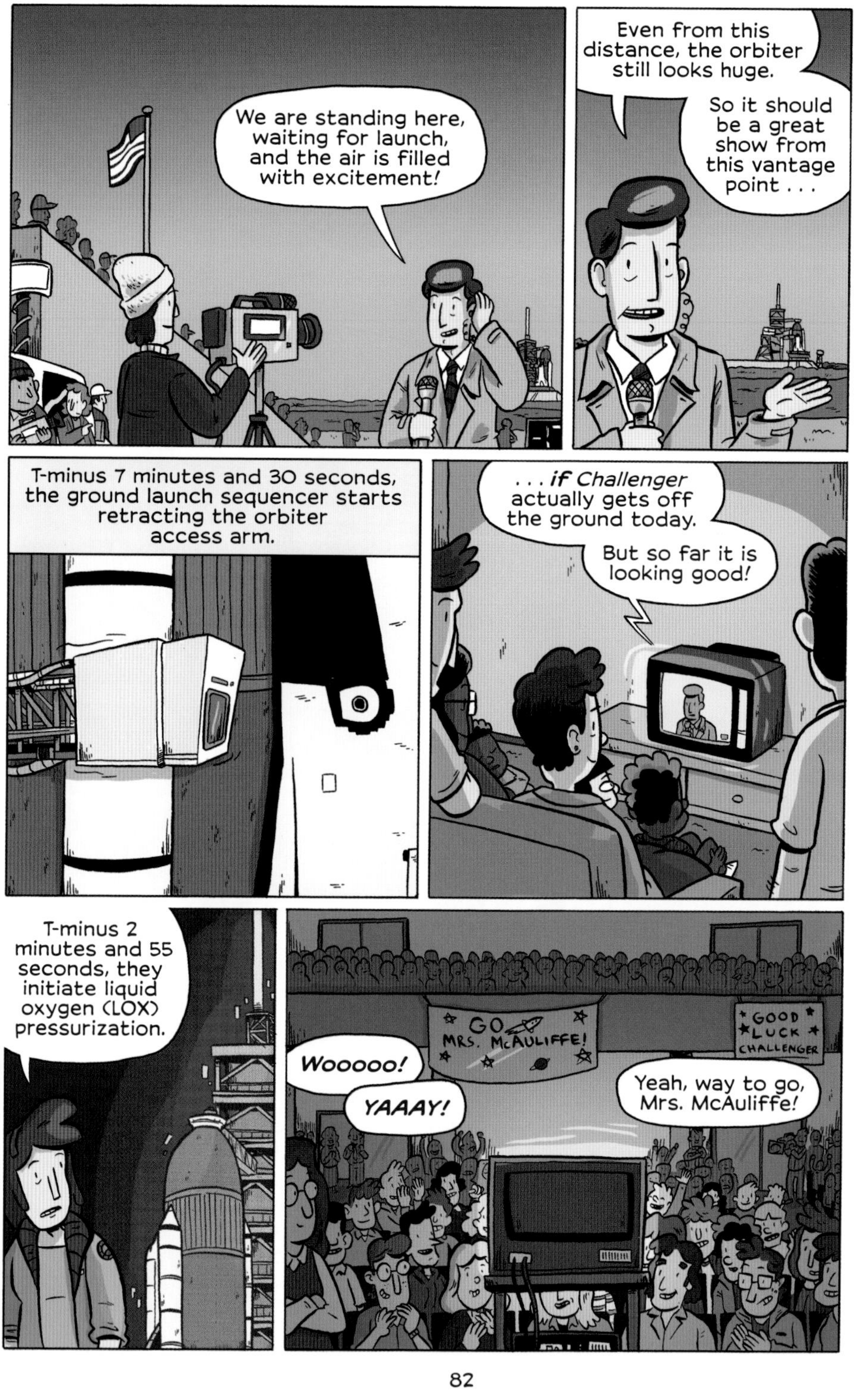

We are standing here, waiting for launch, and the air is filled with excitement!
Even from this distance, the orbiter still looks huge.
So it should be a great show from this vantage point . . .
T-minus 7 minutes and 30 seconds, the ground launch sequencer starts retracting the orbiter access arm.
. . . *if Challenger* actually gets off the ground today.
But so far it is looking good!
T-minus 2 minutes and 55 seconds, they initiate liquid oxygen (LOX) pressurization.
GO MRS. McAULIFFE!
GOOD LUCK CHALLENGER
Wooooo!
YAAAY!
Yeah, way to go, Mrs. McAuliffe!

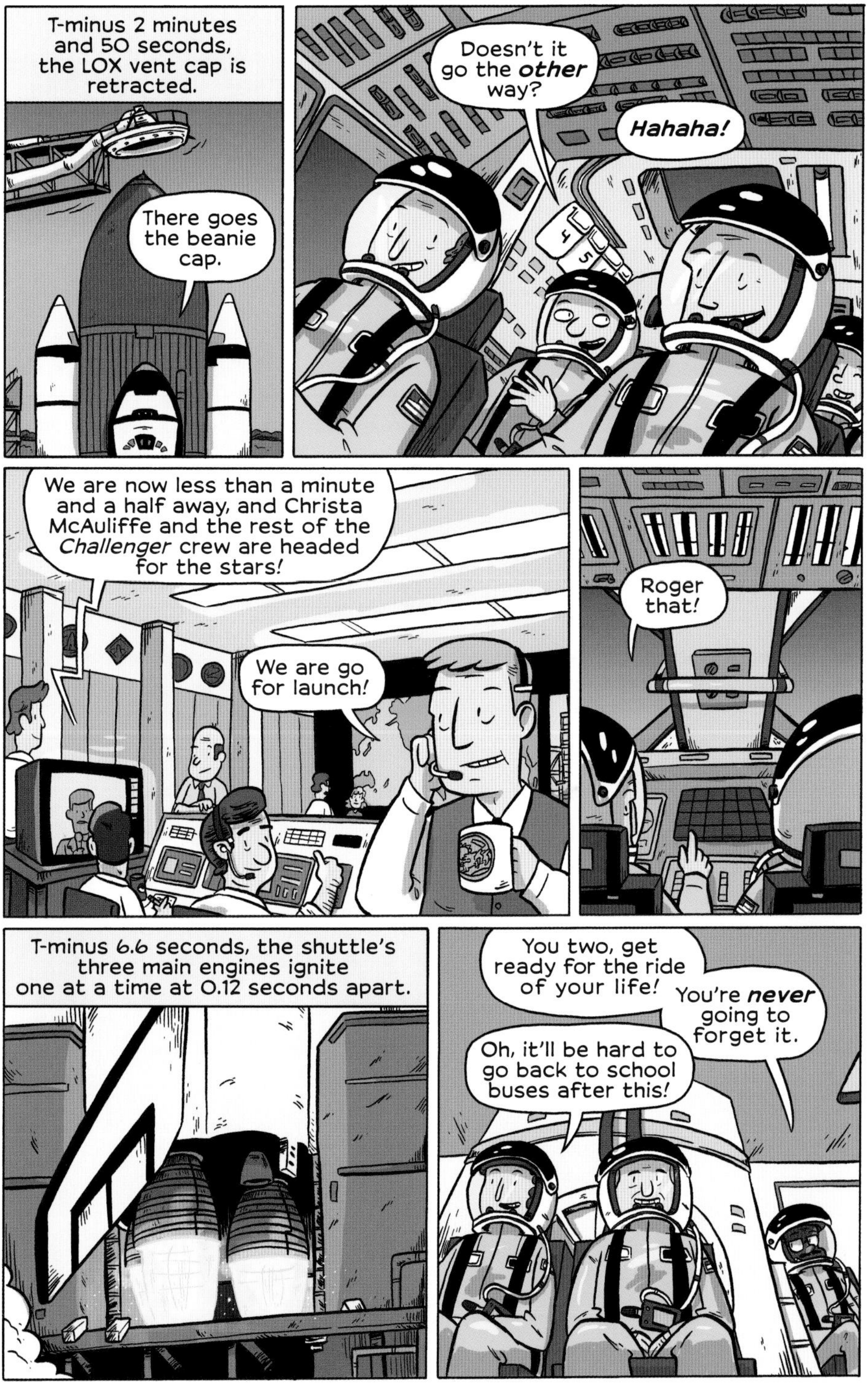
T-minus 2 minutes and 50 seconds, the LOX vent cap is retracted.
There goes the beanie cap.
Doesn't it go the **other** way?
Hahaha!
We are now less than a minute and a half away, and Christa McAuliffe and the rest of the *Challenger* crew are headed for the stars!
We are go for launch!
Roger that!
T-minus 6.6 seconds, the shuttle's three main engines ignite one at a time at 0.12 seconds apart.
You two, get ready for the ride of your life!
You're **never** going to forget it.
Oh, it'll be hard to go back to school buses after this!

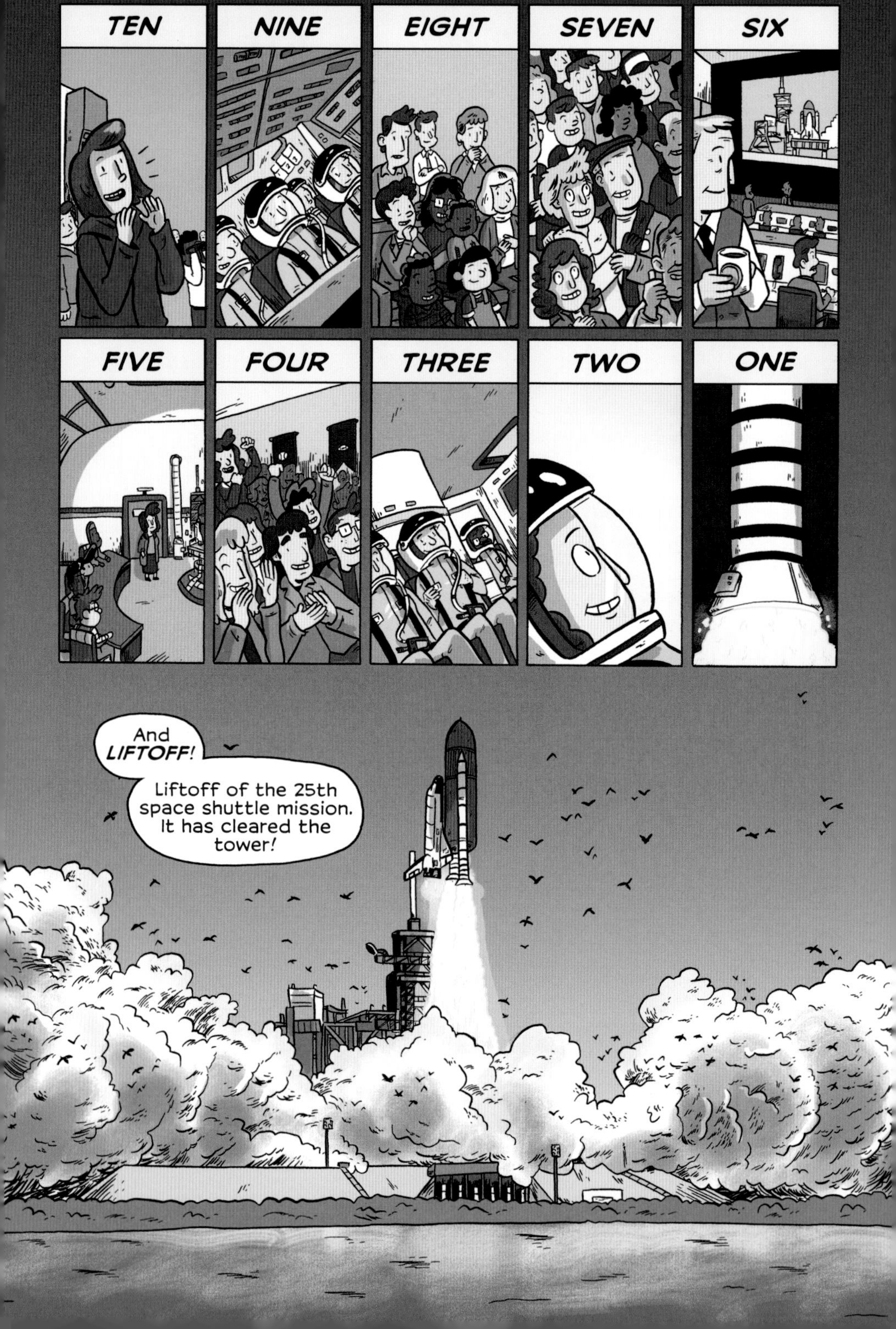
TEN
NINE
EIGHT
SEVEN
SIX
FIVE
FOUR
THREE
TWO
ONE
And LIFTOFF!
Liftoff of the 25th space shuttle mission. It has cleared the tower!

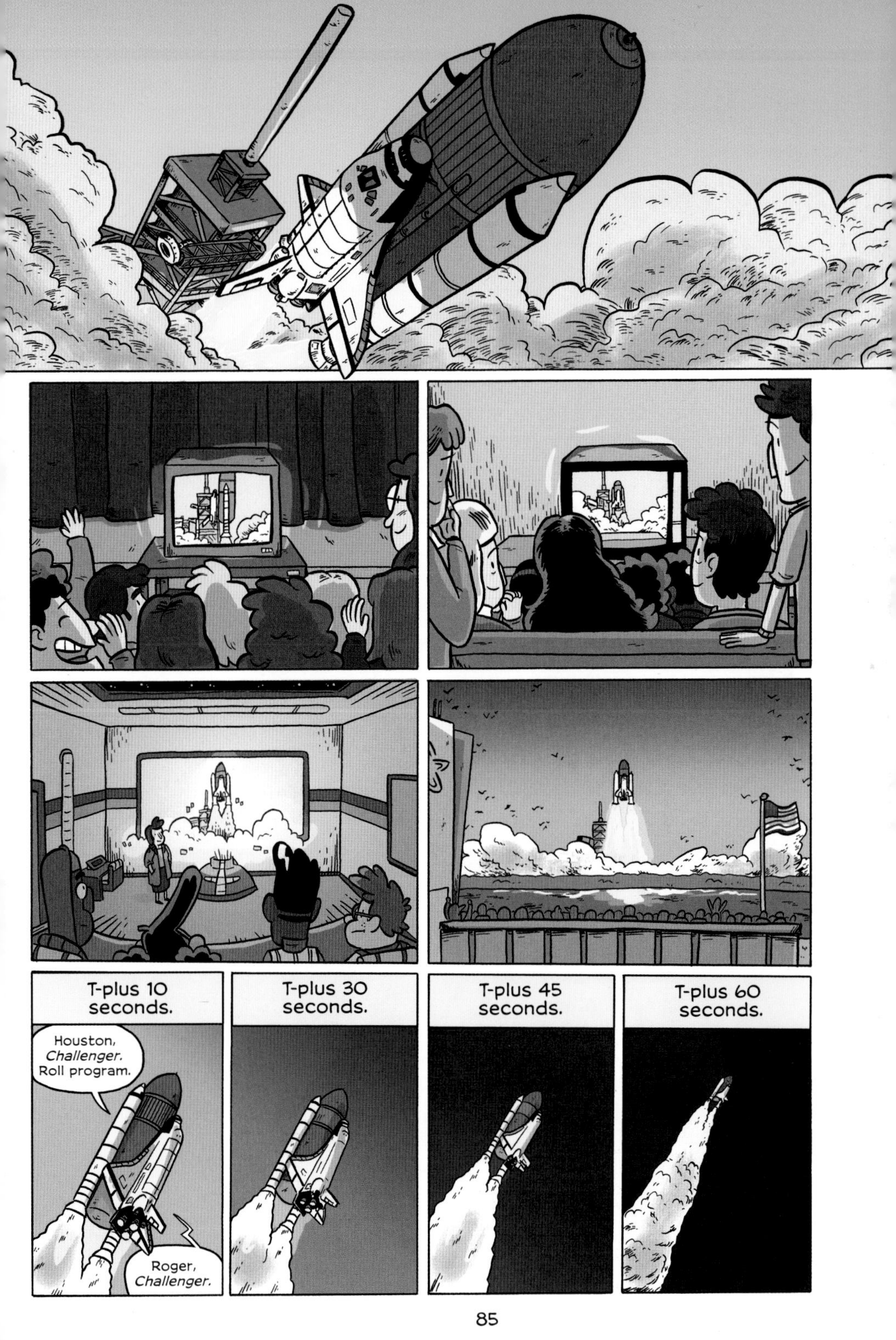
T-plus 10 seconds.
Houston, *Challenger*. Roll program.
Roger, *Challenger*.
T-plus 30 seconds.
T-plus 45 seconds.
T-plus 60 seconds.

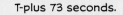

T-plus 73 seconds.

Okay. All operators, watch your data carefully.

Something went wrong here. Uh, we've got a problem with what looks like a second plume of, *uh* . . . smoke!

It . . . it looks like it may have lost a solid rocket booster. It's hard to tell! I don't . . .

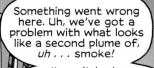

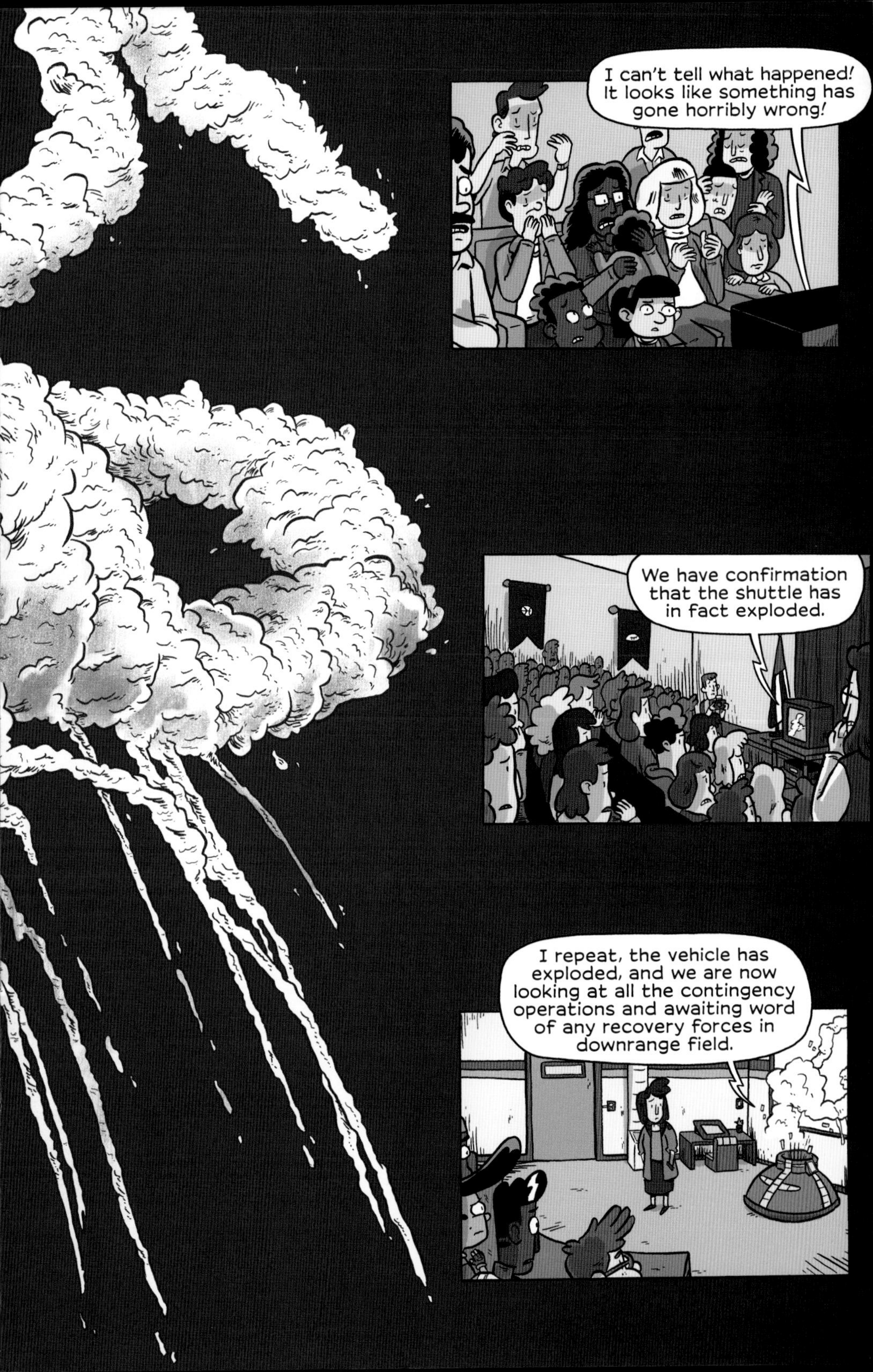
I can't tell what happened! It looks like something has gone horribly wrong!
We have confirmation that the shuttle has in fact exploded.
I repeat, the vehicle has exploded, and we are now looking at all the contingency operations and awaiting word of any recovery forces in downrange field.

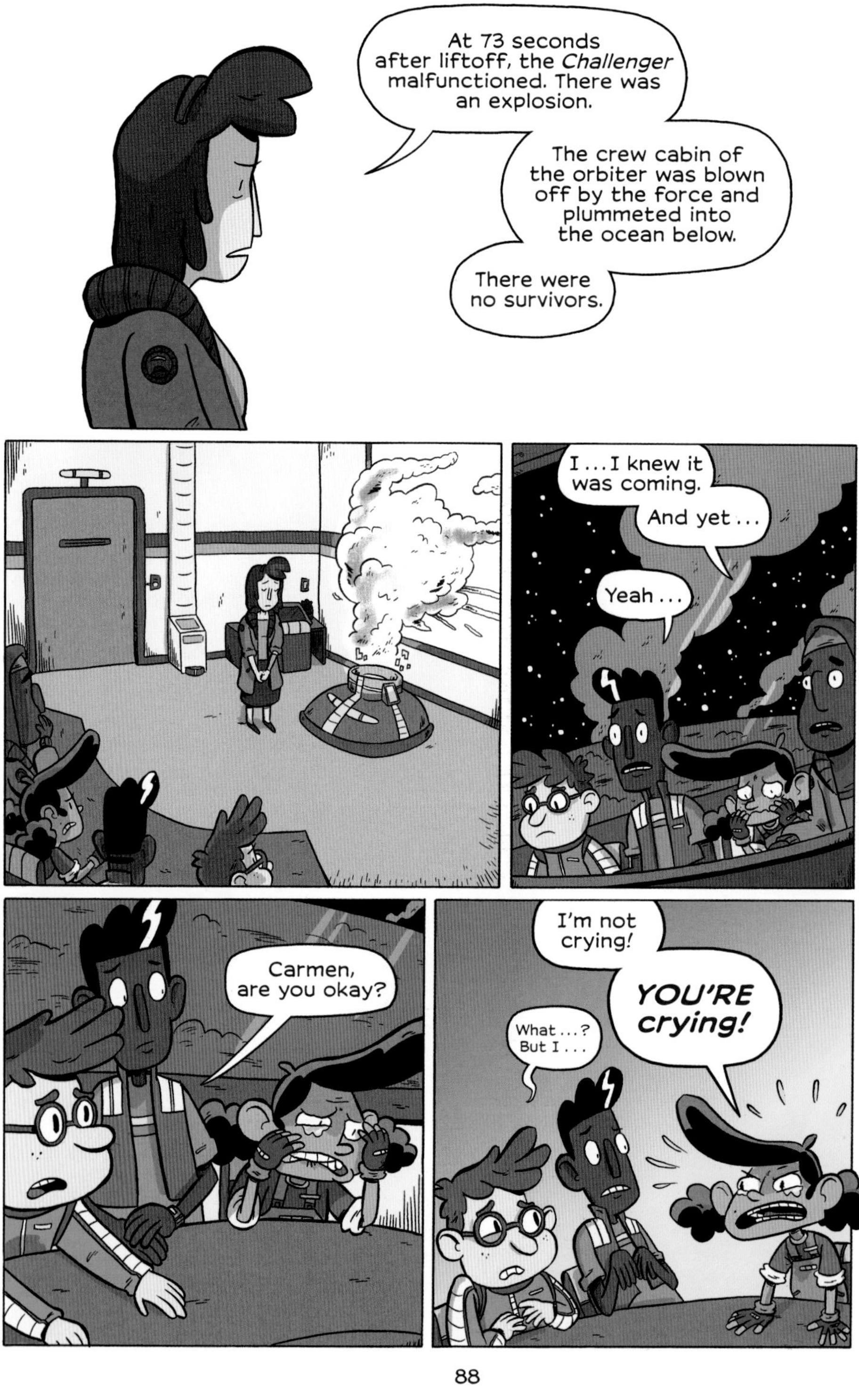
At 73 seconds after liftoff, the *Challenger* malfunctioned. There was an explosion.
The crew cabin of the orbiter was blown off by the force and plummeted into the ocean below.
There were no survivors.
I...I knew it was coming.
And yet...
Yeah...
Carmen, are you okay?
I'm not crying!
What...? But I...
YOU'RE crying!

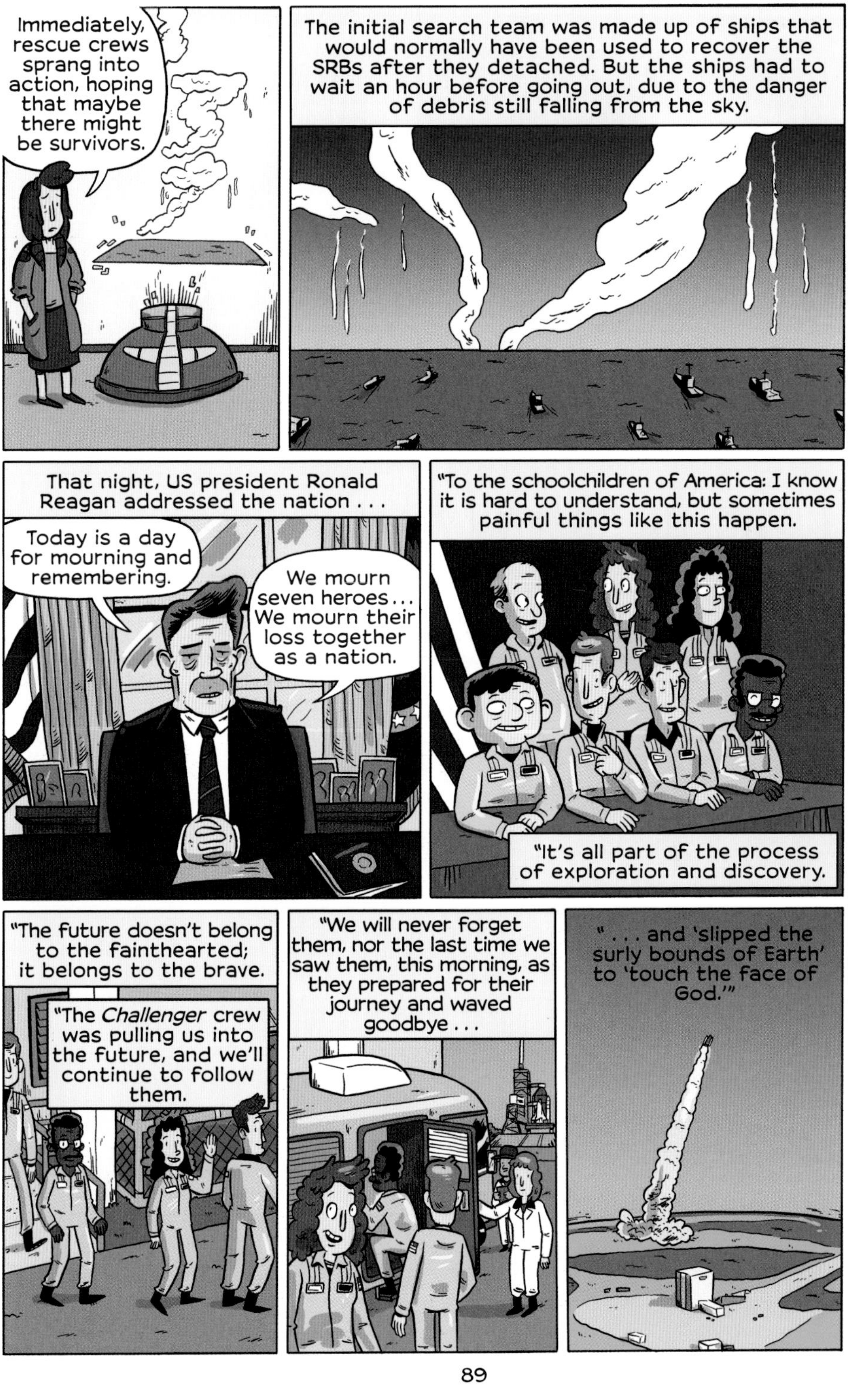
Immediately, rescue crews sprang into action, hoping that maybe there might be survivors.
The initial search team was made up of ships that would normally have been used to recover the SRBs after they detached. But the ships had to wait an hour before going out, due to the danger of debris still falling from the sky.
That night, US president Ronald Reagan addressed the nation . . .
Today is a day for mourning and remembering.
We mourn seven heroes . . . We mourn their loss together as a nation.
"To the schoolchildren of America: I know it is hard to understand, but sometimes painful things like this happen.
"It's all part of the process of exploration and discovery.
"The future doesn't belong to the fainthearted; it belongs to the brave.
"The Challenger crew was pulling us into the future, and we'll continue to follow them.
"We will never forget them, nor the last time we saw them, this morning, as they prepared for their journey and waved goodbye . . .
" . . . and 'slipped the surly bounds of Earth' to 'touch the face of God.'"

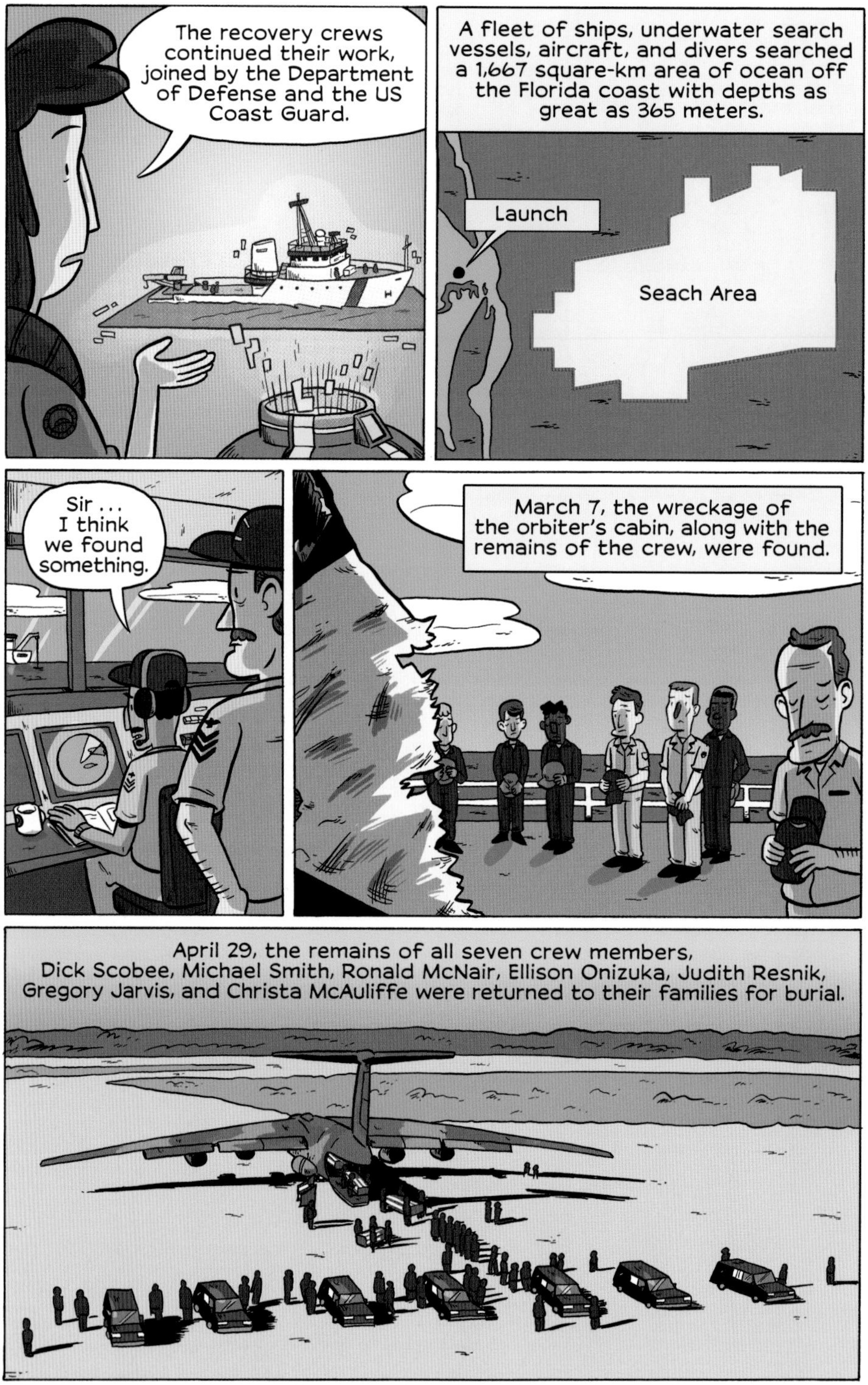
The recovery crews continued their work, joined by the Department of Defense and the US Coast Guard.
A fleet of ships, underwater search vessels, aircraft, and divers searched a 1,667 square-km area of ocean off the Florida coast with depths as great as 365 meters.
Launch
Seach Area
Sir ... I think we found something.
March 7, the wreckage of the orbiter's cabin, along with the remains of the crew, were found.
April 29, the remains of all seven crew members, Dick Scobee, Michael Smith, Ronald McNair, Ellison Onizuka, Judith Resnik, Gregory Jarvis, and Christa McAuliffe were returned to their families for burial.

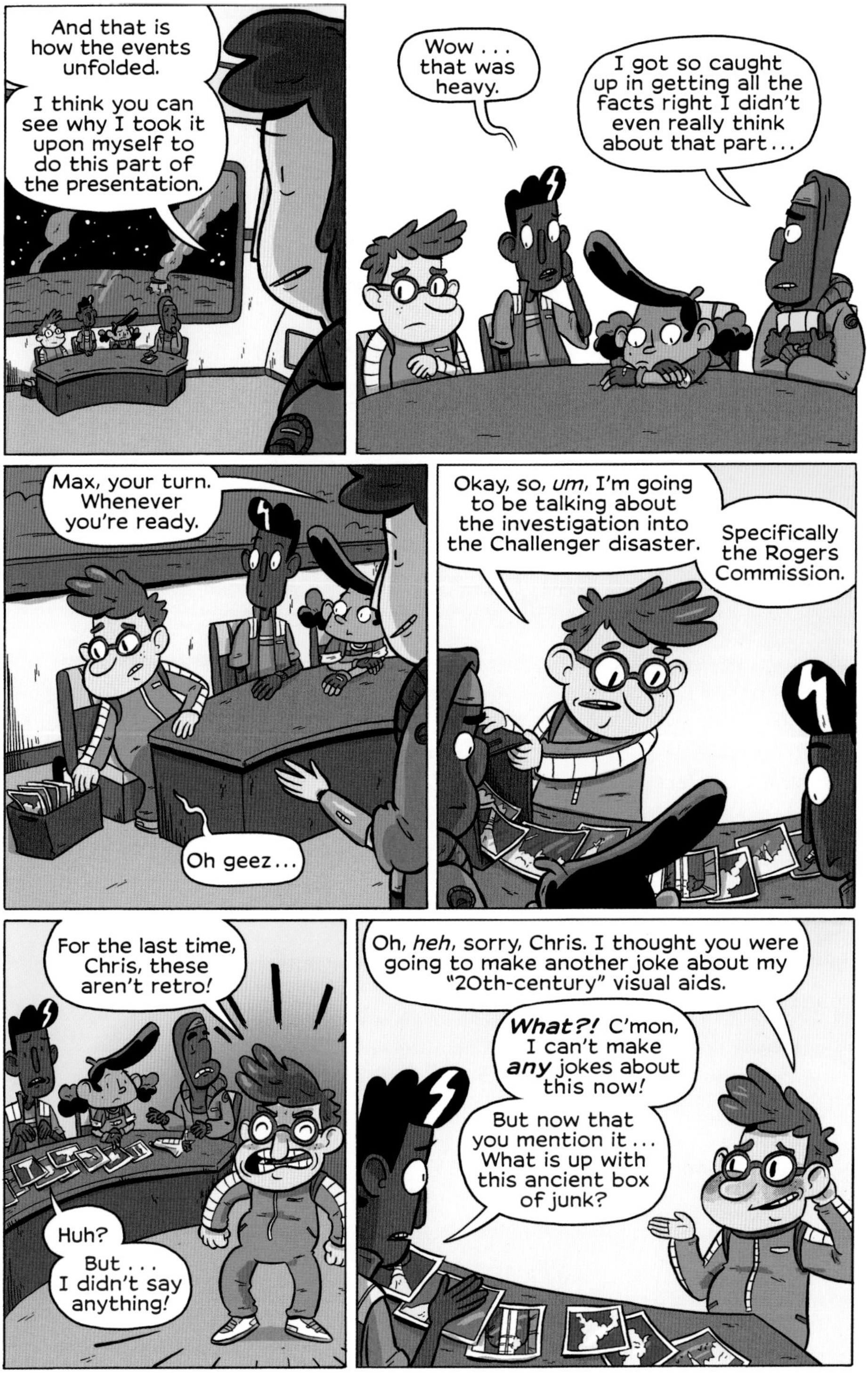

And that is how the events unfolded.
I think you can see why I took it upon myself to do this part of the presentation.
Wow . . . that was heavy.
I got so caught up in getting all the facts right I didn't even really think about that part . . .
Max, your turn. Whenever you're ready.
Oh geez . . .
Okay, so, *um*, I'm going to be talking about the investigation into the Challenger disaster.
Specifically the Rogers Commission.
For the last time, Chris, these aren't retro!
Huh? But . . . I didn't say anything!
Oh, *heh*, sorry, Chris. I thought you were going to make another joke about my "20th-century" visual aids.
What?! C'mon, I can't make ***any*** jokes about this now!
But now that you mention it . . . What is up with this ancient box of junk?

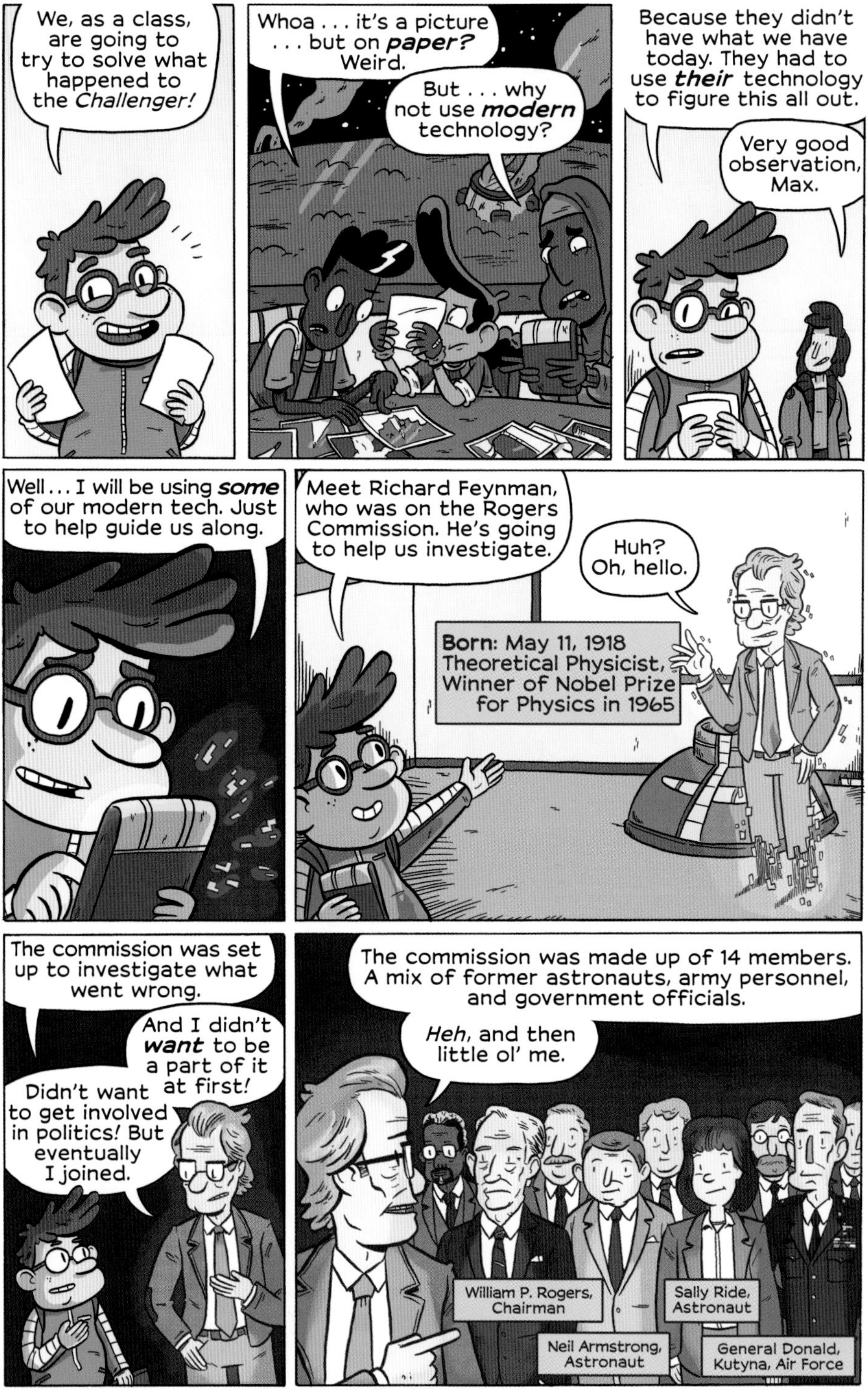
We, as a class, are going to try to solve what happened to the *Challenger!*
Whoa . . . it's a picture . . . but on ***paper?*** Weird.
But . . . why not use ***modern*** technology?
Because they didn't have what we have today. They had to use ***their*** technology to figure this all out.
Very good observation, Max.
Well . . . I will be using ***some*** of our modern tech. Just to help guide us along.
Meet Richard Feynman, who was on the Rogers Commission. He's going to help us investigate.
Huh? Oh, hello.
Born: May 11, 1918 Theoretical Physicist, Winner of Nobel Prize for Physics in 1965
The commission was set up to investigate what went wrong.
And I didn't ***want*** to be a part of it at first!
Didn't want to get involved in politics! But eventually I joined.
The commission was made up of 14 members. A mix of former astronauts, army personnel, and government officials.
Heh, and then little ol' me.
William P. Rogers, Chairman
Sally Ride, Astronaut
Neil Armstrong, Astronaut
General Donald, Kutyna, Air Force

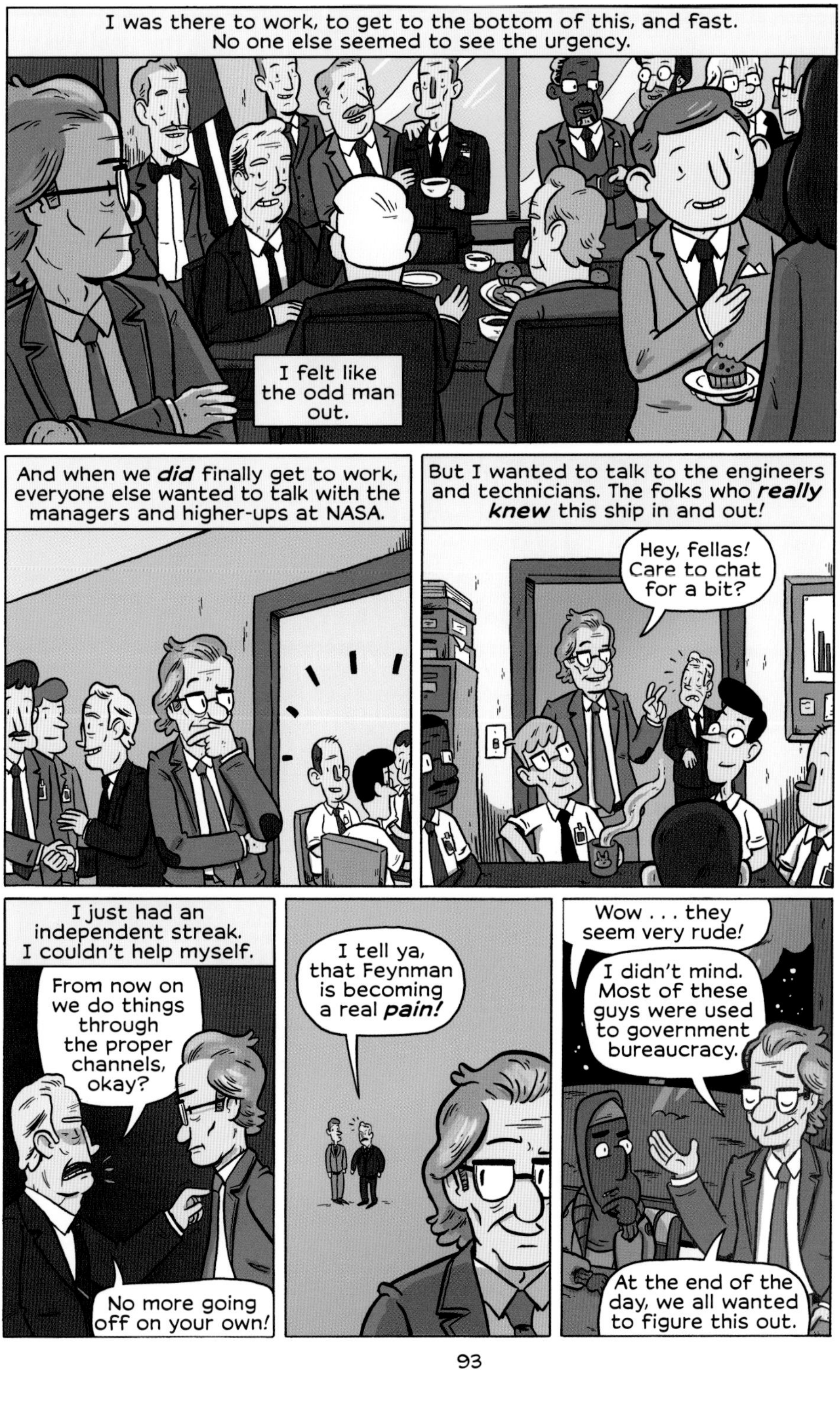

I was there to work, to get to the bottom of this, and fast. No one else seemed to see the urgency.
I felt like the odd man out.
And when we *did* finally get to work, everyone else wanted to talk with the managers and higher-ups at NASA.
But I wanted to talk to the engineers and technicians. The folks who *really knew* this ship in and out!
Hey, fellas! Care to chat for a bit?
I just had an independent streak. I couldn't help myself.
From now on we do things through the proper channels, okay?
No more going off on your own!
I tell ya, that Feynman is becoming a real *pain!*
Wow . . . they seem very rude!
I didn't mind. Most of these guys were used to government bureaucracy.
At the end of the day, we all wanted to figure this out.

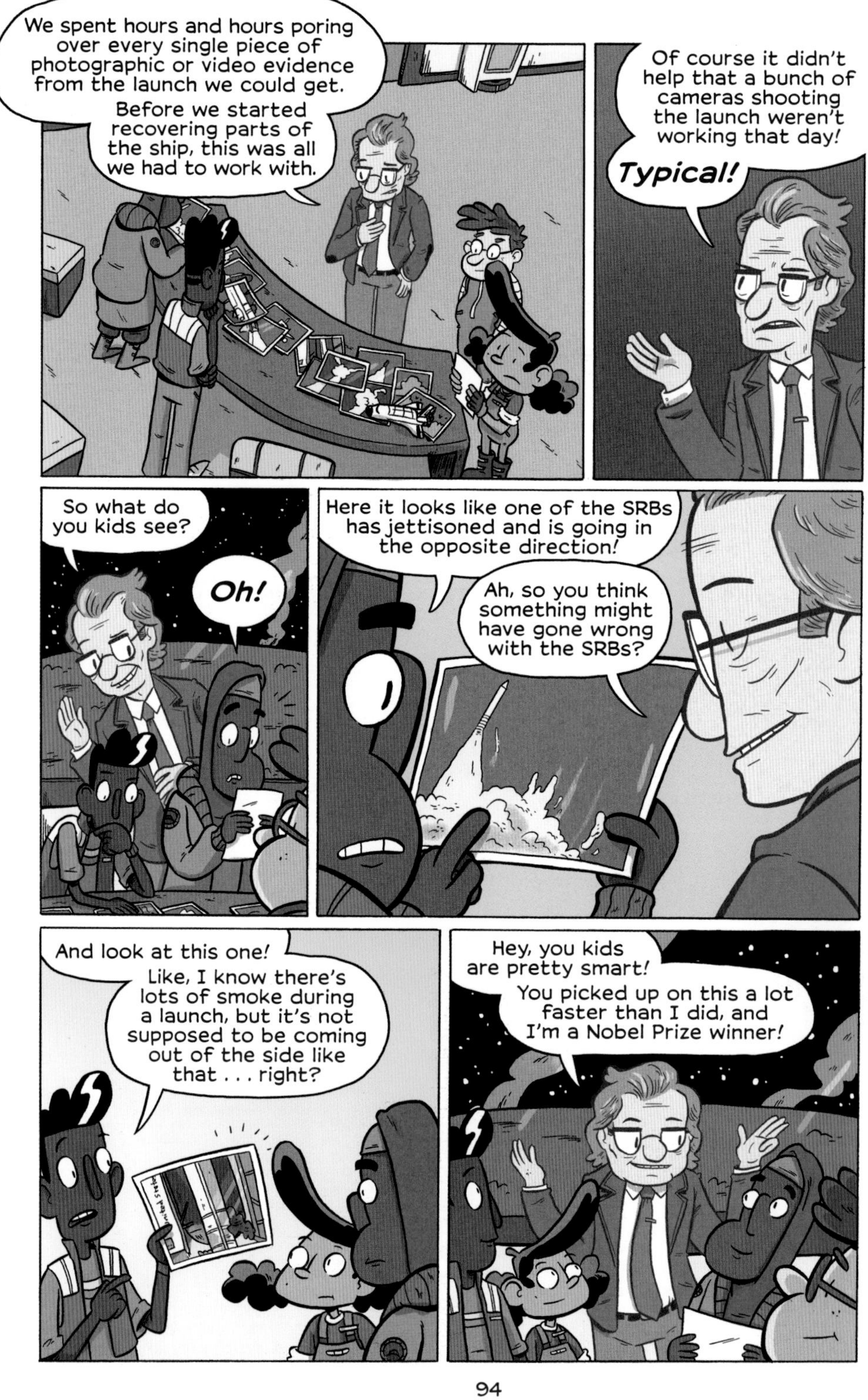
We spent hours and hours poring over every single piece of photographic or video evidence from the launch we could get.
Before we started recovering parts of the ship, this was all we had to work with.
Of course it didn't help that a bunch of cameras shooting the launch weren't working that day!
Typical!
So what do you kids see?
Oh!
Here it looks like one of the SRBs has jettisoned and is going in the opposite direction!
Ah, so you think something might have gone wrong with the SRBs?
And look at this one!
Like, I know there's lots of smoke during a launch, but it's not supposed to be coming out of the side like that . . . right?
Hey, you kids are pretty smart!
You picked up on this a lot faster than I did, and I'm a Nobel Prize winner!

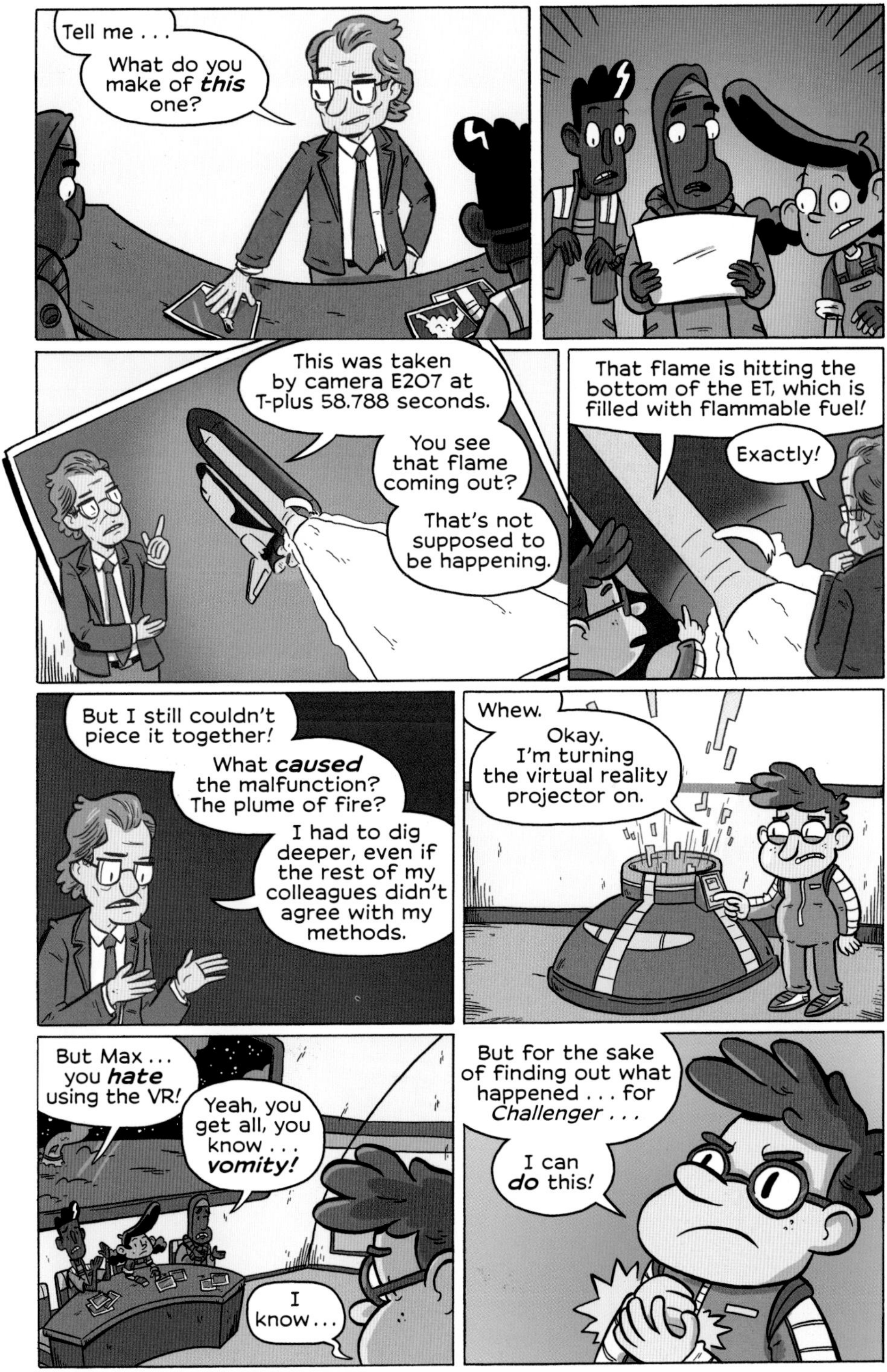
Tell me . . .
What do you make of *this* one?
This was taken by camera E207 at T-plus 58.788 seconds.
You see that flame coming out?
That's not supposed to be happening.
That flame is hitting the bottom of the ET, which is filled with flammable fuel!
Exactly!
But I still couldn't piece it together!
What *caused* the malfunction? The plume of fire?
I had to dig deeper, even if the rest of my colleagues didn't agree with my methods.
Whew.
Okay. I'm turning the virtual reality projector on.
But Max . . . you *hate* using the VR!
Yeah, you get all, you know . . . *vomity!*
I know . . .
But for the sake of finding out what happened . . . for *Challenger* . . .
I can *do* this!

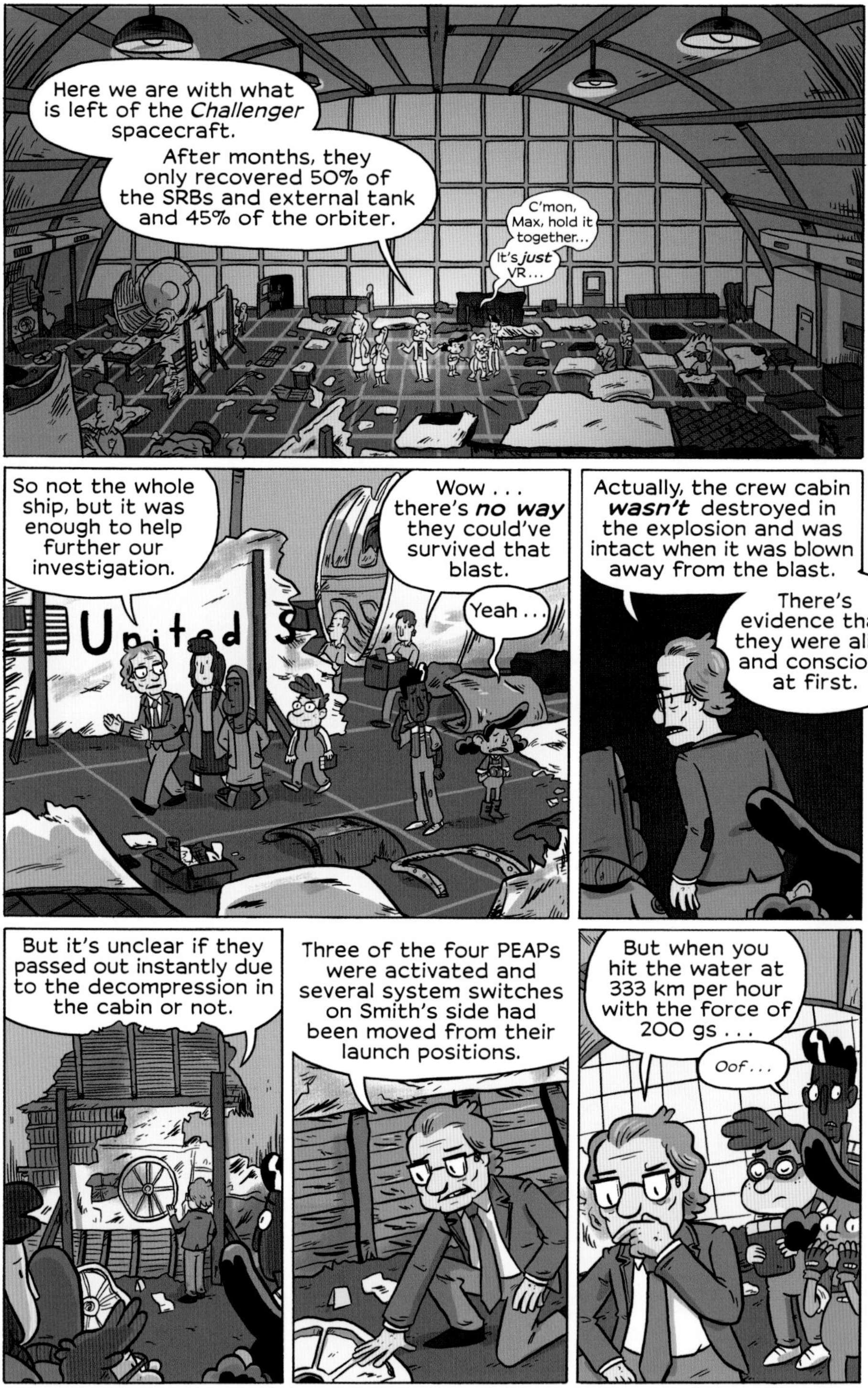
Here we are with what is left of the *Challenger* spacecraft.
After months, they only recovered 50% of the SRBs and external tank and 45% of the orbiter.
C'mon, Max, hold it together...
It's *just* VR...
So not the whole ship, but it was enough to help further our investigation.
Wow . . . there's ***no way*** they could've survived that blast.
Yeah . . .
Actually, the crew cabin ***wasn't*** destroyed in the explosion and was intact when it was blown away from the blast.
There's evidence that they were alive and conscious at first.
But it's unclear if they passed out instantly due to the decompression in the cabin or not.
Three of the four PEAPs were activated and several system switches on Smith's side had been moved from their launch positions.
But when you hit the water at 333 km per hour with the force of 200 gs . . .
Oof . . .

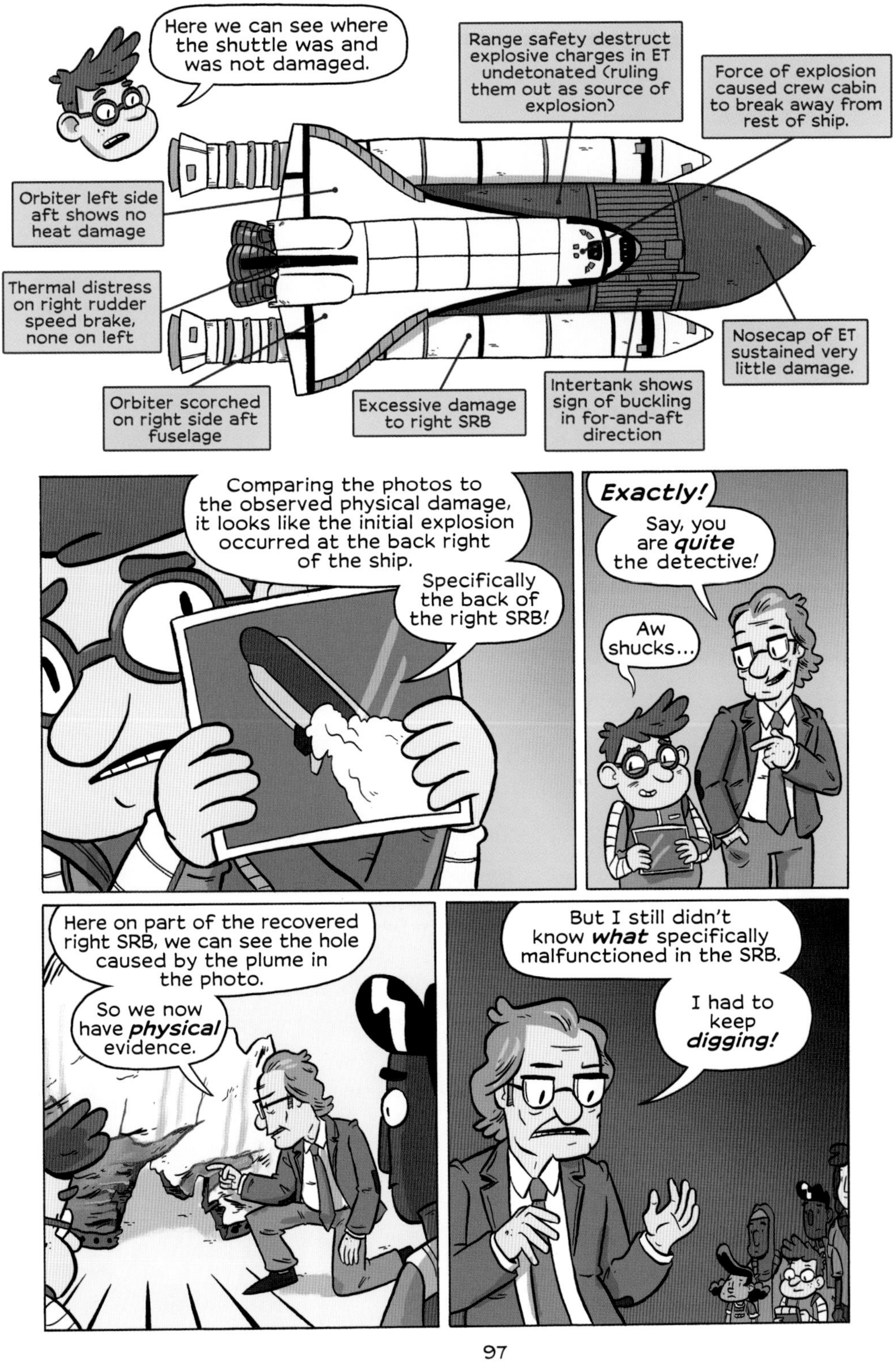
Here we can see where the shuttle was and was not damaged.
Range safety destruct explosive charges in ET undetonated (ruling them out as source of explosion)
Force of explosion caused crew cabin to break away from rest of ship.
Orbiter left side aft shows no heat damage
Thermal distress on right rudder speed brake, none on left
Nosecap of ET sustained very little damage.
Orbiter scorched on right side aft fuselage
Excessive damage to right SRB
Intertank shows sign of buckling in for-and-aft direction
Comparing the photos to the observed physical damage, it looks like the initial explosion occurred at the back right of the ship.
Specifically the back of the right SRB!
Exactly!
Say, you are ***quite*** the detective!
Aw shucks...
Here on part of the recovered right SRB, we can see the hole caused by the plume in the photo.
So we now have ***physical*** evidence.
But I still didn't know ***what*** specifically malfunctioned in the SRB.
I had to keep ***digging!***

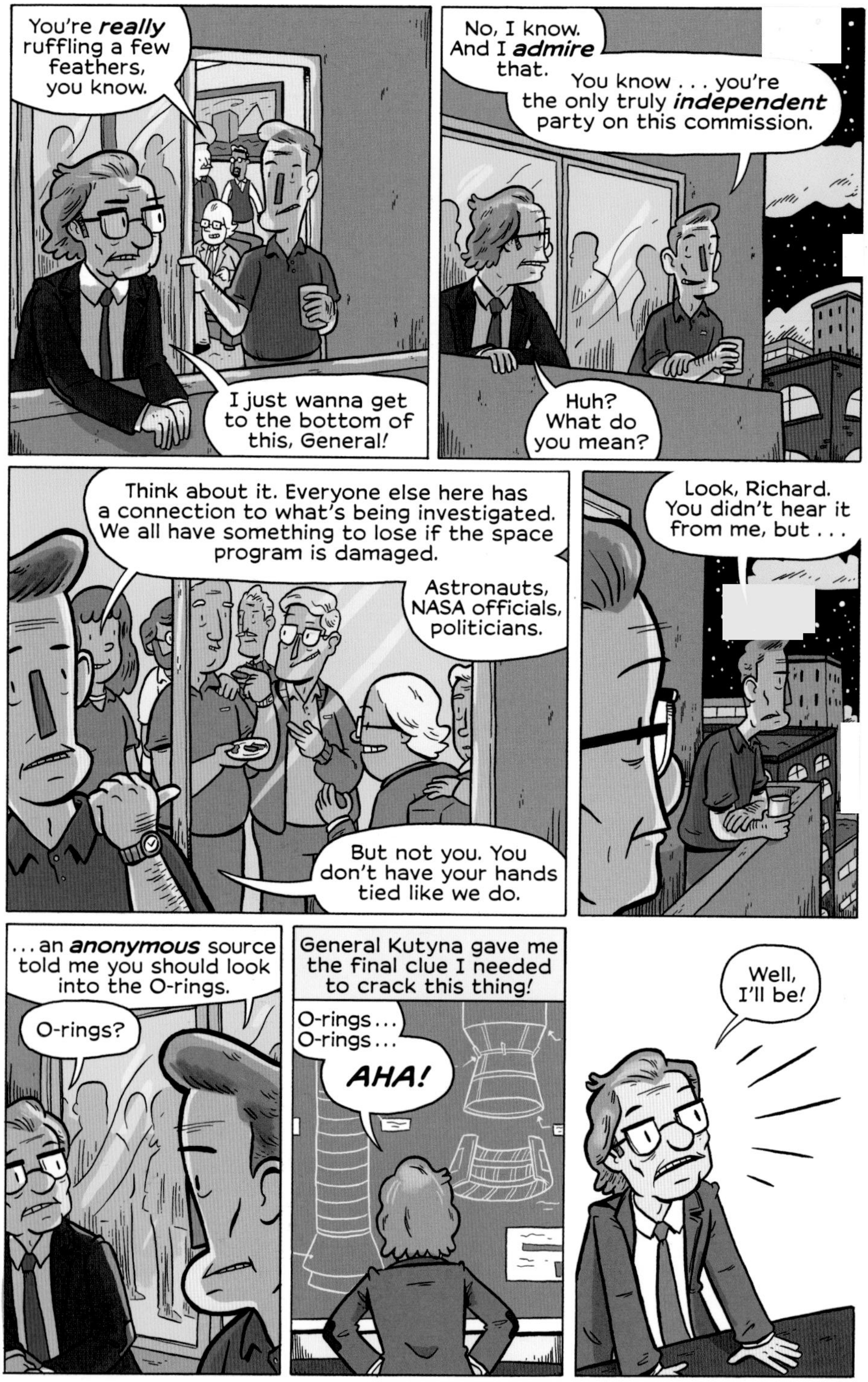

You're *really* ruffling a few feathers, you know.
I just wanna get to the bottom of this, General!
No, I know. And I *admire* that.
You know . . . you're the only truly *independent* party on this commission.
Huh? What do you mean?
Think about it. Everyone else here has a connection to what's being investigated. We all have something to lose if the space program is damaged.
Astronauts, NASA officials, politicians.
But not you. You don't have your hands tied like we do.
Look, Richard. You didn't hear it from me, but . . .
. . . an *anonymous* source told me you should look into the O-rings.
O-rings?
General Kutyna gave me the final clue I needed to crack this thing!
O-rings . . . O-rings . . .
AHA!
Well, I'll be!

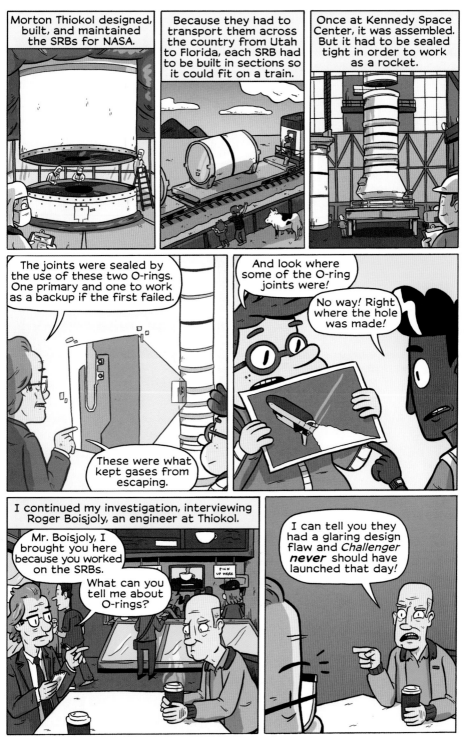

Morton Thiokol designed, built, and maintained the SRBs for NASA.

Because they had to transport them across the country from Utah to Florida, each SRB had to be built in sections so it could fit on a train.

Once at Kennedy Space Center, it was assembled. But it had to be sealed tight in order to work as a rocket.

The joints were sealed by the use of these two O-rings. One primary and one to work as a backup if the first failed.

These were what kept gases from escaping.

And look where some of the O-ring joints were!

No way! Right where the hole was made!

I continued my investigation, interviewing Roger Boisjoly, an engineer at Thiokol.

Mr. Boisjoly, I brought you here because you worked on the SRBs.

What can you tell me about O-rings?

I can tell you they had a glaring design flaw and *Challenger never* should have launched that day!

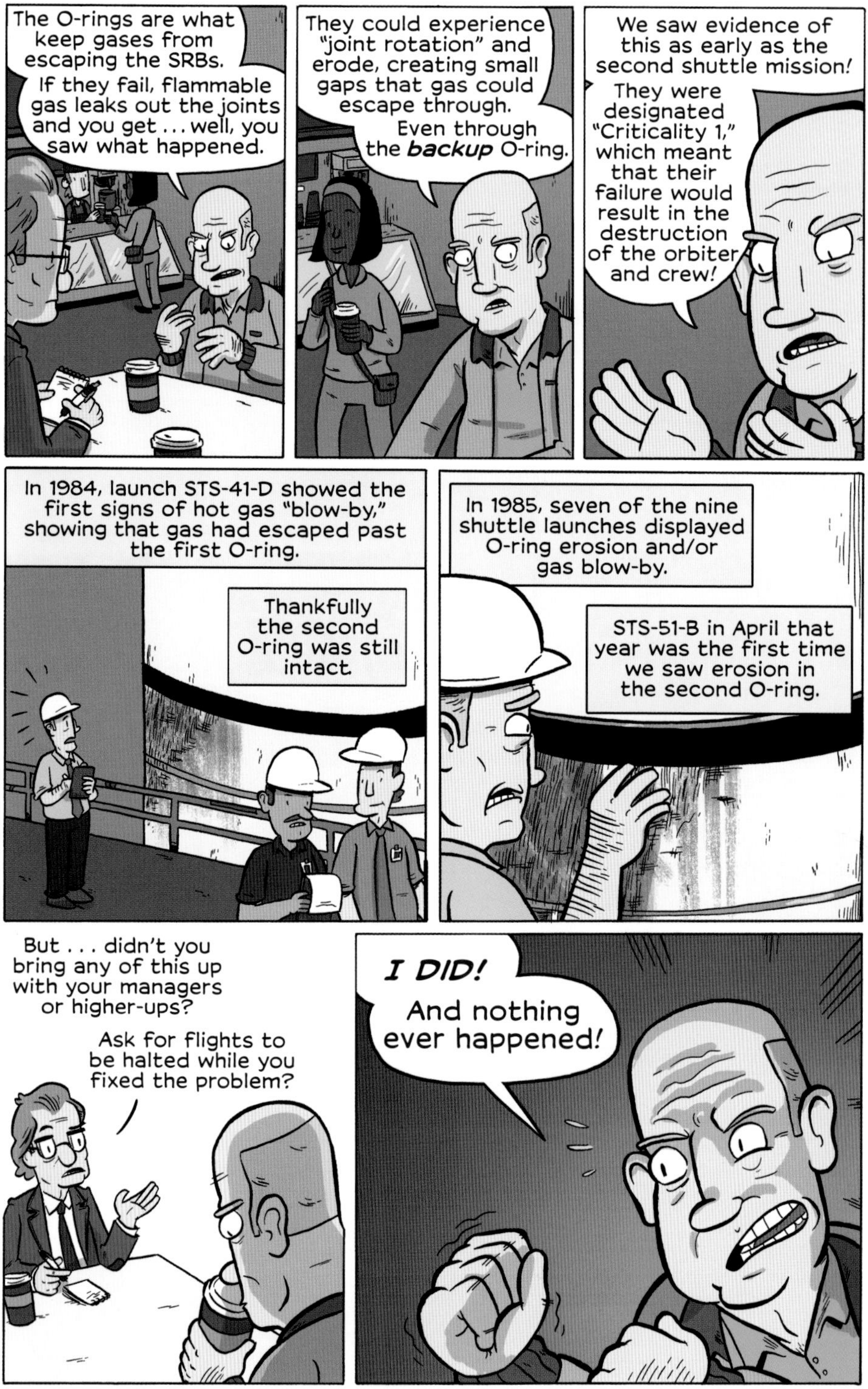
The O-rings are what keep gases from escaping the SRBs.
If they fail, flammable gas leaks out the joints and you get . . . well, you saw what happened.
They could experience "joint rotation" and erode, creating small gaps that gas could escape through.
Even through the ***backup*** O-ring.
We saw evidence of this as early as the second shuttle mission!
They were designated "Criticality 1," which meant that their failure would result in the destruction of the orbiter and crew!
In 1984, launch STS-41-D showed the first signs of hot gas "blow-by," showing that gas had escaped past the first O-ring.
Thankfully the second O-ring was still intact.
In 1985, seven of the nine shuttle launches displayed O-ring erosion and/or gas blow-by.
STS-51-B in April that year was the first time we saw erosion in the second O-ring.
But . . . didn't you bring any of this up with your managers or higher-ups?
Ask for flights to be halted while you fixed the problem?
I DID!
And nothing ever happened!

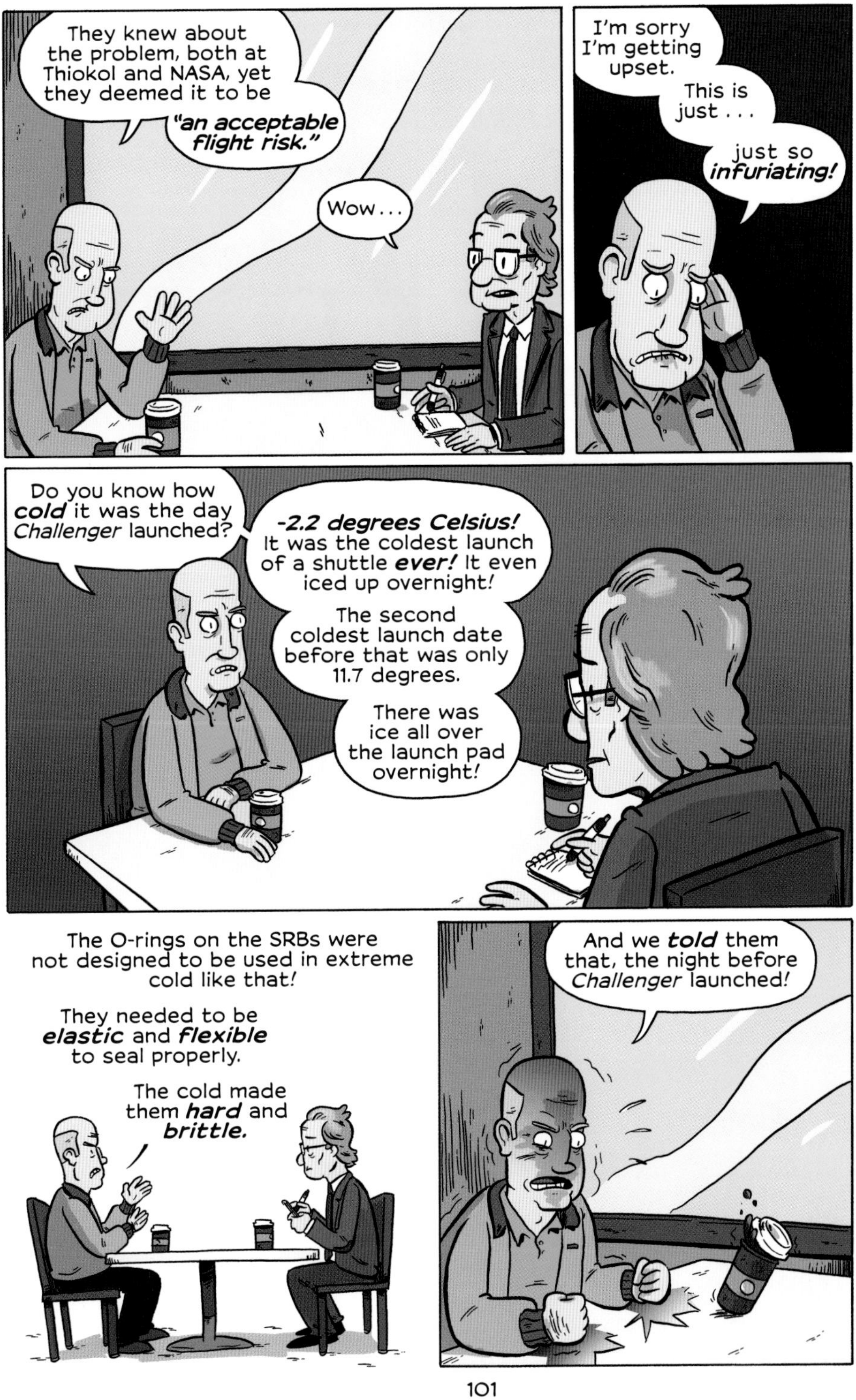
They knew about the problem, both at Thiokol and NASA, yet they deemed it to be
"an acceptable flight risk."
Wow...
I'm sorry I'm getting upset.
This is just . . .
just so *infuriating!*
Do you know how *cold* it was the day *Challenger* launched?
-2.2 degrees Celsius! It was the coldest launch of a shuttle *ever!* It even iced up overnight!
The second coldest launch date before that was only 11.7 degrees.
There was ice all over the launch pad overnight!
The O-rings on the SRBs were not designed to be used in extreme cold like that!
They needed to be *elastic* and *flexible* to seal properly.
The cold made them *hard* and *brittle.*
And we *told* them that, the night before *Challenger* launched!

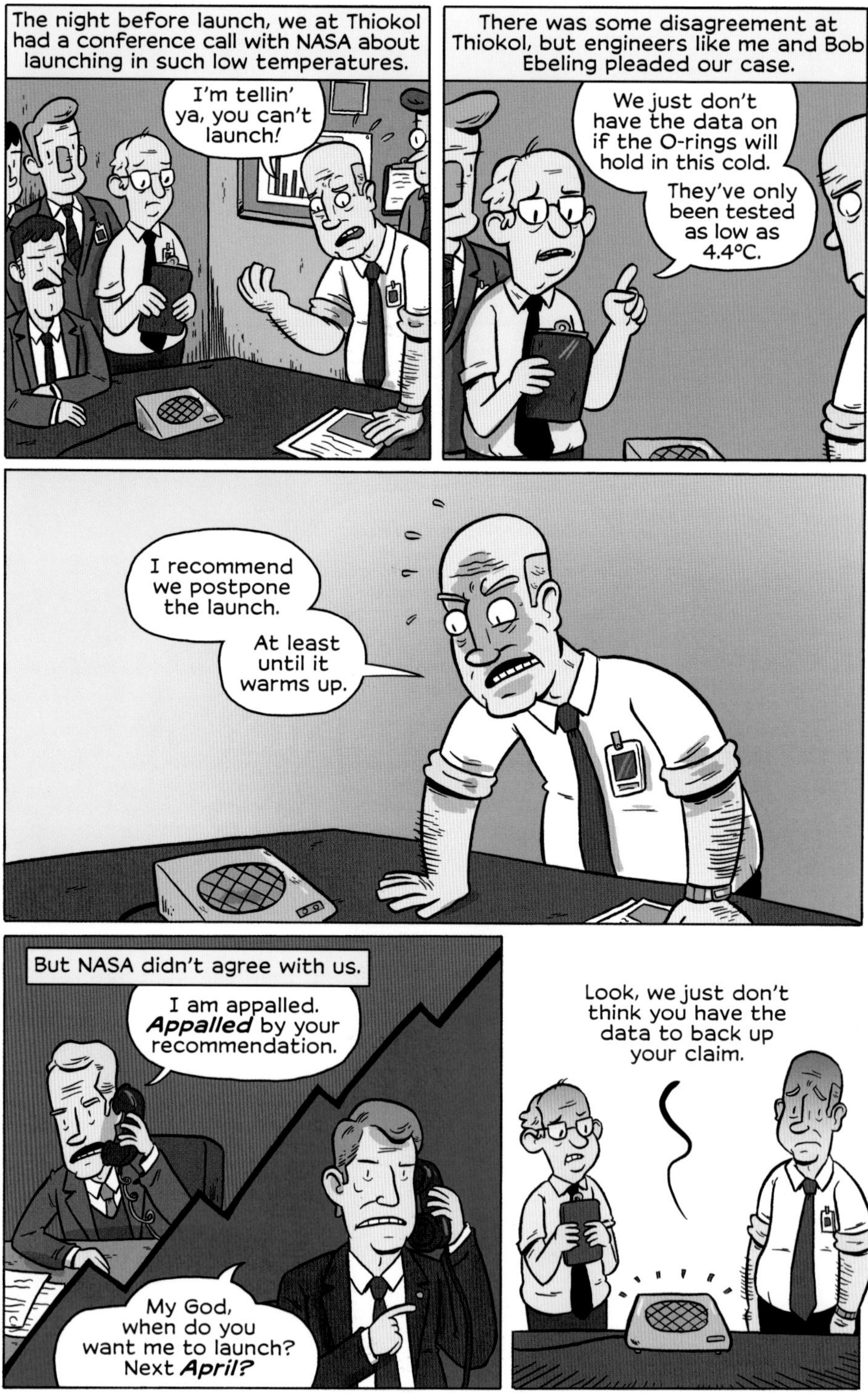

The night before launch, we at Thiokol had a conference call with NASA about launching in such low temperatures.
I'm tellin' ya, you can't launch!
There was some disagreement at Thiokol, but engineers like me and Bob Ebeling pleaded our case.
We just don't have the data on if the O-rings will hold in this cold.
They've only been tested as low as 4.4°C.
I recommend we postpone the launch.
At least until it warms up.
But NASA didn't agree with us.
I am appalled. *Appalled* by your recommendation.
My God, when do you want me to launch? Next *April?*
Look, we just don't think you have the data to back up your claim.

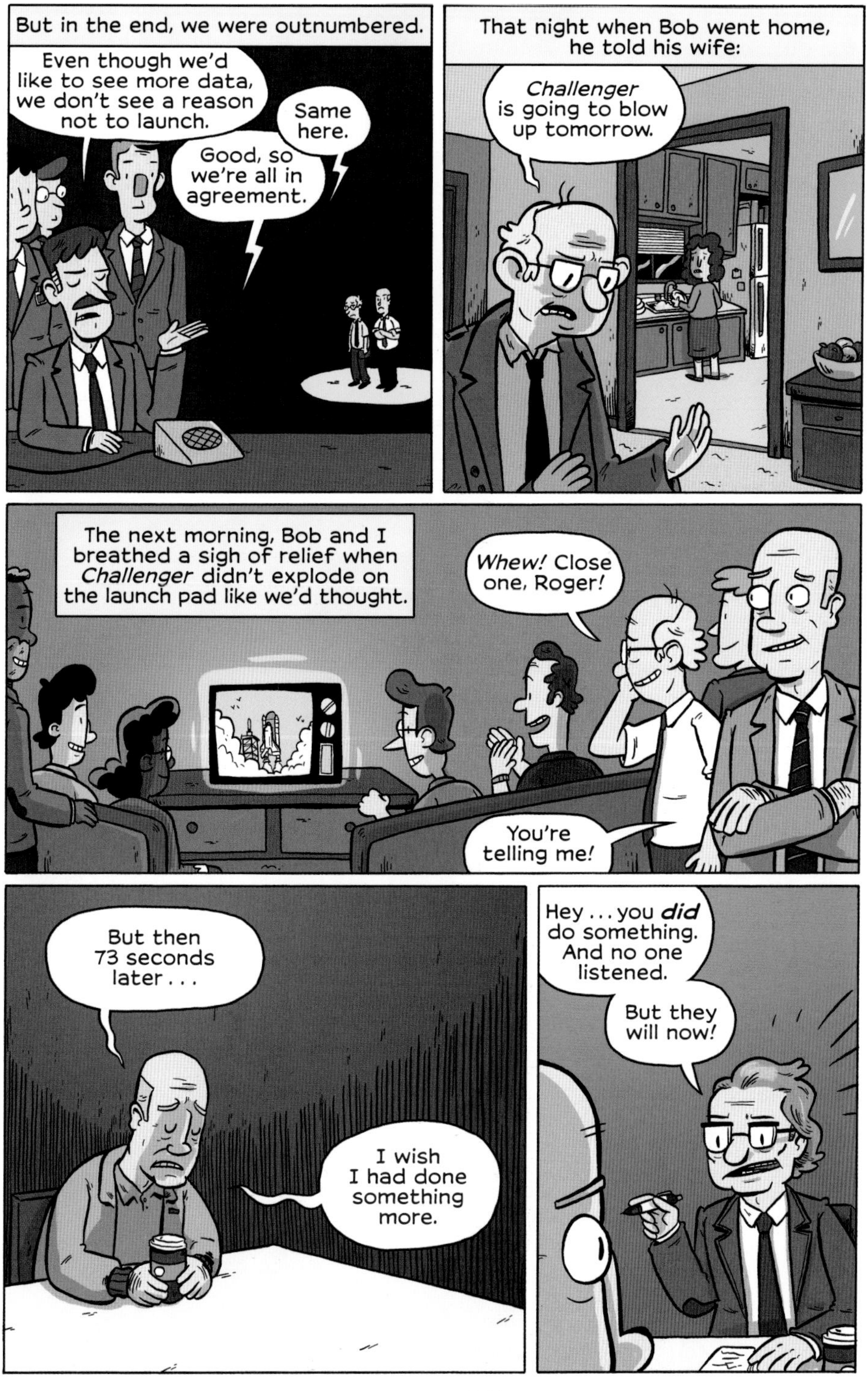
But in the end, we were outnumbered.
Even though we'd like to see more data, we don't see a reason not to launch.
Same here.
Good, so we're all in agreement.
That night when Bob went home, he told his wife:
Challenger is going to blow up tomorrow.
The next morning, Bob and I breathed a sigh of relief when *Challenger* didn't explode on the launch pad like we'd thought.
Whew! Close one, Roger!
You're telling me!
But then 73 seconds later . . .
I wish I had done something more.
Hey . . . you ***did*** do something. And no one listened.
But they will now!

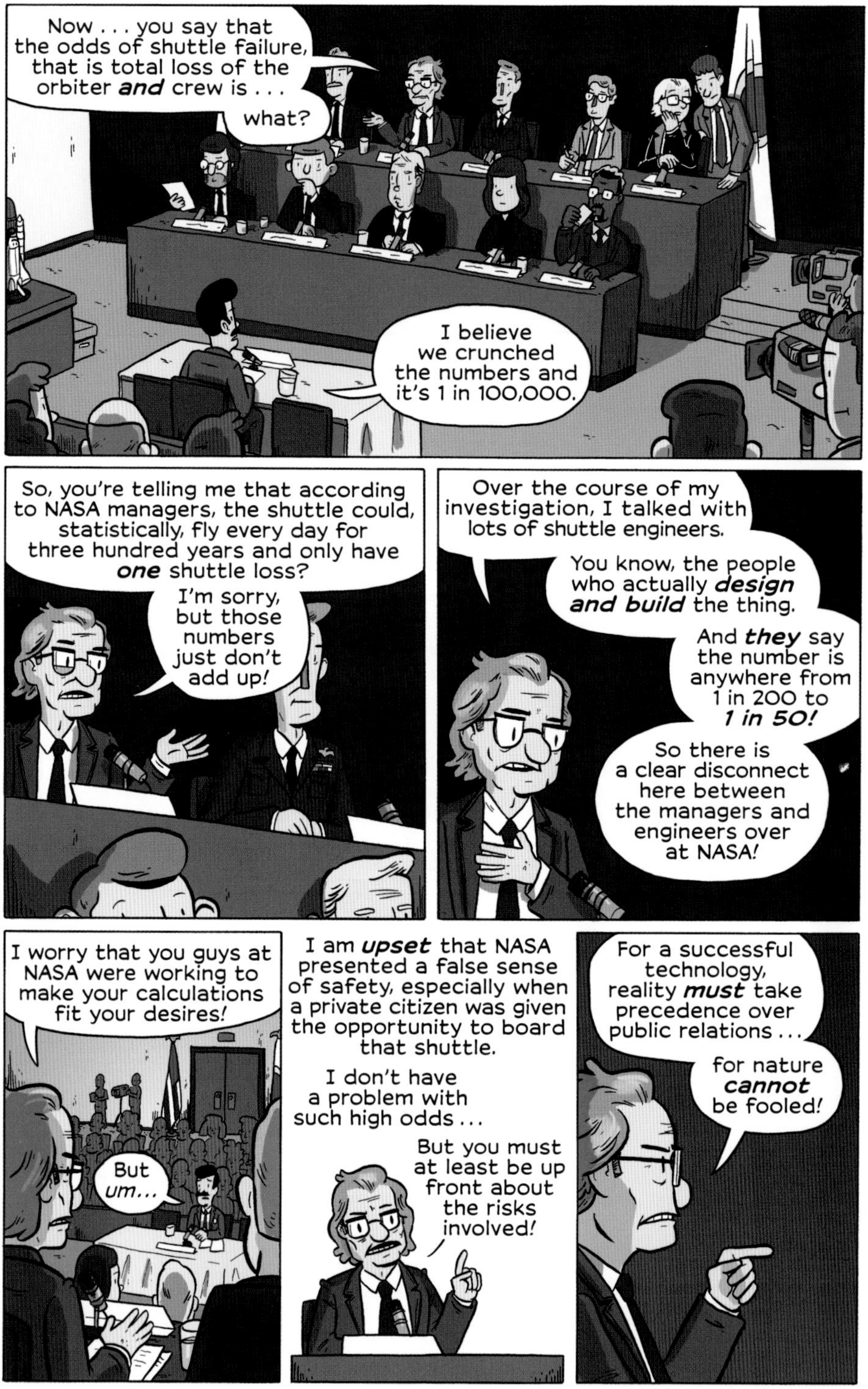
Now . . . you say that the odds of shuttle failure, that is total loss of the orbiter **and** crew is . . .
what?
I believe we crunched the numbers and it's 1 in 100,000.
So, you're telling me that according to NASA managers, the shuttle could, statistically, fly every day for three hundred years and only have **one** shuttle loss?
I'm sorry, but those numbers just don't add up!
Over the course of my investigation, I talked with lots of shuttle engineers.
You know, the people who actually **design and build** the thing.
And **they** say the number is anywhere from 1 in 200 to **1 in 50!**
So there is a clear disconnect here between the managers and engineers over at NASA!
I worry that you guys at NASA were working to make your calculations fit your desires!
But *um...*
I am **upset** that NASA presented a false sense of safety, especially when a private citizen was given the opportunity to board that shuttle.
I don't have a problem with such high odds . . .
But you must at least be up front about the risks involved!
For a successful technology, reality **must** take precedence over public relations . . .
for nature **cannot** be fooled!

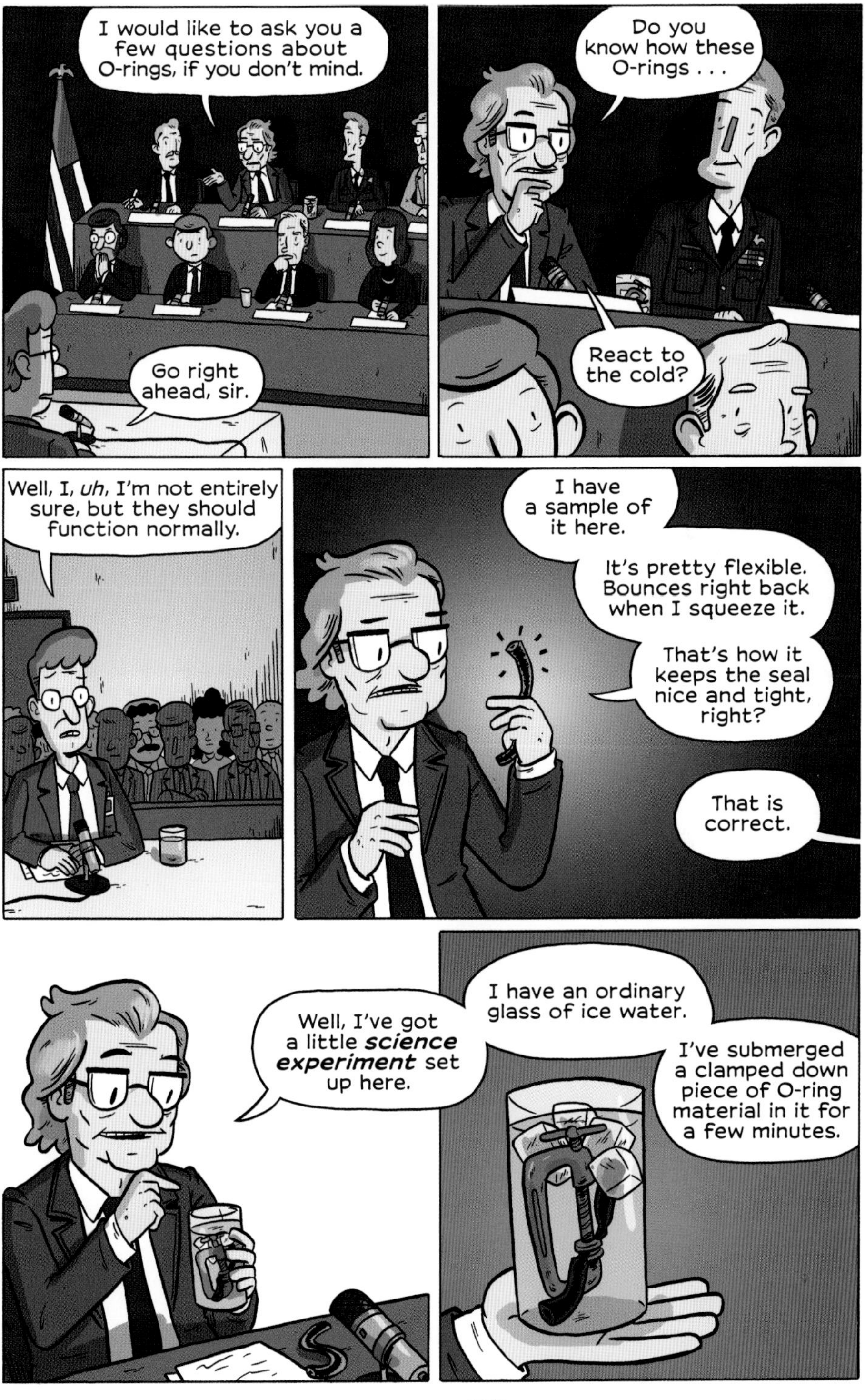
I would like to ask you a few questions about O-rings, if you don't mind.
Go right ahead, sir.
Do you know how these O-rings . . .
React to the cold?
Well, I, *uh*, I'm not entirely sure, but they should function normally.
I have a sample of it here.
It's pretty flexible. Bounces right back when I squeeze it.
That's how it keeps the seal nice and tight, right?
That is correct.
Well, I've got a little ***science experiment*** set up here.
I have an ordinary glass of ice water.
I've submerged a clamped down piece of O-ring material in it for a few minutes.

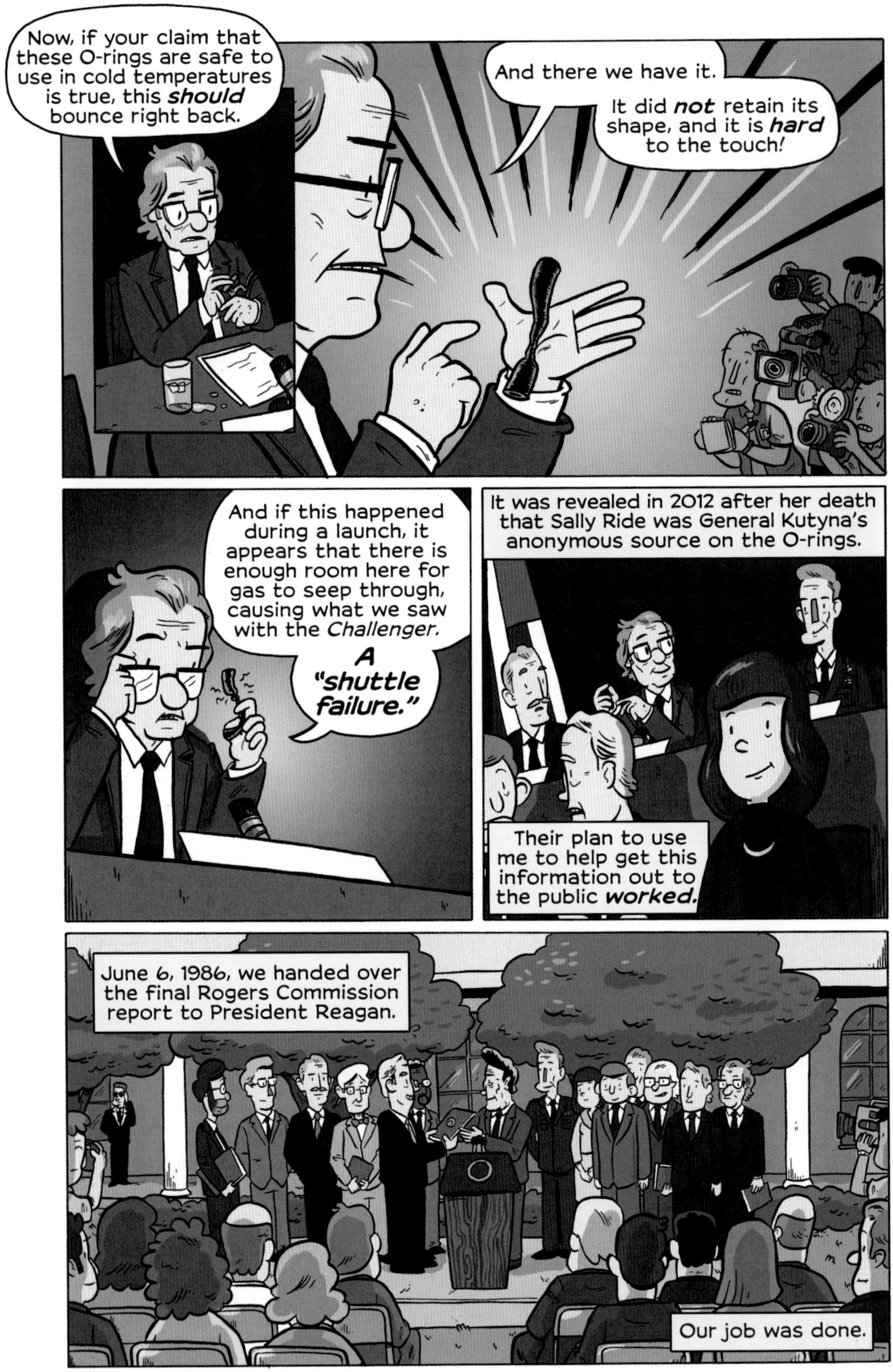
Now, if your claim that these O-rings are safe to use in cold temperatures is true, this *should* bounce right back.
And there we have it.
It did *not* retain its shape, and it is *hard* to the touch!
And if this happened during a launch, it appears that there is enough room here for gas to seep through, causing what we saw with the *Challenger.*
A "shuttle failure."
It was revealed in 2012 after her death that Sally Ride was General Kutyna's anonymous source on the O-rings.
Their plan to use me to help get this information out to the public *worked.*
June 6, 1986, we handed over the final Rogers Commission report to President Reagan.
Our job was done.

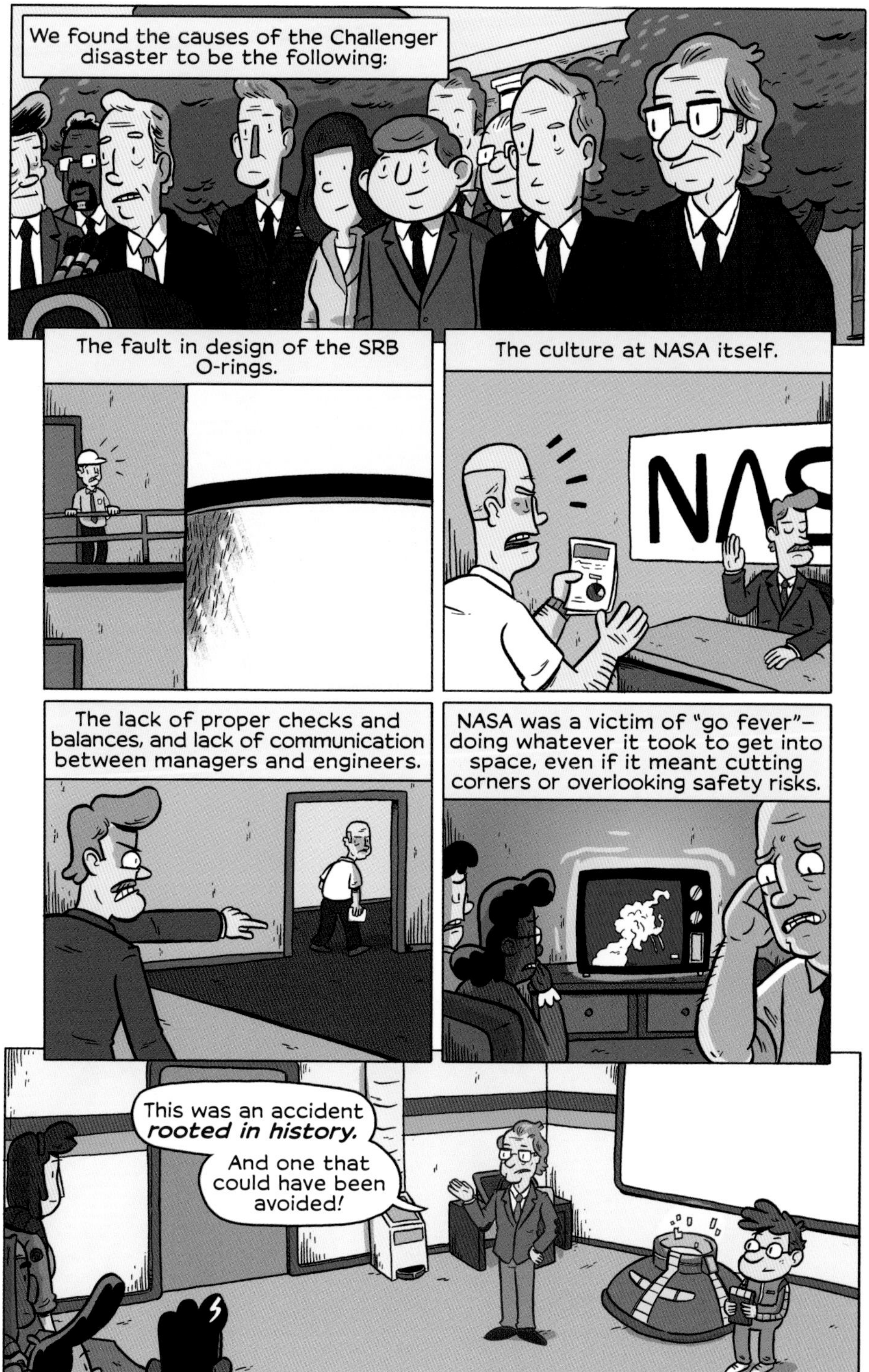
We found the causes of the Challenger disaster to be the following:
The fault in design of the SRB O-rings.
The culture at NASA itself.
NAS
The lack of proper checks and balances, and lack of communication between managers and engineers.
NASA was a victim of "go fever"–doing whatever it took to get into space, even if it meant cutting corners or overlooking safety risks.
This was an accident ***rooted in history.***
And one that could have been avoided!

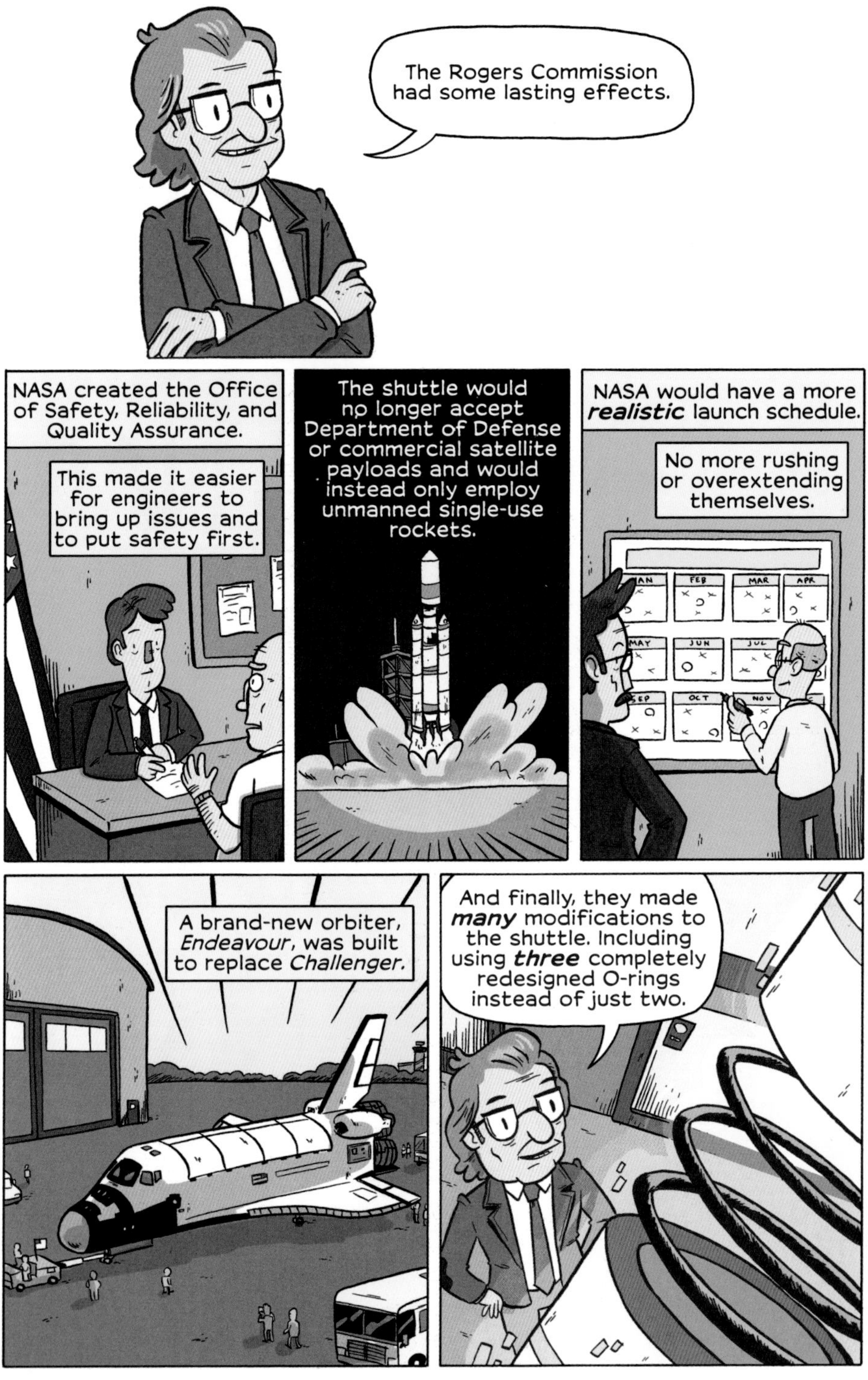
The Rogers Commission had some lasting effects.
NASA created the Office of Safety, Reliability, and Quality Assurance.
This made it easier for engineers to bring up issues and to put safety first.
The shuttle would no longer accept Department of Defense or commercial satellite payloads and would instead only employ unmanned single-use rockets.
NASA would have a more ***realistic*** launch schedule.
No more rushing or overextending themselves.
A brand-new orbiter, *Endeavour*, was built to replace *Challenger*.
And finally, they made ***many*** modifications to the shuttle. Including using ***three*** completely redesigned O-rings instead of just two.

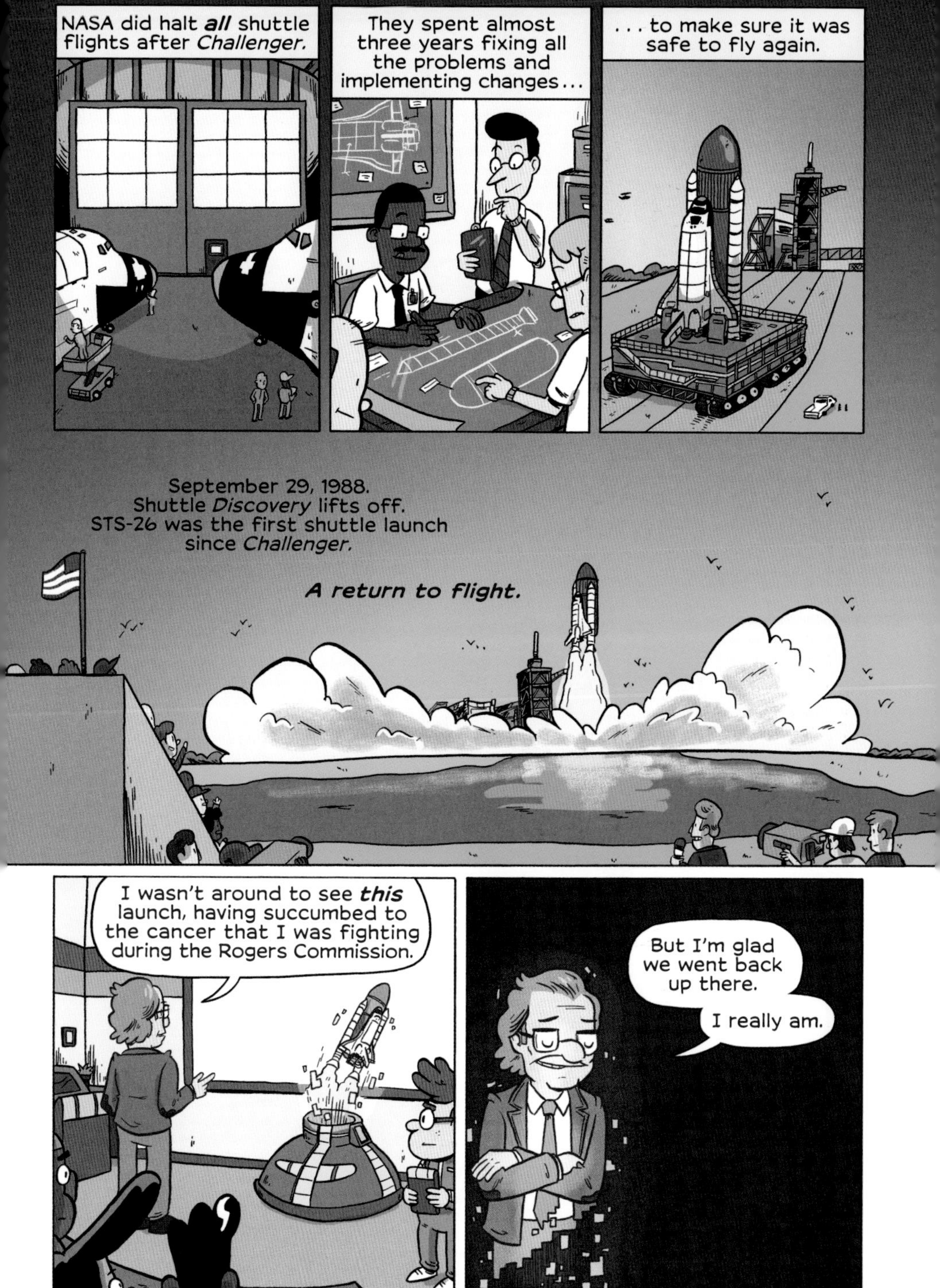
NASA did halt *all* shuttle flights after *Challenger*.
They spent almost three years fixing all the problems and implementing changes...
...to make sure it was safe to fly again.
September 29, 1988. Shuttle *Discovery* lifts off. STS-26 was the first shuttle launch since *Challenger*.
A return to flight.
I wasn't around to see *this* launch, having succumbed to the cancer that I was fighting during the Rogers Commission.
But I'm glad we went back up there.
I really am.

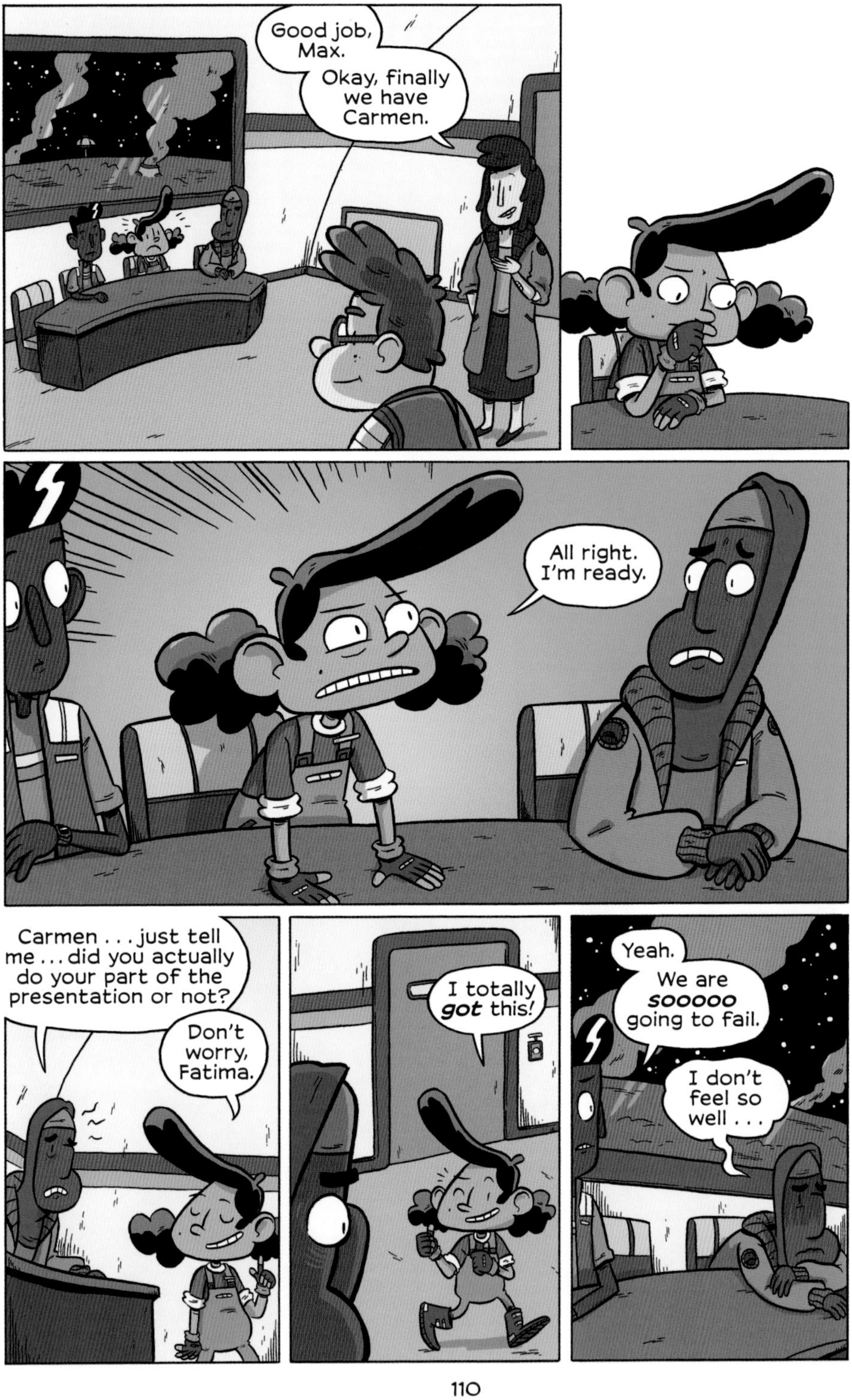

Good job, Max.
Okay, finally we have Carmen.
All right. I'm ready.
Carmen . . . just tell me . . . did you actually do your part of the presentation or not?
Don't worry, Fatima.
I totally **got** this!
Yeah.
We are ***sooooo*** going to fail.
I don't feel so well . . .

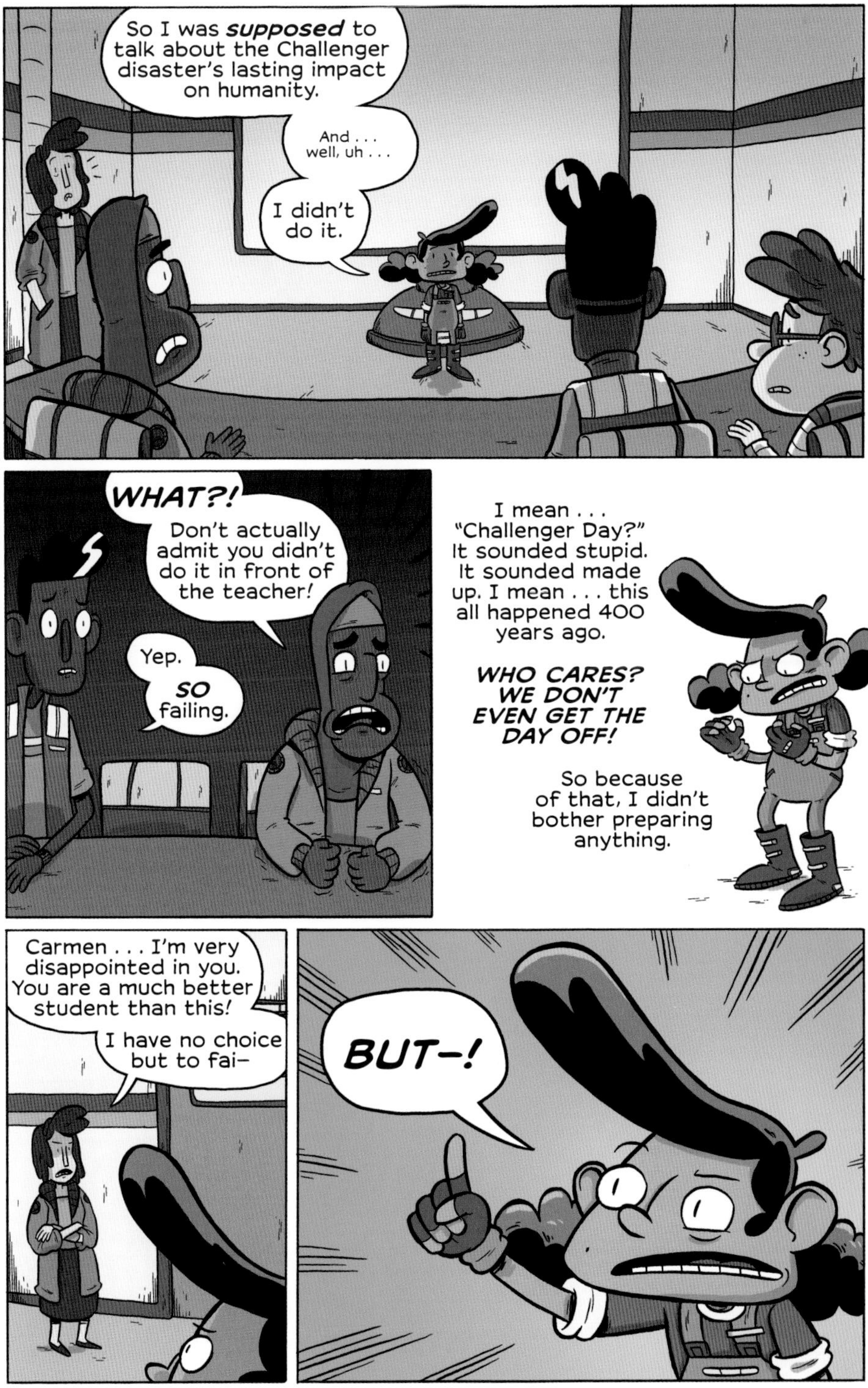
So I was *supposed* to talk about the Challenger disaster's lasting impact on humanity.
And . . . well, uh . . .
I didn't do it.
WHAT?!
Don't actually admit you didn't do it in front of the teacher!
Yep.
SO failing.
I mean . . . "Challenger Day?" It sounded stupid. It sounded made up. I mean . . . this all happened 400 years ago.
WHO CARES? WE DON'T EVEN GET THE DAY OFF!
So because of that, I didn't bother preparing anything.
Carmen . . . I'm very disappointed in you. You are a much better student than this!
I have no choice but to fai–
BUT–!

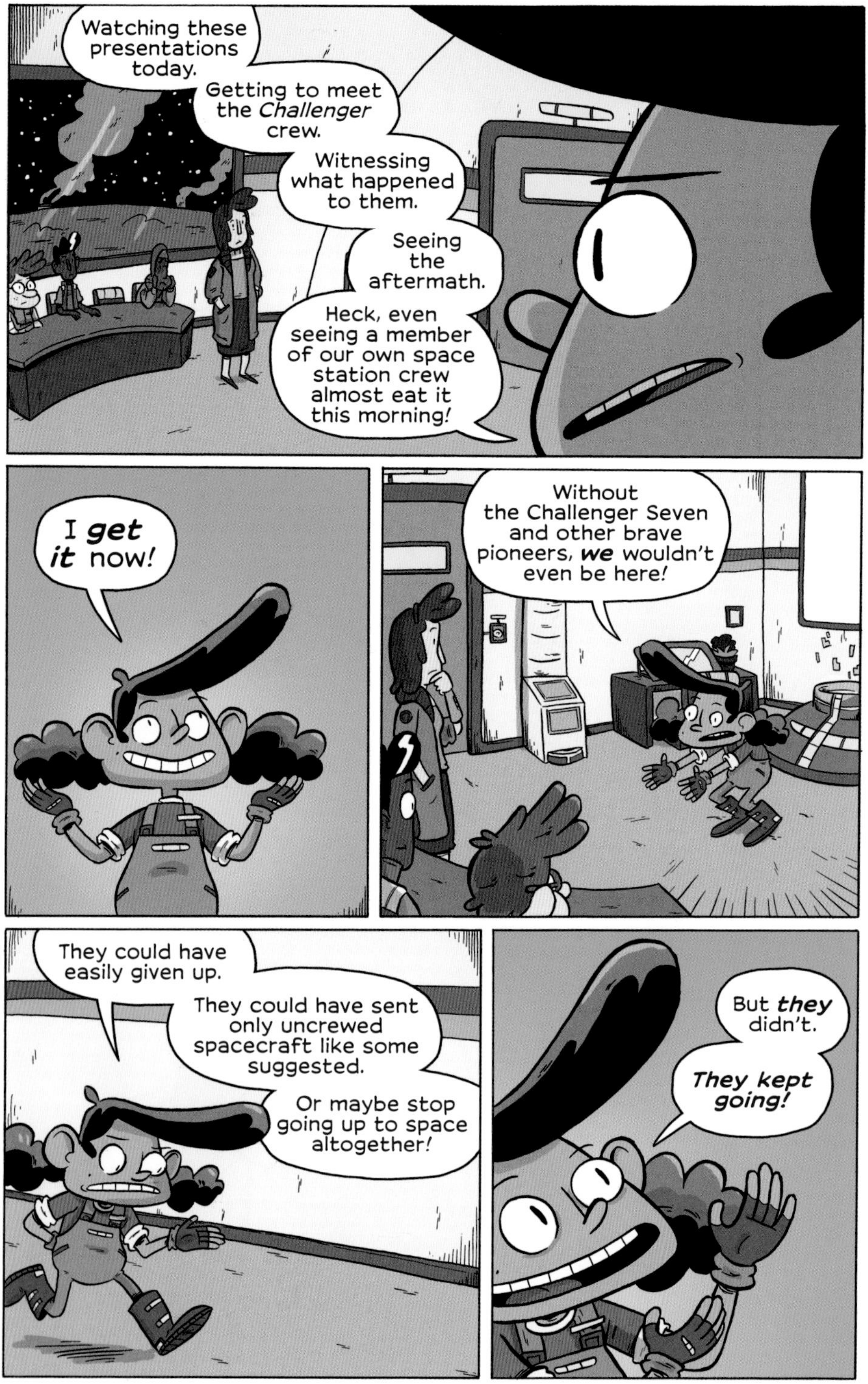
Watching these presentations today.
Getting to meet the *Challenger* crew.
Witnessing what happened to them.
Seeing the aftermath.
Heck, even seeing a member of our own space station crew almost eat it this morning!
I ***get it*** now!
Without the Challenger Seven and other brave pioneers, ***we*** wouldn't even be here!
They could have easily given up.
They could have sent only uncrewed spacecraft like some suggested.
Or maybe stop going up to space altogether!
But ***they*** didn't.
They kept going!

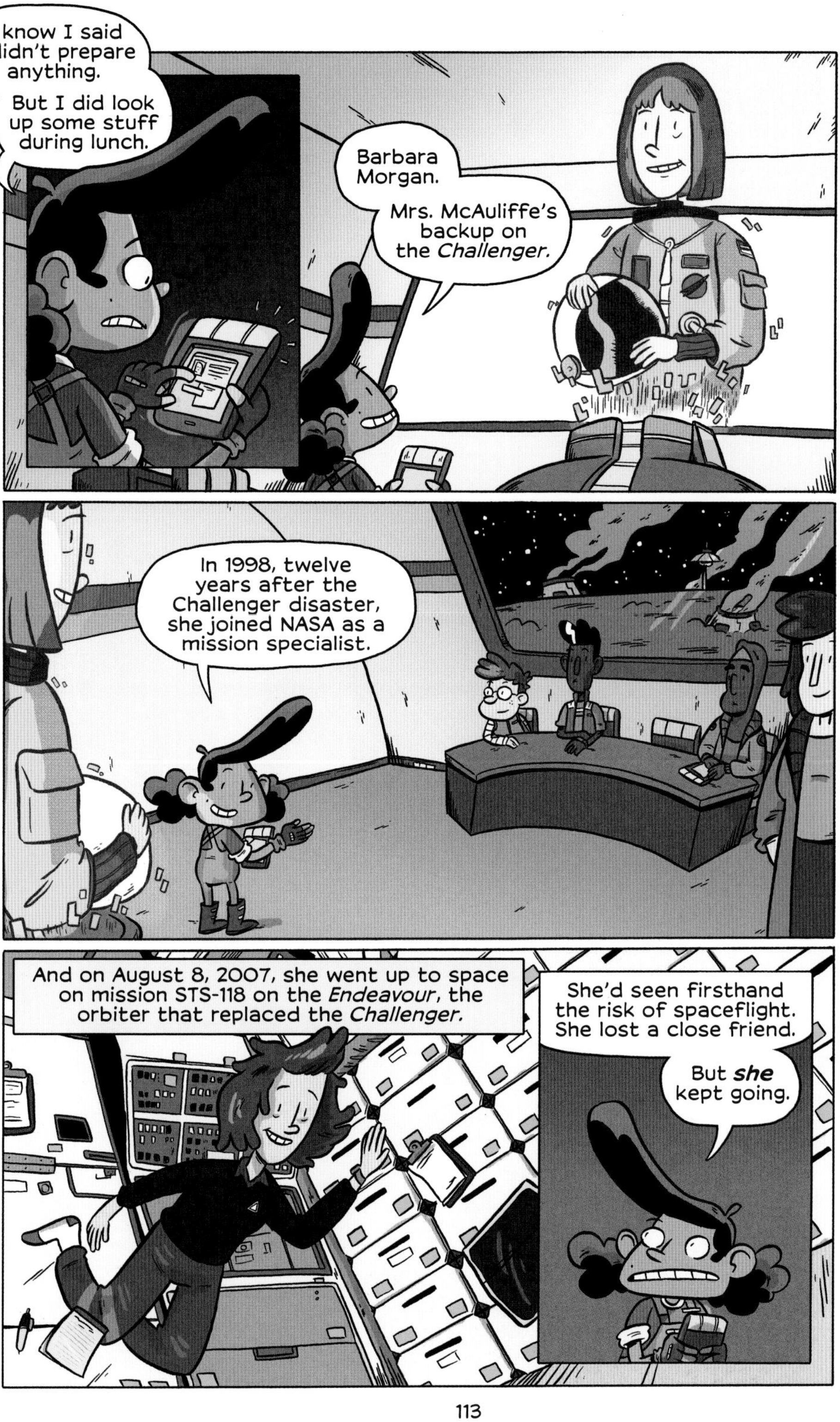
I know I said I didn't prepare anything.
But I did look up some stuff during lunch.
Barbara Morgan.
Mrs. McAuliffe's backup on the *Challenger.*
In 1998, twelve years after the Challenger disaster, she joined NASA as a mission specialist.
And on August 8, 2007, she went up to space on mission STS-118 on the *Endeavour*, the orbiter that replaced the *Challenger.*
She'd seen firsthand the risk of spaceflight. She lost a close friend.
But ***she*** kept going.

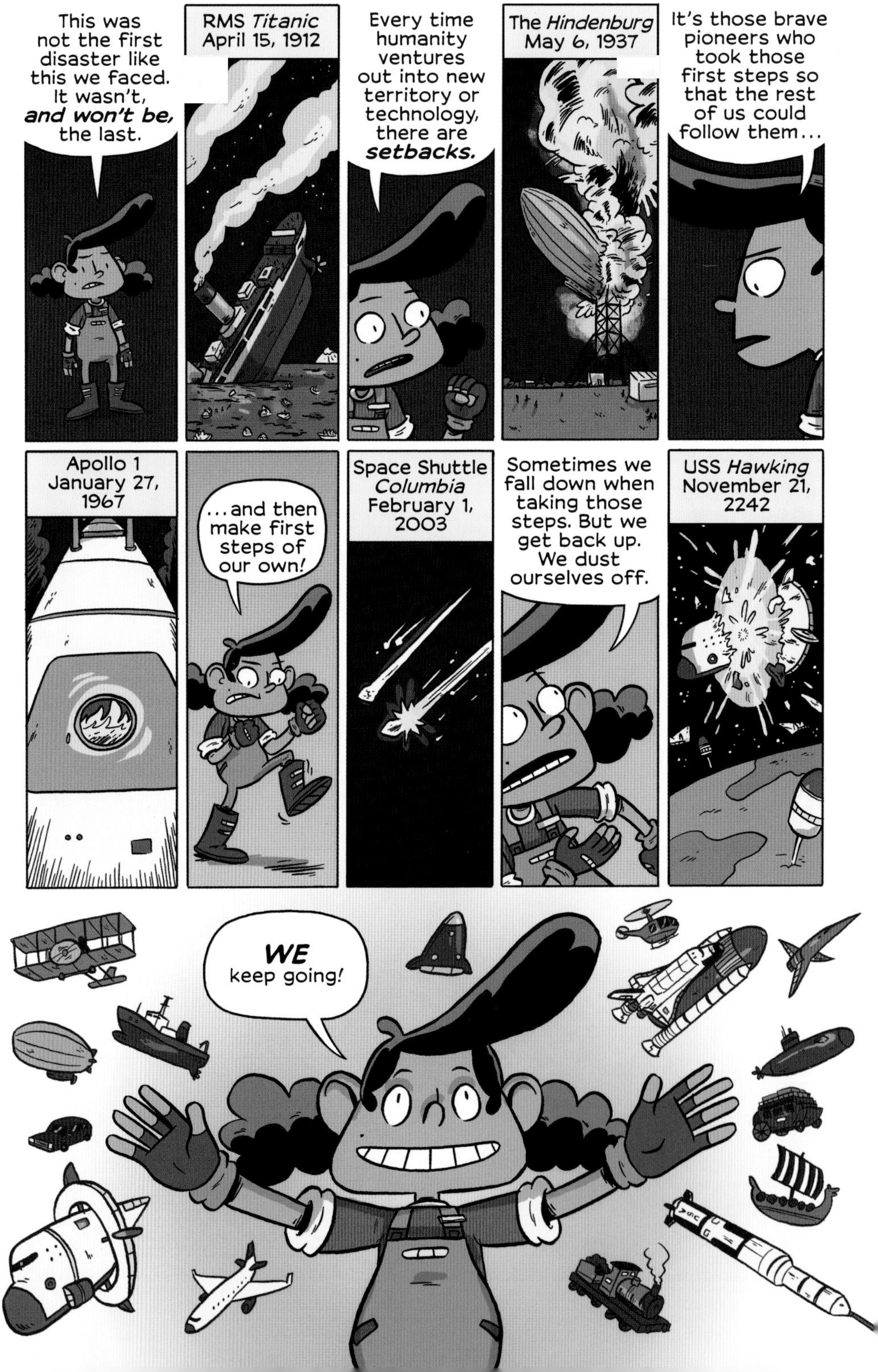

This was not the first disaster like this we faced. It wasn't, ***and won't be,*** the last.
RMS *Titanic* April 15, 1912
Every time humanity ventures out into new territory or technology, there are ***setbacks.***
The *Hindenburg* May 6, 1937
It's those brave pioneers who took those first steps so that the rest of us could follow them...
Apollo 1 January 27, 1967
...and then make first steps of our own!
Space Shuttle *Columbia* February 1, 2003
Sometimes we fall down when taking those steps. But we get back up. We dust ourselves off.
USS *Hawking* November 21, 2242
WE keep going!

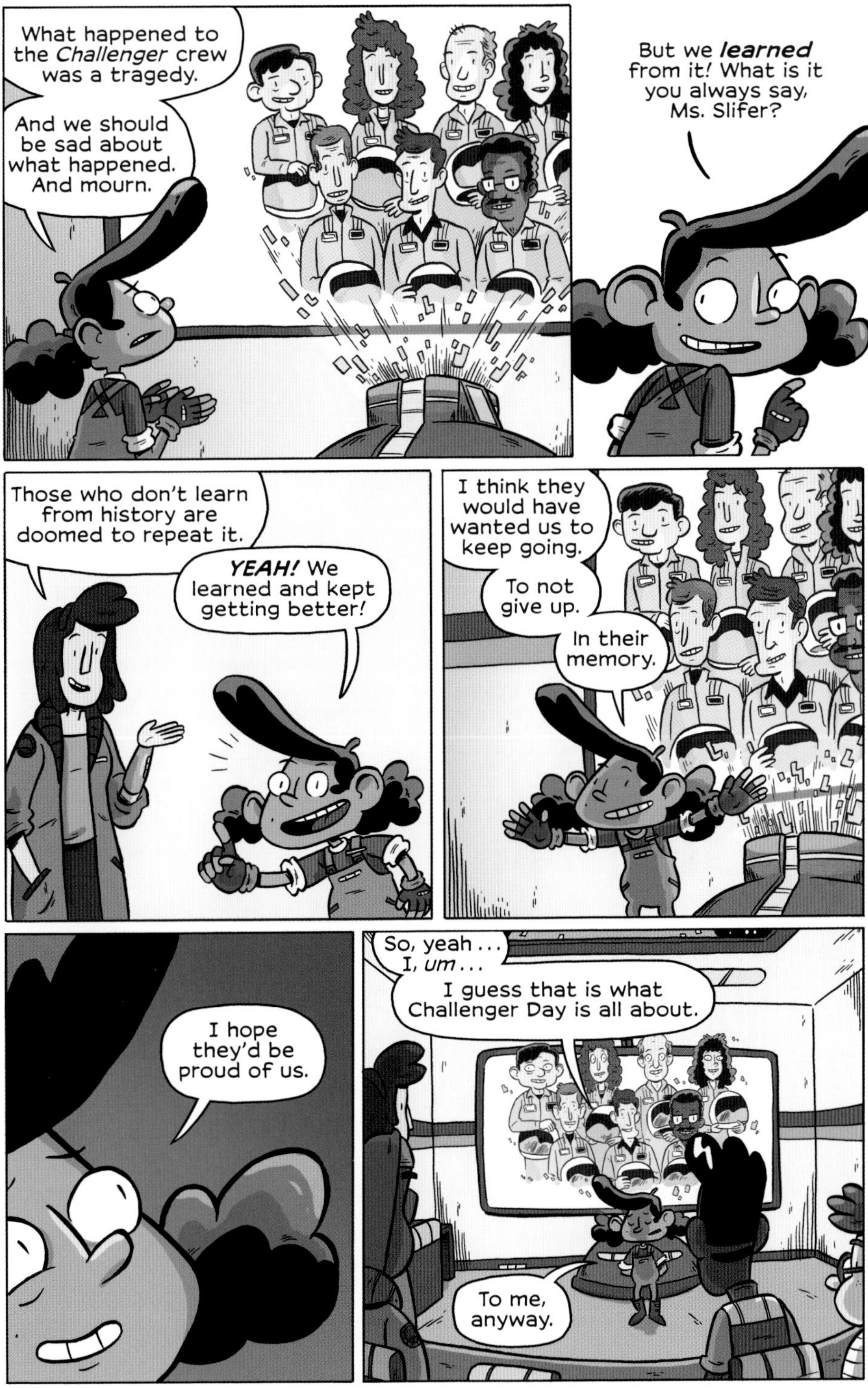
What happened to the *Challenger* crew was a tragedy.
And we should be sad about what happened. And mourn.
But we ***learned*** from it! What is it you always say, Ms. Slifer?
Those who don't learn from history are doomed to repeat it.
YEAH! We learned and kept getting better!
I think they would have wanted us to keep going.
To not give up.
In their memory.
I hope they'd be proud of us.
So, yeah . . . I, *um* . . .
I guess that is what Challenger Day is all about.
To me, anyway.

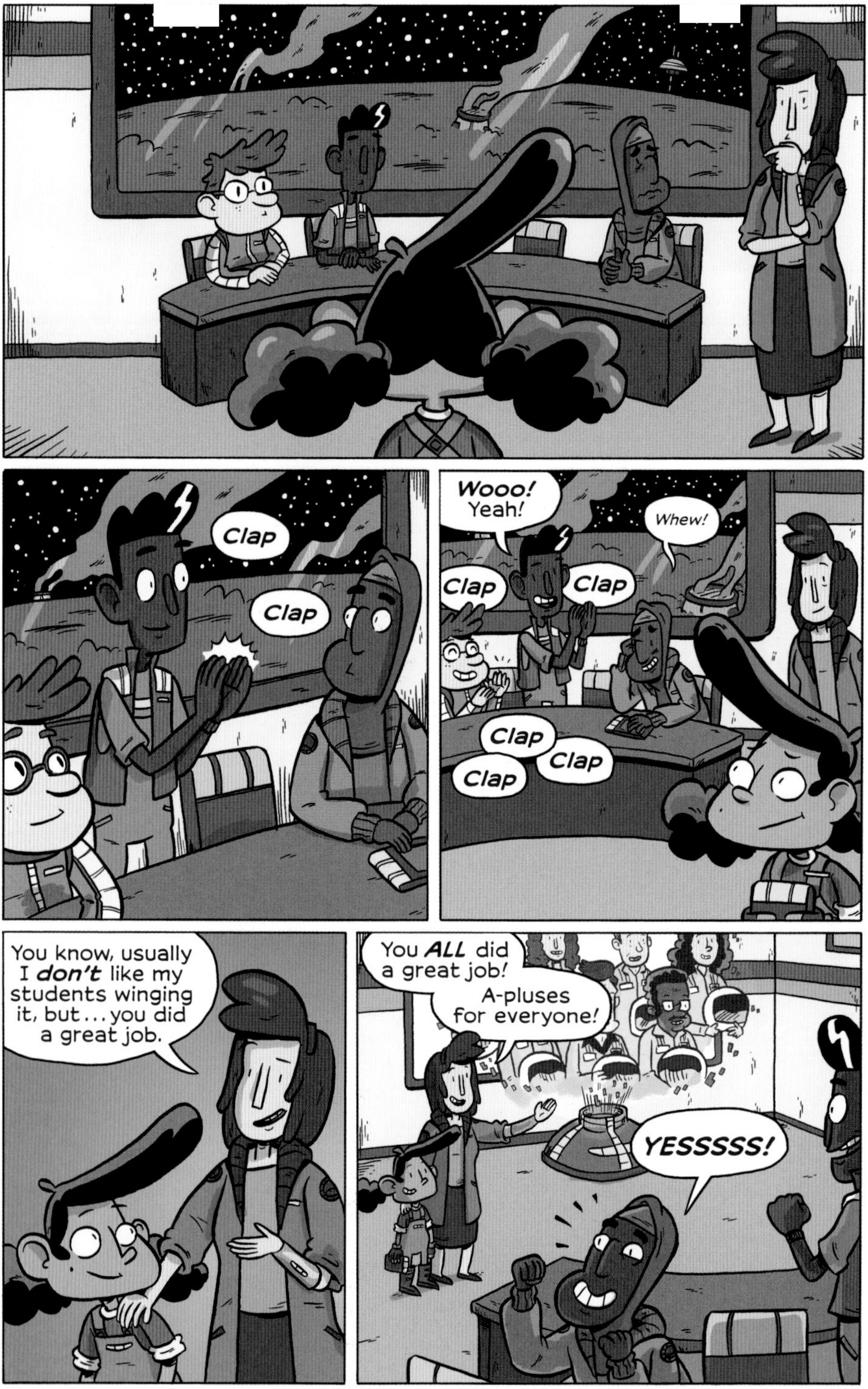
Clap
Clap
Wooo! Yeah!
Whew!
Clap
Clap
Clap
Clap
Clap
You know, usually I don't like my students winging it, but... you did a great job.
You ALL did a great job!
A-pluses for everyone!
YESSSSS!

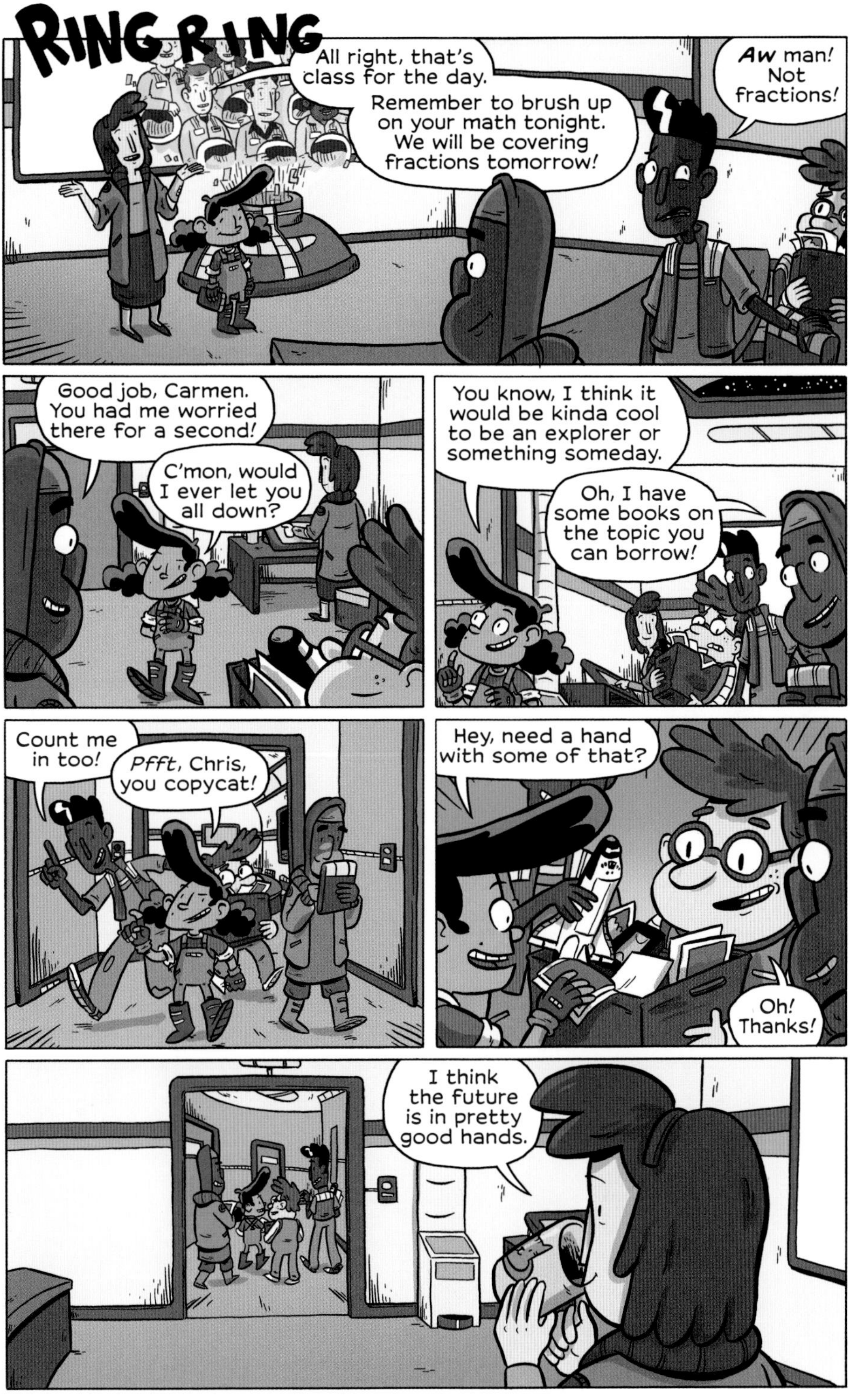
RING RING
All right, that's class for the day.
Remember to brush up on your math tonight. We will be covering fractions tomorrow!
Aw man! Not fractions!
Good job, Carmen. You had me worried there for a second!
C'mon, would I ever let you all down?
You know, I think it would be kinda cool to be an explorer or something someday.
Oh, I have some books on the topic you can borrow!
Count me in too!
Pfft, Chris, you copycat!
Hey, need a hand with some of that?
Oh! Thanks!
I think the future is in pretty good hands.

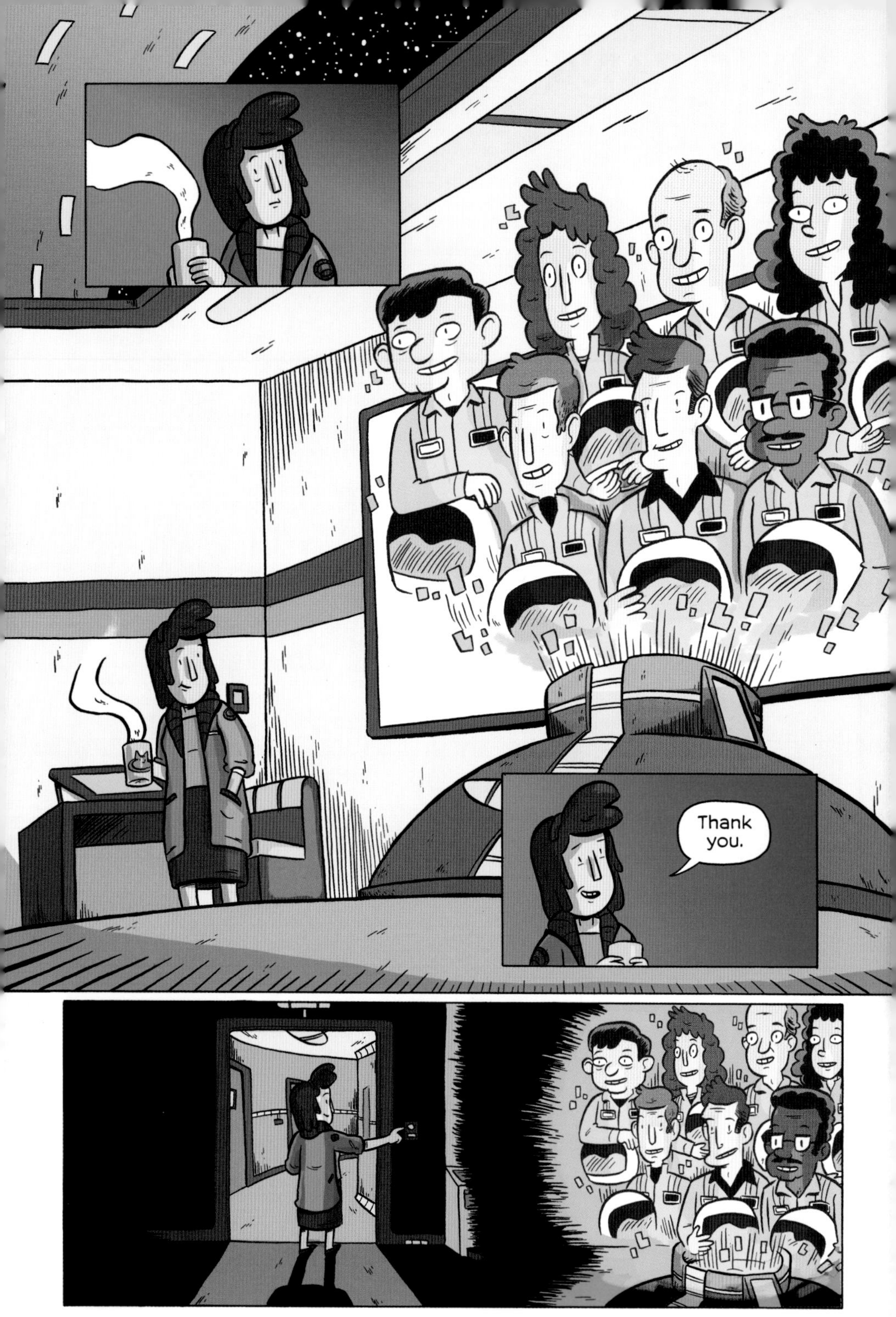
Thank you.

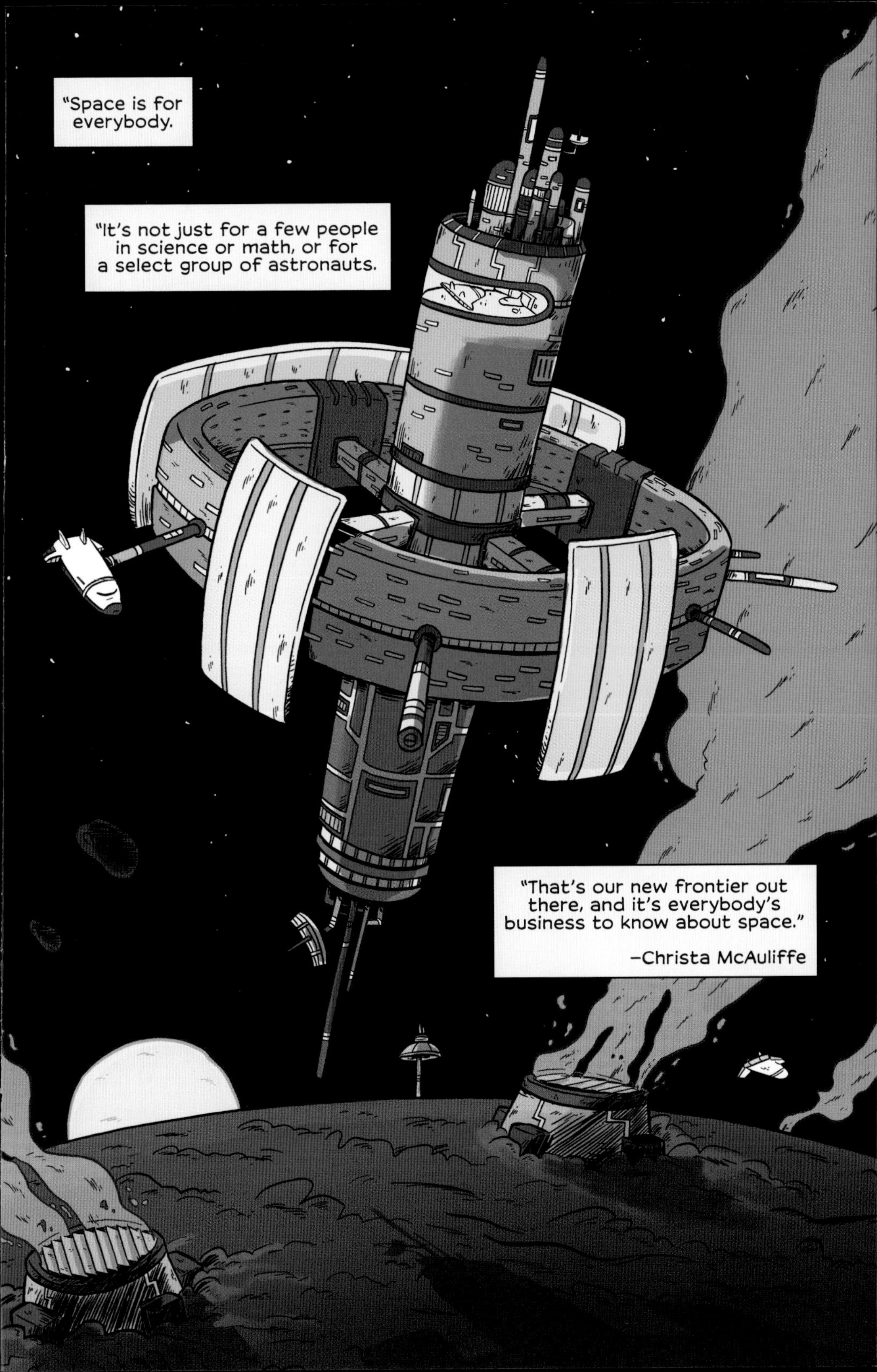
"Space is for everybody.
"It's not just for a few people in science or math, or for a select group of astronauts.
"That's our new frontier out there, and it's everybody's business to know about space."
–Christa McAuliffe

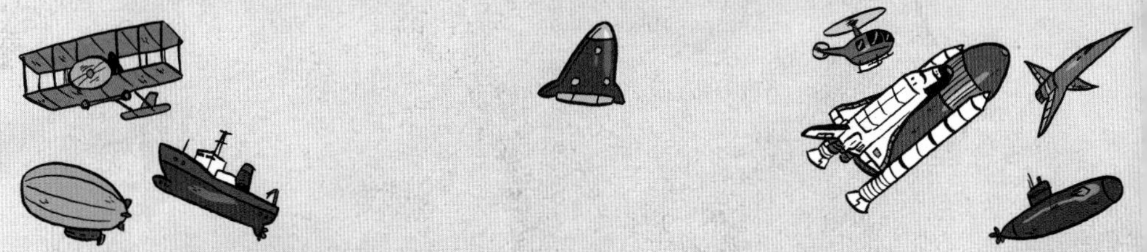

An afterword from author
Pranas T. Naujokaitis

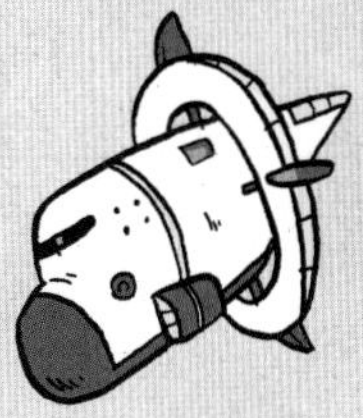

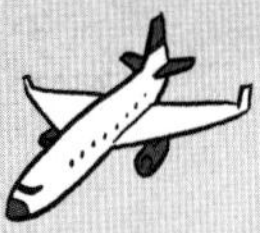

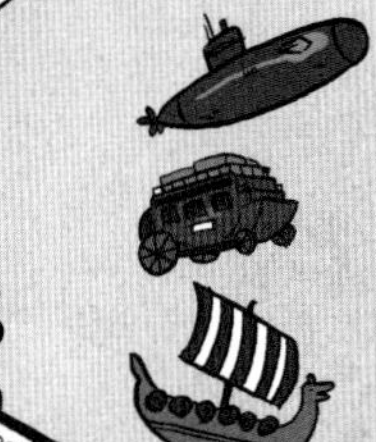

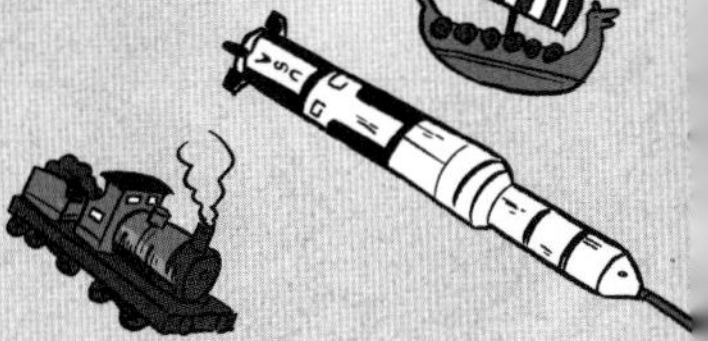

On the day of the Challenger disaster I was only two months old. That morning, my mom, a former schoolteacher herself, dropped me off at day care for the first time, as she had to go back to work. She told me how when she picked me up that evening she hugged me just a little bit tighter, thinking of the kids who had just tragically lost their parents. Obviously I don't remember any of this. I was a baby, after all.

So while I don't remember the disaster itself, I do remember life after *Challenger.*

I remember growing up with the disaster in the public consciousness. That now-iconic image of the plume of smoke and debris hanging in the air over the Florida coast would soon find its way into school textbooks and our collective memory. I remember there seemed to be this newfound fascination with space. I remember being super jealous of all the lucky kids who'd be on a basic cable game show and win a trip to Space Camp. I remember every time my family would go to the local science museum and I'd beg and plead and cry to get a new space shuttle toy (and some of the time my tears actually worked). Space was the place.

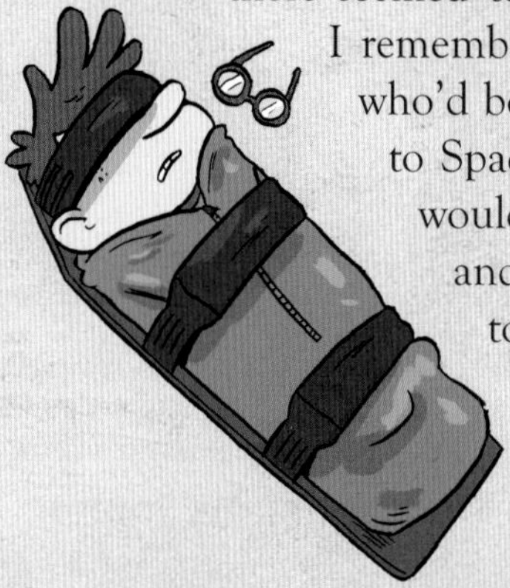

I remember February 1, 2003. Waking up that morning to be met with nonstop coverage, the TV showing the image of the space shuttle *Columbia* breaking up as it hit the atmosphere, twinkling like bright stars in the early dawn light. The weeks of recovery, the months of investigations, the years before we returned to space. Some people questioning if space travel was even worth it anymore. This is what it must have been like for people in 1986 who were older than two months old. I was living through yet another space tragedy but this time I'd be able to actually remember it.

I hope this book will help us all, whether we were alive then or not, remember and pay tribute to Dick, Mike, Ron, Ellison, Judy, Greg, and Christa. For the sake of those who came before us, we should keep their memory alive. And for the sake of those who will come after us, we should always keep looking up toward the stars.

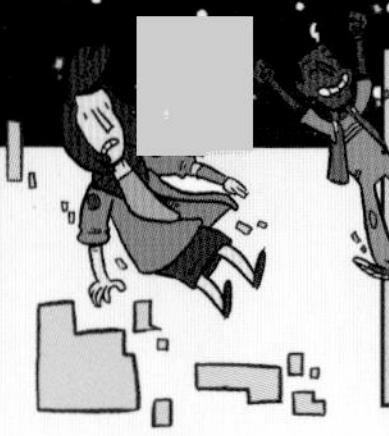

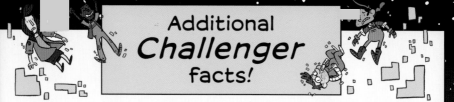

Additional *Challenger* facts!

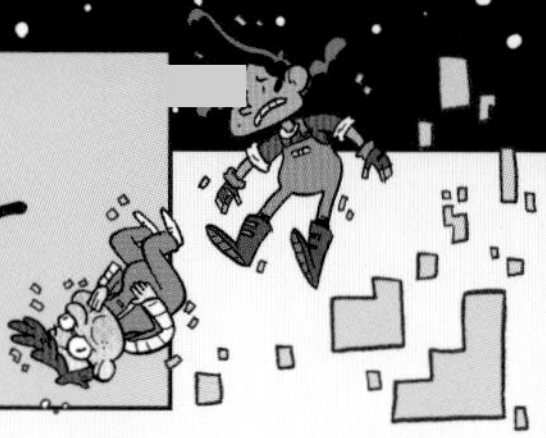

- The *Challenger* was originally built as a test vehicle and later refitted to be a fully functioning shuttlecraft. It was the second orbiter in NASA's fleet, after *Columbia.*

- Over its nine successful flights, *Challenger* was home to many famous firsts. First shuttle space walk, first American woman in space (Sally Ride), first African American in space (Guion Bluford), first shuttle night launch and night landing, first untethered spacewalk, first Canadian in space (Marc Garneau), and first mission to carry two women.

- Before coming up with the Teachers in Space program, NASA brainstormed many different ideas to boost public interest in the shuttle program. According to Caroll Spinney, the actor/puppeteer who played Big Bird on *Sesame Street,* NASA approached him about going into space while in costume, but the idea was dropped.

- In 2004, all seven crew members, along with the crew of the *Columbia* disaster, were posthumously awarded the Congressional Space Medal of Honor.

- The Challenger Center for Space Science Education was founded by the families of the *Challenger* crew as a learning center for kids interested in science, space, and engineering. It has centers in twenty-seven states and four countries, spanning three continents.

- Post-*Challenger* NASA stopped using light blue flight suits and switched to bright orange partially pressurized suits called Launch-Entry Suits. By 1998, all suits were replaced with a fully pressurized model called the Advanced Crew Escape Suit. This was done for added safety to the crew during launch and reentry.

- A soccer ball that Onizuka brought up on behalf of his oldest daughter's high school soccer team survived the explosion and was recovered in almost perfect condition. In 2016 it was taken up into space to the International Space Station.

- Many celestial bodies and objects are named after the crew, including asteroids, craters on the Moon, and a mountain range on Pluto named "Challenger Colles." More down to Earth things were named in their honor, including schools, libraries, and streets.

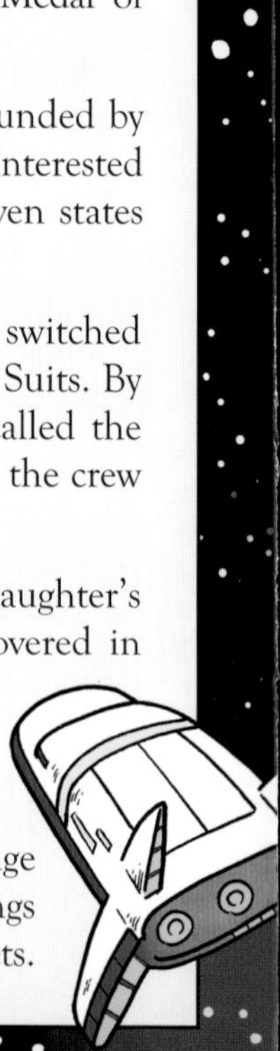